A MALAYSIAN JOURNEY

REHMAN RASHID

Published by
Rehman Rashid
1 Jalan 14/26, 46100 Petaling Jaya
Selangor Darul Ehsan, Malaysia.

Second Edition

Perpustakaan Negara Malaysia
Cataloguing-in-Publication Data
Rehman Rashid
A Malaysian Journey/Rehman Rashid
Biblio: p. 293
ISBN 983-99819-1-9
1. Rehman Rashid—Journeys.
2. Malaysia—Description and travel.
I. Title.
915.959

Printed by
Academe Art & Printing Services Sdn Bhd
Lot 14082, Jalan Kuchai Lama
58200 Kuala Lumpur, Malaysia.

For my brothers, Rafique and Razif;
and our mother, Rosna;
and the memory of our father, Rashid Ismail;

and for Rosemarie Chen Peck Yee,
my candle in the night.

The Author

REHMAN RASHID became a journalist in 1981. After seven years as a Leader Writer and Columnist with the *New Straits Times*, Malaysia's leading English-language daily, he joined *Asiaweek* magazine in Hong Kong as a Senior Writer. From there he left for a year in Bermuda, as a Senior Writer with *Bermuda Business* magazine, before returning home to Malaysia to complete *A Malaysian Journey,* his first book. He was the Malaysian Press Institute's Journalist of the Year for 1985, and Bermuda's Print Journalist of the Year for 1991. Rehman Rashid lives in Petaling Jaya, Malaysia. ❑

A Note on the Names of Places

AFTER more thought than the matter probably merits, I have decided to spell the names of places the way they are pronounced.

Malaysians still say "Penang" (the second syllable rhyming with the English "hang"), rather than "Pinang" (as rhymes with, say, "Minang"). The Penang Malays themselves still use "Tanjung"—the traditional name for Georgetown—in generic reference to their island; to refer to "Pulau Pinang" in everyday conversation seems to many a trifle precious.

As for "Terengganu": I have yet to hear anyone, anywhere, pronounce that first syllable.

"Melaka" it is and always has been: I have always much preferred the crisp traditional rendition to the somewhat effete version of the imperialists. (Two genuflecting little "c"s in place of one stalwart "k", legs akimbo).

"Johor" is Johor: Nothing is lost by shedding the colonials' silent and superfluous tail-end "e".

As for the eternal confusion over "Bahru" or "Bharu" (or even the stammering atrocity "Baharu") as regards Johor, Kota, Kampung or Kuala Kubu—I give up. The spellings seem to vary with every signpost. As far as I'm concerned, they'll all be "baru" plain and simple. ❑

Contents

PROLOGUE
The Border
April 25, 1992

"NICE HAT," said the money-changer. "Where did you get it?"

It was a broad-brimmed felt fedora, from a streetside vendor in New York's Little Italy. I'd always wanted a hat like that, ever since the first Indiana Jones movie. The money-changer sat in his little barred cubicle, the rust on the bars so deep it looked like paint. An ancient clock arthritically ticked on the wall behind him. Next to it the pages of a calendar, graced with the vapid smile of the inevitable Hong Kong starlet, rustled in the breeze from his table fan. The money-changer was an elegant old Chinese man. He wore a striped shirt and grey trousers. His iron-grey hair was perfectly combed. Despite the noonday sun blasting down upon the railway station, he looked cool and fresh. And quizzical.

"New York," I told him, feeling ineffably discomfited. What manner of person buys a fedora in New York City, then turns up at the Padang Besar border crossing, off the Smugglers' Special from Thailand? He nodded sagely. "You need a hat like that in this weather," he said. He spoke with precision, as befitted a man of his vocation. "You can't get a hat like that here."

"I'm sure you can," I said. "It's just a simple hat." This was in the Padang Besar railway station, a few hundred metres south of the Thai border. I was home, for the first time in years. This was one of my first conversations with a fellow Malaysian on our home soil. We were discussing my hat; or perhaps the utility of hats in general. "It's good for a man to wear a hat," said the money-changer. "It keeps his head cool. It's good to keep your head cool."

"How long have you been here, Uncle?" I asked, happily slipping into the polite honorific of general Malaysian discourse. He chortled.

"Longer than you've been alive, I think. Forty years."

"FORTY YEARS!" My surprise was in no way feigned. Forty years in this little cubicle, changing baht to ringgit and back again, a twice-daily business timed to the tidal passage of the Butterworth-Bangkok express. Those bars must have gleamed when he first took his seat behind them.

Apu Murugiah stepped in off the platform and said, "Ah, there you are! My luck is good today. The train got Indian driver today. I can ride in the cab." Apu was a signalman with Malayan Railways. He was thirty-two years old but looked much younger. We'd met four hours earlier on the platform of Haadyai railway station. Apu, toting a small plastic holdall, macho to the point of thuggishness in a red singlet and jeans, was going home after a weekend break in Thailand. "This time Bangkok. Last time, I went to Chiangmai. I like to travel, see other countries, compare with Malaysia." And being a railway worker, Apu made the most of his eligibility for discounted tickets. But he was growing bolder. "Next time, maybe Indonesia. Can take ferry to Medan. I hear there got many Indian people."

Apu and I had waited for the southbound train together, sitting in the Haadyai station canteen in the early morning. I had flown down from Bangkok the day before; he had taken the overnight train. I bought him a coffee; he bought me sweets. As the train pulled in, Apu reached into his holdall and extracted a new shirt. "See I bought shirt. I bought two. Better wear one. Those UPP buggers so bad." (UPP: *Unit Pencegah Penyeledup;* the Anti-Smuggling Unit.) "They just take people's things and throw." He pulled on the shirt. It was of good heavy denim, liberally appliqued with American Army insignia and a Master Sergeant's stripes on the sleeves. "I bought in Bangkok. Only ten dollars our money. Very cheap, ah? Quite style also." The shirt fit him well. Apu was indeed quite style. In his new shirt, a distinct swagger began to undulate in his bearing.

We sat together on the hour's ride south to the Malaysian border. This was the legendary Smugglers' Special. The morning train out of south Thailand is reputedly filled with Malaysian trippers going home with sacks of cheap rice, bundles of cheap clothing, hoards of cheap anything. Stories abound of inventive illegality on this train. Carriage wall-panels filled with new screwdrivers. Boxes of ballpoint pens wrapped in plastic and stashed in toilet cisterns. Sacks of rice strapped to the bellies of ostensibly pregnant women. As soon as the train crosses the border, the sides of the track are supposed to be suddenly littered with illicit packages tossed out of the windows for collection by accomplices.

But there seemed nothing especially untoward about our fellow passengers on this train that morning, although that may well be the way it is with smugglers. A loud Chinese family occupied the two rows in front of us, apparently determined to eat their way to Malaysia. The floor around them was rapidly hidden beneath mounds of peanut skins, fruit peels, eggshells and plastic wrappers. Further along, a Malay couple attempted in vain to quell the squallings of their two infant children. Here a brace of Western backpackers; there a portly middle-aged Indian with a briefcase and a livid razor cut on his cheek from an inadvertently late awakening in Haadyai that morning.

The train rattled past a tract of newly cleared land, where the rudiments of new housing had begun to appear, and our coach was instantly filled with clouds of gritty red dust. There was a rush to bang shut the windows, which only ensured that the dust remained trapped inside the carriage. I remarked on the folly of this to Apu, suggesting we keep our own window open. He agreed, diplomatically, and thereafter kept his eyes gamely squinted against subsequent invasions of dust. By the third such blizzard, I was contrite. "Er, Apu?" I ventured. "Perhaps we should shut the window after all."

"No. You are right. Open window the breeze will blow out the dust. But must take care of eyes," he said, squinting.

Changing the subject, I asked Apu how things were in Malaysia. "Can do, lah. Better than before. Anytime better than Thailand. You see these people. Little children working in the fields. Selling mineral water in the train. Little children! Not like back home. We can relax more. Mahathir saying 2020, all will be good." He was referring to the prime minister's latest blueprint for national development, which postulated a fully developed Malaysia by the third decade of the new millennium.

"But still," said Apu, "depends on the colour of your skin, lah. You know what I'm saying." I knew what he was saying, but I wondered if he did. It seemed too glib, too pat. Apu was responding to received wisdom.

Apu lived in the railway's bachelor quarters by the Bukit Mertajam station. He divided his time between there and his mother's house in Prai, where she was cared for by his sisters. His father died a couple of years ago, but before Murugiah went he managed to buy that little house for Apu's mother. "At least this much he did," said Apu. "We live in the world must give something back. Take care of wife and family. Money we spend every day. A house. Good."

The train crossed the border, and minutes later pulled into Padang Besar station. The passengers disembarked and flocked to the Thai immigration booth for their exit stamps. Then they inundated the Malaysian immigration booth for their entry stamps. Apu went in search of a cup of tea to wash the dust from his throat. I stood on the platform between the Thai and Malaysian counters, savouring the sensation of being home. It was, after all the years away, a moment of quiet joy, unmarred by the self-conscious posturing of the young policemen who stalked about the platform. Uncertainly poised between their conflicting roles—were they to be a reassuring presence for tourists, or were they to intimidate potential criminals?—smiles and frowns tussled for ownership of their faces, which were consequently reduced to an indeterminate twitching.

"Where you from?" asked the uniformed officer who suddenly appeared before me. He spoke English. He was tall, paunchy and moustached. He wore the uniform of a Customs official: black trousers, white shirt with epaulettes and silver buttons. His name tag read: SHAFIE. His tone was not unfriendly.

"Taiping," I said.

"Oh, our people, ya?" he said, breaking into Malay and a simultaneous smile. "Had a good time in Haadyai?" Ah yes, the infamous fleshpots of that southern Thai town ....

"I was only there a night."

"A night is all it takes." A guffaw.

" I have no idea what you're talking about. I came down from Bangkok ...."

"Even worse."

"... and before that from Hong Kong. I've been away a long time."

"And now you've come home," said Shafie.

"Now I've come home."

"That's good. This is a good country."

"I know."

"Where are you going?"

"I don't know. I want to wander around, see the place again, talk to people, see how my homeland is these days."

"That's good. What sort of people?"

"People like you."

He laughed. "I can't tell you much!" But he clearly didn't mind the prospect. "So you going to wait around here for a while? I have to attend to my duties ...."

"What sort of duties?"

"Just looking at people's bags twice a day. It's a really boring job, but there's lots of free time. I'll see you after the train goes."

"Sure, I have no plans. But I have to change some money."

"No problem," said Shafie. "The money-changer's over there, near the canteen. He's Chinese, but he gives good rates."

And he did. "The Malaysian ringgit's growing stronger and stronger," said the money-changer. "Every day, one or two cents up." But he let me have five cents extra on the baht. I was folding the Malaysian currency into my wallet—and even the sight of those notes amplified the thrill of being home—when Apu reappeared bearing a plastic bag of tea and the news that the train driver was an Indian and therefore a friend and confidante, which meant he could ride up front for the rest of the trip to Butterworth. "Hey, nice meeting you man," said Apu, transferring the bag of tea to his left hand and extending the right to me. "If you come to Bukit Mertajam you come see me, okay? You can stay my house. Just go to the railway station and ask for Apu Murugiah. Everyone knows. You come, okay?"

And off he went, loping up the platform in his sergeant's shirt, swinging up into the engine cab with practised ease. Apu Murugiah, the engine driver, the American soldier, the world traveller, the Signalman: "If not for me the trains all go crazy."

The train whistle blew—I was certain I knew who pulled the cord—and the engine revved, spitting a plume of black smoke into the sky. The carriages jerked forward in a clatter of couplings; the train pulled out of Padang Besar. Silence washed over the station. A cock crowed. Distant trees rustled in the hot afternoon breeze. Dust-devils swirled briefly over the construction site across the tracks, where an impressive new immigration office was being built. I remembered Padang Besar as it had been five years before: huge raintrees on either side of the tracks; a rusty iron pedestrian bridge linking the Thai and Malaysian sides of the border. Now there was a wide expanse of levelled orange earth, upon which backhoes and bulldozers lumbered hither and yon.

I went to the station canteen for a glass of iced-coffee. I was still deep in the thrill of being home in Malaysia, in the so-familiar surroundings of a small-town railway station. The worn wooden benches, the faded schedules on the wall, the signs advising patrons not to spit in any of four languages. And there in its eternal corner: the canteen, with its glass jars of biscuits and sweets, its cardboard panels of packeted peanuts, its dangling bags of crackers, its Chinese-starlet calendar, its rattling old refrigerator, its smell of kerosene and charcoal and tea on endless brew.

Shafie came in, duties done, shirt unbuttoned. He folded his gangly frame onto a stool beside me and gruffly ordered a cup of tea from the Chinese proprietor. The man gruffly delivered it. Their mutual irascibility seemed well practised; part of the theatre of their daily routine. One was a Chinese shopkeeper, and the other a Malay government officer. They were not unfriendly towards each other, but that didn't mean they might ever be friends.

We were joined by a third man: short, rotund, clad in a tee-shirt and jeans low beneath his belly and bagging at the crotch, aviator sunglasses ostentatiously dangling from his collar. Shafie introduced him as Osman, of the UPP. "Oh, you're one of those guys who throws stuff from the trains," I joked. Osman laughed, mirthlessly. "Just doing my duty," he said, and said nothing else thereafter.

But Shafie wanted to talk. Things were going well in this country, he said. "Mahathir's mellowed. He really is a good administrator. He has the long view." He talked about commodities and industry; about Malaysians abroad and whether they knew what was going on back home. We talked about politics and corruption—but it was a conversation that merely mentioned these words. Shafie seemed not to have a personal sense of such matters; he was content to mirror the views of the establishment of which he was a loyal servant. I could not hold this against him. "The economy has grown well," said Shafie, "and now the Bumiputras are well off. This was the point of it. We had to take care of the Bumiputras, the Malays, so that everyone can look forward to a better future."

"We seem to have become optimists," I said.

"Now is the time for optimism," Shafie said. "Inflation may be a problem, but the stronger ringgit is something we can be proud of, don't you think? Now foreigners won't think our country is worthless."

Shafie was an earnest man. At thirty-eight, he could measure Malaysia today against what it had been two decades or more ago, and recognize that he owed his entire life to the preferential policies that had come to define him. But he was not dismissive of the non-Malay communities; it troubled him that they were troubled by the need for Malay preference and political supremacy. But the difficult years were over, he was sure. The country was rich now, and all Malaysians had a bigger share of the national wealth. "They understand us better now," said Shafie.

I wished he had said: We understand each other better now. But it was still, in this Malaysia I had not seen for so long, in the Malaysia of this hot and sunny April afternoon in 1992, a matter of "us" and "them". Perhaps it truly would take another thirty years to bridge that gulf.

The money-changer locked up his desk and lowered the grille. He stepped out of his cubicle and carefully bolted its ancient wooden door. "That's it for the day?" I asked. He nodded. "So what do you do the rest of the time?"

"Other things," he shrugged. "Sit at home. Plant vegetables. A simple life," he said. "This is the answer. Don't say you're Number One. Say you're last. You'll be happy."

"I agree," I said. "All my troubles began when I said I was Number One."

"That was when you were foolish," he said, turning to go. He paused, cast me a glance, granted me the hint of a smile. "Welcome home," he said. "Watch out you don't lose your hat." ❑

1

DURING THE YEARS OF EXILE, my thoughts of Malaysia were memories of night.

... the soft, moist, fluid Malaysian night; the darkness that draped in velvet folds upon the land; the levelling, blanketing, unifying night. I would recall its sensuality, and its silence, and I would come to think of it as the single most enduring backdrop to everything I knew of my homeland. The Malaysian night held for me promises and secrets, assignations, encounters, illicit liaisons. Forever my thoughts would be illumined by the soft yellow glow of carbide lamps in curbside stalls, or of sodium streetlamps in the distance, or of the moon ....

This is to romanticize, of course, but perhaps not unconscionably; for I thought of Malaysia a very great deal during those years. There were few greater pleasures than to discover, in a musty old bookstore in London or Madras, some obscure tome that shed some wan imperial light on the long-gone people and events that had, to greater or lesser degrees, shaped the land of my birth. London was, of course, the richer lode for such prospecting. There I discovered, in a nondescript building south of the Thames, in a room sibilant with librarians, on parchment brittle with age, in careful copperplate calligraphy, ink almost illegibly faded, the original treaties signed by the original Malay sultans with the original British.

I diligently copied some of those passages into my notebooks, which would have been the appropriate pretence of the scholar I fancied myself to be, but all too often the sheer weight of their history would leave me awed and reverential, and I would merely gaze at them, run my fingers gently over their vellum and inhale the sweet, unearthly fragrance of paper two centuries old. Besides, there were always comprehensive transcriptions of these documents in the standard texts.

No, I was no scholar, but a wanderer, an explorer; a young Malaysian on a long journey, itinerary uncertain and duration unknown, determined only by circumstances beyond myself. Occasionally, as in the archives of the East India Company in London, or in Higginbotham's splendidly anachronistic bookstore in Madras, I would be rewarded with some recorded glimpse of the journey my country had itself taken, and I would add yet another mouldy old silverfished and wormholed book to my collection. They never cost very much, for these were records and accounts and polemics that had been destined to vanish into the swirl of changing times, their authors unremarked and soon forgotten. Eventually they would resurface on humble wooden shelves in Long Acre or Tottenham Court Road or Delhi, upon the clearance of someone's attic of some adventurous life's accumulated exotica and debris. To me, however, they were like faint voices from unmarked graves, urging me to continue as they had, heedless of the likelihood that my own passions and efforts would ultimately meet much the same fate as theirs.

For here was indeed a story: a story of a place, a crescent of land at the south-eastern extremity of the planet's vastest continent, a slender appendage leading to a scattering of islands at the confluence of oceans and hemispheres; a peripheral sort of place, at the furthest outposts of sprawling empires; an incidental place, where in the beginning only outlaws and adventurers had ever roamed, but where lives had been lived and a nation had been born and was being, even as I wandered, assiduously built.

It was, to my mind, a nation unlike any other. This uniqueness, this singularity, seemed to me all the stranger as I wandered about a world in which history seemed so often to have functioned as a production-line, a factory, a mill; first of exploration, then of conquest, then of empires, then of upheaval, then of nationalism. Each stage drew from the one that preceded it and inexorably gave rise to the one following. There was a grand inevitability about the process; one sensed that the things that happened *had* to have happened, given what had preceded them, and that what ensued could not have happened differently. History seemed to me to have functioned like a mass producer, making an utter mockery of the conceit of "free will", filling the world with cookie-cutter nations differing only in texture and flavour, in the elements of their raw material. And for this we should cherish "nationalism"? Absurd!

The country that had come to call itself Malaysia was no different—it too had been flung free into the world as an orphan of Empire and left to fend for itself as best it could, picking through the rubble of its colonial identity in search of clothes that might still fit, or the material with which to fashion new ones—yet, it *was* different. There was something special about its ingredients; something unusual in the clay which the potter's wheel of history would spin into so apparently familiar a form.

As a young journalist in Kuala Lumpur, I had believed it simple to see what was special about Malaysia: it was multiracial, multi-cultural, multilingual, what could be clearer than that? But then, as I was to learn, so was virtually everywhere else. Salman Rushdie had written, and I was to quote him often: "The immigrant is the central figure of our time." This had indeed been the anthem of the 20th Century: the sound of ships' horns and jet engines, the susurrus of arrival halls and departure lounges; the great discordant chorale of commingled humanity. Rivers of people, adventurers and refugees, flowing to and fro, rushing swollen with hope or shrunken in despair, breaking their banks and spilling over borders and boundaries, endlessly seeding new lands or inundating old ones, irrevocably reshaping their human geographies, raising again and again the conflict of old and new, "here" and "there", "us" and "them", imposing on ancient lands new realities, new social orders .... It had become a hybrid, grafted, cross-fertilized world, and diversity alone explained little.

But gradually Malaysia's peculiarly distinctive mosaic pieced itself together for me, and the picture pulled into focus. I had been born into a nation that, upon the withdrawal of one imposed overlay of identity, had not been immediately subsumed beneath another. Something in Malaysia resisted too pat an imposition of a post-colonial New Order, insistently making of it something more. Malaysia had greeted Independence as a nation *equally divided* between Indigene and Immigrant, and this had made all the difference.

There was in Malaysia, as nowhere else, a *balance* between these two great defining icons of the 20th Century. The Indigene had not been hounded to the brink of cultural extinction by the Immigrant, as he had been in Australia or America. Nor had the Immigrant been bludgeoned into capitulation by the Indigene, as in Indonesia, or swallowed whole, digested and absorbed, as in the Philippines and Thailand.

No: in Malaysia, Indigene and Immigrant were more evenly matched than anywhere else in the world—it was, when the British went home in 1957, literally a 50:50 split. Being in balance they resisted each other's defences, and each was compelled to recognize the other as an inescapable, ineradicable element of his own reality. This was what had made Malaysia special. Here was the truest of all confluences: of hemispheres, oceans, monsoon winds, and equally of histories, cultures, and destinies.

Great streams of history, and of peoples, had for centuries met at that spit of land at Asia's south-eastern extremity. Sometimes they merged; often they clashed. But always they would move from then on *together*, whether they liked it or not, and something new and wonderful would emerge as they did so. They would be transformed, these immiscible partners and uneasy bedfellows, this chalk and cheese, oil and water, this Tiger and Dragon, this Yin and Yang, into something neither could ever have been without the other—and nothing would be destroyed in either but their ignorance of each other, and all that was good and great in both would survive, and thrive.

It was, to the young journalist in Kuala Lumpur, a beautiful and heartening theory to contemplate, and I consequently saw evidence for it everywhere, in everything. I was aware that there had been a price to pay for it, but I believed the price had been paid a generation earlier. In this, of course, I was foolish, and naive, and very young. And that is why, during the years of exile, my thoughts were of night.

It was at night, often over frothy tumblers of Indian tea, that the more lasting revelations had made themselves clear to me, and talk would distill down to essences and immutable truths. In the smallest hours between midnight and dawn, when our conflicts would melt into irrelevance, and the beat policeman would join the worn-out thug at the curbside stall for a tumbler of Indian tea, and each would recognize enough of himself in the other to make no matter of their differences. The night would unite and enfold us, and that is why I chose to have the night define my memories of home.

And for another reason: they came at night when they wanted to take us away; sliding through the darkness like thieves to suddenly appear at our gates in their nylon jackets and jogging shoes, with their weapons and arrest warrants, using the night, and our vulnerability within its narrow, shadowed confines, to attend to the wider view only they could clearly see.

The Malaysian night: beguiling, seductive, treacherous.

And so I became an exile. I left the night behind as I winged out over the world, now here, now there, breathing for many years a rarefied and alien air, laden with strange fragrances. I worked for a time in Hong Kong, then lived for a year in Bermuda. I visited Britain and America, India, the

Philippines and China. I watched my country from varying distances, from condominiums in Hong Kong and mountaintops in Maharashtra and a sliver of coralline limestone in the middle of the Atlantic, paying for my passage with my writing. There were times when I wished I could see myself as less of an exile, or more—whatever it might have taken for the endless motion, the restlessness and impermanence, to abate. But then, always, would come a moment of stillness and silence, and within it I would see the sodium-yellow light of a carbide lamp or the moon, and sense on every quarter of my skin the moist caress of the Malaysian night, and in my exile I would dream of home.

I grew older, the years of my thirties falling away, and I wondered if I had not been impetuous in my departure. Perhaps it would have been better if I had stayed and rolled with the blows, retreating perhaps, momentarily, but remaining a present element of my country's turbulent quest for identity. Perhaps.

In the fourth year of my exile I began to realize that what I had truly done was to freeze a frame of my Malaysian journey, the better to allow myself the passage of a few years before hopefully re-introducing myself to the scene. I had hoped that time would grant me a new clarity of vision. I had wanted to shed my youth, a moulting of sorts, and during the interim I would trim my sails to the winds of circumstance, trusting to time the exculpation of youth's inadequacies—the impotent rage and humiliation that had clouded its spectacular, evanescent joys.

But as I grew older the frame stayed frozen. It was a frame of the Malaysian night, and within it was everything I cherished, and everything I feared. When the time came to go home, then, it seemed appropriate that I should want to do so in shadow, slipping back across the border self-effacing as a thief. ❑

The Room of Dancing Horses

IT WAS WELL after midnight when the noise finally abated in Kangar, and this surprised me.

Kangar was the smallest of Malaysia's state capitals; the principal town of the country's smallest state. I had last known it as a quiet place of greensward and tidy shophouses, cooled by a constant breeze bearing the fragrance of padi. But now Kangar was bustling and sodium-lit; the blank yellow light of new streetlamps casting a waxy pallor into what used to be softly melting shadows. I sat at the window of my hotel room and watched the traffic on the street below. Motorcycles screamed. Articulated lorries coughed and belched and lumbered around corners. Cars yelped and hooted; pedestrians leapt for safety.

There came a crash and a clatter, a tinkle of breaking glass: a motorbike had been sideswiped into the roadside ditch by a particularly malevolent car. The rider was assuredly uninjured—he fairly danced across the road in a welter of rage, calling out to passers-by for witnesses, screaming at the heavens, yanking off one rubber slipper to hurl in the direction of his rapidly vanishing assailant.

The two-wheeled fraternity came to his rescue—there is honour among the meek. A group of fellow cyclists stopped to help the livid victim haul his 80cc Yamaha Cub out of the ditch. The bike was well enough, despite the clearly expensive loss of its headlight. It started on the first kick (but it was quite a kick, to be sure), and the victim and his newfound companions wailed off in pursuit of the bully. The strident chorus of their exhausts faded; coils of blue smoke rose greasily into the glow of the streetlights. Had that avenging posse ever caught up with him, the car driver might have learned what crash helmets swung in resolute unison could do to his bodywork. That, and the error of his ways in assuming that heroism, valour and sheer brute strength had anything to do with the size of the vehicle commanded.

Street theatre in Kangar, which used to be so placid and docile a town. Times had changed. The days had extended. The nights had receded.

As had the land. There having been no hotel in Padang Besar, I had chartered a taxi to drive me the score of kilometres to Kangar. The driver was a lugubrious old Chinese, weary beyond his fifty years, and he spent the duration of the drive advising me of the folly of believing it was possible to make money in this country without money to begin with. He needed a new taxi. (I readily agreed.) Someone had offered him a reconditioned Toyota for $9,000. He could come up with a third of that sum. He could get a loan for the balance, but "you borrow $6,000, after five years you pay $10,000. How can?"

The government had done well for the Malays, said the taxi driver, but for the non-Malays things were still difficult. I wasn't to misunderstand, he urged: he liked the Malays a lot. After all, he had been born and bred in that very Malay part of the country. The Malays were his friends. Still, these days, it was far better to be a Malay than not.

There was no malice in his voice. These were not accusations; they were simply observations. He bore no grudge. He was just very tired.

As he spoke—and he spoke interminably—we drove past wide expanses of cleared land. New factories and housing estates were coming up all over Perlis, he said. "I don't know what they're going to make here. Someone told me ceiling fans. Air-conditioners."

But in the distance the ancient limestone hills of Perlis bulked elephantine and indigo against the horizon, and before them still swept the viridian fields of padi that had once made this region famous as the Rice Bowl of the country. The sky through the scarred windshield of this sad old man's battered Opel Gemini was the palest of eggshell blue, and diaphanous clouds drifted slowly inland on the softest of zephyrs. The road before us was a ribbon of grey, sparsely trafficked. The red laterite of cleared land was still frequently punctuated by stretches of gold-green foliage: the brackens and ferns of secondary jungle; the occasional palisade of rubber trees or oil palm. I inhaled deeply the hot wind blowing in through the taxi's open windows, and I told my driver this was still a most beautiful country.

He did not pause in his lament.

He deposited me in the centre of Kangar, pointing out two hotels where I might find a room for the night. Both were classic cheap Chinese hotels: rooms above, a coffee-shop below. I gave the driver my thanks and a generous tip. "What's this for?" he asked, staring at the extra dollar bills in his palm, his incredulity genuine and quite charming. "To help you buy that new taxi," I said, which helped restore his spirits to their customary mien.

There was no vacancy in the first hotel. There was in the second. A room on the top floor with an attached bathroom for $18 a night. The proprietor hauled out an enormous ledger and asked me for my identity card. Of course! Again, the unexpected thrill of being home. I rummaged in my satchel for my filofax, pulled out my Malaysian IC from the compartment in which it had languished for four years, and passed it to him. He studiously transcribed its details into the ledger, then handed it back to me. I restored this document, my unassailable proof of citizenship and identity, to its legitimate berth in my wallet. And thought once more: I'm home.

The room was spartan but clean enough. There was a bed, a cupboard, a clothes rack and two armchairs covered in yellow vinyl. There was a washbasin and a serviceable bathroom with a squat toilet and a trough for bucket baths. All pretty much standard for this level of establishment. But some thought had gone into the decoration of one wall. Having dumped my bags on the bed and slumped into an armchair to light a cigarette and take my bearings, I found myself staring in fascination at the room's main wall. The white plaster was covered with a repeated pattern, traced in red paint, of leaping horses.

Considerable artistry had gone into the design; the horses were lithe and lively, their manes and tails flying as at full gallop. Their hooves flailed; their heads tossed. A hundred red horses flew down the wall of a room in a cheap Chinese hotel. And not one of them was exactly like any other. I wondered how this mural had been done—surely not freehand! But there was a distinctly freehand fluidity about the pattern. Perhaps it had been done with a block stencil. Very well done, in that case, for there was no tell-tale sign of sutures or joins or paint-runs between what might have been the stencil panels.

A small, yet engaging, mystery: unsung artistry in the most humble milieu—and such artistry! The horses leapt and pranced and danced; each one subtly different from the others, yet all leaping in harmony down the wall of my room. I fancied I could hear their hooves, their whinnies, the snort of their nostrils.

And thus I rolled onto the bed, beneath my parade of red horses, and slept.

I AWOKE IN THE LATE AFTERNOON, fur on my tongue, a dull ache behind my eyes. But exhilaration still stirred within me; it had stayed with me in my sleep, in a dream of winged horses. I swung my legs off the bed, padded over to the bathroom for a quick rinse. I dressed and ventured out for a walk and some food. I was ravenously hungry.

Now Kangar was quiet—it was the last hour of the afternoon siesta—and in the slumberous silence of the hot afternoon I detected a hint of the way it used to be in small Malaysian towns: the post-lunch Total System Shutdown. Traffic was sparse and whispery, the coffee-shops were almost empty, the occasional mendicant dozed in the shade of trees.

Down one street, a Malay woman sat tending her food stall, reading a fashion magazine. She hadn't much left to sell, but even the remnants looked good to me. In my years away, nothing I'd eaten had ever tasted like food to me. But here it was: bean-sprouts and chillies in coconut milk, spinach and soya beans, fish curry, spiced beef ... the northern cooking I'd loved since childhood. I ordered, sat down and feasted.

A group of four Malay schoolgirls floated by like ghosts, or angels, depending on how one felt about organized Islam. I watched their round brown faces graced with smiles and framed by white head-coverings that fluttered about their shoulders as they trilled along. They noticed me; they fell into silence, swallowing their smiles and casting down their eyes. Their faces, a moment before so lively, became masks of wood carved by a melancholy sculptor. A few paces on, and presumably out of harm's range, animated chatter resumed and bright laughter danced like tinsel on the enervated afternoon air.

It was a curious piece of theatre. Three swift acts; two instant costume changes: schoolgirls-Muslim women-schoolgirls. The transitions seemed practised to the perfection of unconsciousness. One moment, they were four carefree young friends walking home from school. The next, in the presence of the male of their species, they were Muslim women: dour, sullen, silent, fearfully modest, commanded by the burdens and perils of their gender. It was like the tripping of a switch. They had their magnetic field; I had mine. The fields merged, their defences triggered. *There is a man. He can see you. Therefore he is watching you. Therefore you are in danger. Sinfulness is in the air. Be alert. Move swiftly. Do not attract his attention.*

The fields parted, and all was well once more. I shrugged and finished my meal.

As dusk fell, the town began to come alive. Vendors began appearing by streetsides and in parking lots, setting up their carts of fruits and food—fried bananas, lentil cakes, doughnuts, noodles. In the covered market, stalls that had remained shuttered all afternoon opened for business; their wares of household goods or shoes or cloth spilling out for the enticement of browsers. Crowds began to surge, as the heat and light began to drain from the day.

The sun set spectacularly; I watched its iridescent departure from the table of a drinks stall by the bus station. Taxi drivers vied for passengers. The long-distance buses began to gather like elephants at a watering hole. It was possible to ride the length of the Malaysian Peninsula, from Kangar to Singapore, for $36. Such a journey would take all night and half the following day, but in these mammoth air-conditioned coaches it would not be an entirely uncomfortable experience. Families gathered to send off their own. One young woman on a journey to Kuala Lumpur had her father, grandfather and three uncles in attendance. "I've put her bags down below," said one of her menfolk to another. "Not her drinking water," he was cautioned. "Of course not. What good would her drinking water do down there?"

Where was she going? "Kuala Lumpur." What would she do there? "Go to college." What would she be studying? "Business." They followed her into the coach to see her safely to her seat. She would not lack for companions; the bus was full.

All the Kuala Lumpur-bound buses were full; one had to book two days in advance to be sure of a seat. The gravitational pull of the national capital had strengthened in the time I had been away. Kuala Lumpur was once a very long way from Kangar, Perlis. Now, leaving at sundown every night of the week and timed to arrive at dawn, an armada of coaches ferried the people of this far northern state to that great vortex of opportunity down south. Kuala Lumpur, Crown Jewel of the Klang Valley, Navel of the Nation, the metropolitan apotheosis of the Malaysian Dream.

When would she be back? "Don't know. No point in her coming back here to work. Things are better in KL. You can make more money there. Perhaps we'll go down to visit her. It's not that far. It's not that expensive. Where are you from?"

Where indeed? I lay on the bed in the hotel room, regretting my afternoon nap, as the hours slipped past midnight. I listened to the ceaseless traffic below, barking and snarling and whining like dogs. I watched the yellow glow of headlights wash across the wall; each formless passage of light playing on a blood-red host of horses frozen in flight. ❑

2

I WAS BORN soon after midnight, soon after mid-year, soon after mid-century, in a town called Taiping, in the state of Perak, in the north of what was then known as British Malaya.

It was, by then, but a nominal designation. It was the twilight of Empire, and colonialism had but two years left of its sway on the Malay Peninsula. For nearly a decade, a new nationalism had vitalized a hitherto dormant populace. It had had its origins in the immediate aftermath of the Second World War; the war that had finally shattered the British Empire's hallowed illusion of supremacy in Asia.

In the first stages of what would be the Japanese Occupation, Malayans had watched the British cut and run like rabbits as Japanese forces made their swift and largely unimpeded way down the length of the Malay Peninsula to Singapore, the mighty fortress of Empire that was to collapse like a house of cards within hours of the Japanese arrival at the Straits of Johor. Four years later, when the war ended and the Japanese left, the British had come marching back and, if you please, attempted to turn Malaya into even more of their domain than it had been before.

The British had deserted a Malaya that had been sectioned into their outright colonies of Penang, Melaka and Singapore (known collectively as the "Straits Settlements"), and their four "federated states" of Perak, Selangor, Negri

Sembilan and Pahang. Now they proposed a "Malayan Union", which would rope in the five "unfederated states" of Perlis, Kedah, Kelantan, Trengganu and Johor and grant equal citizenship to all Malayans under the Crown. As for the sovereignties of the nine Malay sultanates, hitherto guaranteed as part of the conditions, for British administration of their territories, well, "casualties of war" and all that.

The response to the Malayan Union proposal was phenomenal. British officials watched the wildfire spread of a spectacle so unprecedented they could hardly believe their eyes. Across the peninsula, out of every Malay village, there came a flood of emotion against the Malayan Union. There were rallies and speeches and condemnations—"even the women!" wrote one astounded British observer. And this from the *Malays?* Those gentle, tractable people, no doubt with the occasional tendency to run amok, but so essentially good-natured a folk as to make the occasional stern warning and harsh example all that was really needed to keep them in line? Who would have thought?

It was as a direct result of the anti-Malayan Union movement that Malaya's first political party was formed. On May 12, 1946, in Johor Baru, the state capital of Johor, was born the United Malays Nationalist Organisation. Umno would spearhead the populist thrust for Malayan Independence, and would always remain the country's foremost political party.

Indeed, for quite some time thereafter, the *only* political party. (Discounting the sundry Malay splinter groups that would split from Umno and spiral thence into oblivion.) The Chinese had resisted pledging any lasting fealty to Malaya while it was still part of the British Empire. It took the Independence movement spawned by the Malays to focus their minds on what their fate would be in a Malayan nation. The formation of the Malayan Chinese Association, in 1949, was a testament to the investment of past Chinese generations in this land, and a declaration of their intent to stay and be a part of its future.

Meanwhile, Malaya's Indian communities organized themselves into the Malayan Indian Congress, which joined Umno and the MCA in forming the Alliance, and Malaya thus had its government-in-waiting.

By the time of my birth, it had been agreed that Malaya would be granted its Independence in 1957. The notion of nationhood was seductive indeed, and Malaya was held in thrall to its many variants. As the prospective national government practised its new amities, it had to endure the depredations of those who saw more promise in a Communist future. The forested interior was the redoubt of the Malayan Communist Party, which at the time of my birth was at its murderous zenith.

The communists' targets were, for the most part, British planters and administrators, but many were the hapless plantation workers who got in their way, and the communists were easily portrayed as predators on the new nation being shaped from the old colony; the *musuh dalam selimut*, the Enemies in the Blanket.

Despite the turbulence of the times—the forbidding darkness of rural roads and the plantation nights pregnant with terror—these were, on the whole, happy and optimistic days for Malaya. Nationhood was all but assured, the economy was enjoying its post-war boom, and these would be remembered as years of song and dance as much as of political ferment and communist terrorism. ("The Emergency", it was called, for to have labelled it for the civil war it was would have been to play havoc with the insurance rates set for British interests in Malaya by Lloyds of London.)

A firm national consensus held sway, and it accepted that Malaya's future depended on the continued co-operation of the three main ethnic groups that constituted this mosaic of the country. In its first test of electoral support, in 1955, the Alliance won all but one of the fifty-two seats available. (The one it didn't win went to a party dedicated to creating an Islamic republic of the new nation. This was ominous, as we shall see.) By and large, however, Malayans recognized that their government should be no more nor less than a reflection of themselves, for a certain working concord had by then been defined in their daily lives. This was the pattern: the towns were Chinese, with their shopkeepers and traders; the villages were Malay, with their farmers and fishermen; the plantations were Indian, with their rubber tappers and labourers. Above and amidst them all, filling the interstices between the races with the ceramic insulation of their authority, were the British.

The British were famous for turning to their administrative advantage the social divisions of the lands they colonized, and they kept the races at just the right distance from each other to have the disparate elements of Malaya work in remote harmony. Now the masters were leaving, there was the hope that, with time and judicious management on the part of the country's inheritors, these distinctions would blur, if not disappear altogether. It was, as I have said, an optimistic time.

But first had to come nationhood, and in 1955, the year of my birth, Independence was a cause most clearly defined not so much by pledges of commonality as by two contrasting foes: the communists, and the colonists. Of the two, there was no question which was the greater evil. So clear, so graphic was the communist threat—the frail Indian bodies lashed to rubber trees and hacked to death with hoes—that their cause would remain a national bogy for decades thereafter.

And because the Malayan Communist Party was principally, though by no means exclusively, a Chinese affair, the pursuit of Malayan Independence incubated within it the toxic seeds of future discord. Soon enough, the communist myth would be seen to have been but one manifestation of a deeper and more durable conflict. Malaya, in time, would come to be an arena for the contest of the Tiger ("Sang Rimau": the emblem of the Malay warrior; the embodiment of all that was noble and courageous about the Malay) and the Dragon.

But in 1955 all this was in the future—although not so far off that the more prescient Malayans could not sense the ominous vapours on the horizon. Still, the year I was born was a year of hope; there had even been a meeting of the communist leader Chin Peng and Alliance chief minister Tunku Abdul Rahman—he who would be Independent Malaya's first prime minister—in a small schoolhouse by the edge of the jungle in the north of the country. Nothing had come of their meeting, but the prevailing mood of optimism saw promise in their having met at all; surely, as the day of Independence drew ever nearer, the communists would come to see their cause as meaningless, and irrelevant to the nation's future.

I was born in a town with a Chinese name: "Taiping" means "Peace" in their language.

Nearly a century before, this had been a small mining village on the upper reaches of the great Perak tinfields that had drawn like a magnet to Malaya unprecedented numbers of Chinese fortune-hunters. To this part of the Malay peninsula, they came mainly from China's southern provinces of Fukien and Kwangtung. The tinfields of Perak in the latter years of the 19th Century were brutal, brawling and lawless warrens of pestilence and degradation—miners died like flies in the horrid conditions. But the promise of riches was great and sustaining. As a matter of mutual survival, the Chinese organized themselves into clan associations, as was their wont in all their overseas communities. The British described these as "secret societies", but in truth they held more in common with masonic lodges than with the Triads that were to become infamous in later years.

Two of the principal Chinese societies in Perak were the Ghee Hin, mostly of Cantonese from Kwangtung, and the Hai San, who were mainly Hakkas from Fukien. They incessantly warred with each other in the 1870s, transplanting to Malaya their implacable ancestral quarrels. It was their feuding—or, more to the point, the disruption it wrought on the Straits tin trade—that ultimately impelled the British to emerge from their bailiwick on the island of Penang and extend their authority to the peninsula's west coast.

The British, it must be admitted, had been loath to intervene. They had no great desire to sequester the Malay lands beyond what they had already acquired: Penang had been for almost a century a useful victualling station for their ships in the Bay of Bengal, but Malaya had never been more than a distant and minor outpost of "Greater India", and the Napoleonic wars were dampening the enthusiasm of the eastern administrators of Europe's imperial powers to encroach too closely on each other's turf.

But business was business, and Malaya's was tin, and what would eventually come to be known as "British Malaya" had its origins in a treaty signed in January 1874 on a British steamer moored in the shallows of Pulau Pangkor, a small island not far from where the Perak River opened into the Straits of Malacca. Here the British presided over an agreement to cease hostilities, signed by the leaders of the warring Chinese factions and the Malay rulers of Perak.

(There was intrigue even in this: Perak, a large territory, was divided at the time between three ruling Malay families. Needless to say, they didn't get on well at all. To the ruler who agreed to accept the advice of a permanent British Resident, the British pledged recognition as Sultan of Perak. This turned out to be a foppish man named Abdullah, whose abilities had never quite matched his ambitions, and he would soon come to regret his decision. The first British Resident in Perak was a stern man named Birch, aptly enough, and he was not popular. He was duly murdered—ignominiously stabbed to death while easing himself in an outhouse over the Perak River—and the British promptly installed a rival family to the sultanate and sent Abdullah and his retinue packing to the Seychelles where, in the manner of all good royal stories, their descendants live to this day.)

The Chinese paid little heed to the Pangkor Treaty at the time, but soon enough, worn out by the interminable bloodletting and cognizant of the new administrative machinery gradually being installed in Perak by the British, they accepted peace for themselves. They did so in that little mining post upriver, and that was why it came to be named "Taiping". ❑

My Grandfather's Notebook

THE HOUSE was still there. What would have become of me if it wasn't? I would have stood dumb as a statue and desolate as driftwood by an empty lot on Hale Lane, Assam Kumbang, Taiping, staring into a vacuum ....

But there it was, gazing cataractedly through shuttered windows upon its quadrangle of sand, where the rambutan tree had grown big and wide and the durian tree had been felled. (The durian tree, planted as a seed on the day of my birth, had shot up straight and tall but had never borne fruit worthy of the name. There had been a big storm some years before, and the tree had listed dangerously. It had had to go. But the rambutan tree ... I could not look at it without seeing the sparklers of Hari Raya, the Festival of Aidil Fitri, tracing fiery circles in the luminous night beneath its boughs; round and round they spun, comets around the son, until I tripped in the sand and fell, spraining an eight-year-old ankle ....)

Taiping had been more than recognizable—it seemed hardly to have changed. The first Malaysian town of any size to be bypassed by the north-south trunk road, Taiping had settled into a gentle dotage of old colonial buildings and wooden houses and stately schools: St George's, King Edward's. But the pride of history had long abounded in Taiping—even the local workingmen's club was proudly emblazoned with the year of its founding, 1901—and continued to imbue the town with a strong resistance to change. The people of Taiping liked their town as it was—their botanical gardens were still the loveliest in the land, and the rain of Maxwell Hill (or Bukit Larut, the rain mattered more than the name) continued to keep Taiping fresh and clean and green and the wettest place in Malaysia. Taiping was a sweet place to live, and anyone who didn't think so was free to live elsewhere. Taiping was still the Pensioner's Paradise; the Nicest Hometown in Malaysia.

But the pace of Malaysian change had left me giddy and amazed ever since crossing the border—villages had grown into towns, towns had webbed into conurbations of housing estates and factories, new roads and highways lanced across the land, presenting unfamiliar new landscapes to the eye—and not until I was actually standing in front of my ancestral home did I allow myself to believe it was still there.

And yes, there it was, stolid and imposing as ever, if feeble now in the gloaming of its years. Wooden houses do not last; wood is alive and therefore must die. This house was now ten years older than my grandfather had been at his death, and nearly twice as old as my father at his. It was near the end. The pale blue of its God-knew-how-manyth coat of paint was flaking inexorably into powder and dust as had all the others before it (this house having been in various decades white, yellow, green). Its stilt legs were shaky and grey, the grain of the wood wide and deep as a patriarch's wrinkles. The groundfloor rooms seemed empty and dead, although there was evidence that someone still occupied them. (A child's red bicycle, glimpsed through the cobwebs and dust of a metal-latticed window.) The stairs to the upper floor, their wood worn smooth as river rock, sagged and creaked. (How high those stairs to the child!) The house was silent. (But then, its only noise had been the cries of children.)

"BOOMAAAAAH!!"—a child cried from the quadrangle of sand, clutching a sprained ankle, fighting back the tears ....

From deep within the upper rooms there came an answering holler: "Oi! Who's that?"

"Come and see!"

A window rattled open. In its frame appeared the face of my maiden aunt Sarimah—Pupu Mah. (She had finally experimented with marriage at the age of forty-seven; it hadn't worked.) She was sixty now. The face had grown wide and pudgy, the mouth betel-black and toothless, but she still wore her hair the way she always had: parted in the middle, clasped on either side with a brace of barrettes. Her eyes squinted myopically down at me, then widened in recognition. She emitted the familiar Pupu Mah call, known and loved by her nieces and nephews since the ages of two. It is not easily rendered in writing: a nasal howl, emanating from somewhere above the epiglottis and rebounding through the prefrontal sinuses before emerging from all oral cavities as "AAAAAOOOOWW!!" rising through the octaves to a credible high-C, followed by the name of the blessed child concerned. Which was, in this case, mine.

The doors were flung open; an enormous woman completely filled the space between the jambs, her arms flung wide as Hercules' at the Temple. I shucked off my shoes and clambered up the stairs to disappear in a vast embrace, betel-fragrant kisses on both cheeks. "Where have you been? I haven't seen you for so long! Don't know when I'll see you again!" But she always says that.

The rooms of my ancestors were a mess. Pupu Mah lived there alone now, running a fair business as the neighbourhood seamstress. Sewing machines and cutting tables; bolts of bright cloth draped upon every surface, multicoloured skeins of thread lay coiled like worms on the floor. But still on the walls, where they had hung for three decades, the fading sepia-toned photographs of my generation: my brothers, my cousins, me, as children of two and six and seven. And through the now-open windows and door blew the sweet soft breeze off Maxwell Hill, smelling of river sand and rambutans, rain and childhood, of Taiping.

Pupu Mah sculpted out of the clutter a space for us to sit. "Sorry lah, such a mess! But Bu Mah lives here alone now, so who cares?" She laughed her high-pitched cackle of a laugh, which sounded exactly like her mother's—my grandmother, my Dadee.

"You look well, Bu Mah."

"I'm old and fat and ugly. Only five teeth left. But I'm well enough."

"Business is good?"

"Can do. People have more money these days. So they want more clothes. Sometimes I'm too busy." On cue, the telephone rang. She attended to the customer's needs. "Next week!" she yelled into the receiver, "I said next week! I can't do it any sooner!" She listened for a moment. "Okay," she resumed, "I'll do my best." Replacing the handset, she feigned exasperation. "See? Every few minutes, triiinngg! triiinngg! How to work?"

"Better that than the phone doesn't ring at all."

"Ya lah, Bu Mah is always complaining. Where are you staying? You can stay here. Have you been to see Dadee yet?"

My grandmother lived a fifteen-minute walk away in a somewhat more elegant part of town, in a spacious brick bungalow bought for her some years before by one of her sons. My uncle Halim, a successful businessman, had wanted Bu Mah to move out of the old Hale Lane house too. The house was too rickety and dangerous, he'd said. He had a good point. But Bu Mah would have none of it. "I told Halim they'll have to lift me out of here with a crane," she said. "This house goes, I go with it. I go, this house goes with me. This house was Dada's gift to me."

I'd heard this before, too, although many years ago there had been some ambiguity over what my grandfather had truly intended for this house. But he had died in 1952, three years before I was born, and Pupu Mah's durable insistence over the decades had eventually worn down the collective family resistance. Besides, she was the only one who really wanted to live there; was happy to get by without a flushing toilet. So she had become, triumphantly, custodian of the ancestral abode. I was always grateful to her for that. But the place was a mess, and decidedly fragile, and since childhood I had done my damnedest to avoid ever having to take a shit there, preferring constipation and the subsequent ordeal of castor oil to the horror of the bucket latrine out back. So:

"Thanks, Bu Mah, but I was hoping to stay with Dadee. No, I haven't been to see her yet. I wanted to see the old house first."

"Yes, this old house. Your Dada's house." A mist of memory veiled her eyes. "Your father's room was downstairs." (The child's red bicycle.) "After your grandfather retired he retreated from the world. He said out there it was all wrong. He stayed up here and never left the house. His friends would come to see him. They'd talk for hours. When they weren't around he'd sit on his bed and write and write."

I knew this. It had always been impressed upon us that our grandfather had been a most literate man. It was from him that my father was said to have gained his own erudition, which in turn had been passed along the genetic chain to me. But I'd never seen anything my grandfather had ever written.

"Don't know what he'd write," my aunt continued. "He left a whole stack of notebooks. Don't know where they all are now. Perhaps one of your uncles has them. I only kept one, for remembrance."

"YOU KEPT ONE?!"

"Yes. Haven't I ever shown it to you?"

"NO!"

Pupu Mah heaved herself up and waddled off into her bedroom, emerging a moment later with a slim, hardcover book. She handed it gently to me, with both hands. It was a 1950 diary. "He used the wrong ink," she said. "He should have used good English ink. But he used cheap Chinese ink. Now the paper's all brittle and you can hardly read it."

It was true. The pages crumbled like dry toast. But the handwriting was still legible enough in parts. My grandfather wrote in a strong and elegant hand, in an English formal and antique:

"Every man's task is his life preserver. The conviction that his work is dear to God and cannot be spared defends him.

"There can be no greatness without abandonment. Just to fill the hour—that is happiness. What has been best done in the world—the work of genius — cost nothing. No painful effort, but the spontaneous flowing of thought. Shakespeare made his Hamlet as a bird weaves its nest. Poems have been written between sleeping and waking, irresponsibly. The poet was never the poorer for his song. Those only can sleep who do not care to sleep; and those only write or speak best who do not too much respect the writing or the speaking ....

"Character is the highest name at which philosophy has arrived. Character makes us great in all conditions. It is the only definition we have of freedom and power."

And then there came this tirade, and forty years of silence sundered in the thunder:

"Nothing comes to the bookshops but politics, travel, statistics, tabulation and engineering. Even what is called philosophy and letters is mechanical in structure, as if inspiration had ceased, as if no hope, no religion, no song of joy, no wisdom existed any more. The tone of colleges and of scholars and literary society has this mortal air. They exert every variety of talent on a lower ground, and may be said to live and act in a sub-mind. I seem to walk on a marble floor, where nothing will grow ....

"As they trample on the nationalities to reproduce London and Londoners in Asia, so they fear the hostility of ideas, of poetry, of religion—ghosts they cannot lay; and having attempted to domesticate and dress the Blessed Soul itself in English broadcloth and gaiters, they are tormented with fear that herein lurks a force that will sweep their system away ....

"In the absence of the highest aims, of the pure love of knowledge and surrender to nature, there is suppression of the imagination, the priapism of the senses ... we have the factitious instead of the natural, tasteless expense, arts of comfort, and the rewarding as an illustrious inventor whosoever will contrive one impediment more to interpose between man and his objects.

"Thus poetry is degraded, and made ornamental. We want the miraculous; the beauty which we can manufacture at no mill. Poetry exists to speak the spiritual law."

And then the righteous torrent abated, distilling into an elixir of aphorisms:

"The education of the will is the object of existence."

"Have the courage not to adopt another's courage."

And, most resonantly of all to the eldest grandson of Ismail bin Kassim Ali, feverishly transcribing the words of the grandfather he had never known:

"He has not learned the lesson of life who does not every day surmount a fear."

I put aside my notebook, gazed reverently at his. "Bu Mah," I said, "this is great stuff." She nodded. "Your Dada was a very holy man," she said. Holy? The guy was a nationalist! A revolutionary! At least, at heart. But he was just a schoolmaster born with the century in British Malaya, who chose to retire at fifty and died of bronchitis two years later. Every Hari Raya morning while my father was alive, he would take us to visit his father's unprepossessing grave in the grounds of Taiping's Old Mosque. That grave, and a single old photograph of a stern-faced man in a tweed jacket, sitting in a wicker armchair and holding a cane, was all I'd ever known of my grandfather. But it was a face that had been mirrored in my father's, and now, at last, I could hear at least an echo of the voice that had gone with it.

It was a diligent and impassioned voice, but in all it sang a monotonous song: a simple plea, clothed in elaborate metaphor, for devotion to God. But its power was there, and undeniable: after forty years, his sentiments remained valid. Were his language judiciously edited into modern idiom, my grandfather's thoughts would almost certainly command a receptive audience today.

I seem to walk on a marble floor, where nothing will grow ....

The last entry in that diary:

"This book contains philosophy and advice for the guidance of young people in particular who wish to gain some knowledge which matters a good deal. Taiping. 29/3/1950."

Ismail Kassim Ali had been a teacher to the very last. ❑

3

I WAS BORN the first child of a young Malay teacher and his teenage bride, only one of whom was present at the time.

My father was the scion of a venerable family, and his paternal ancestry led back through northern India, the Punjab and Afghanistan to, the family legend had it, Arabia in the time of the Prophet Muhammad. My earliest Malayan ancestors on my father's side, according to this myth, came to the Peninsula in the wake of the Indian Mutiny of 1857. They were staunch Muslims, steeped in Sufi mysticism. They bore for generations the title "Sheikh", distinguishing themselves as descendants of the Prophet's Companions. My father was the last to bear this honorific, however, or rather the first to relinquish his claim to it, because in his view the connection had grown far too remote and diluted by legend to set much store by, especially when its effect was to elevate one above the mass of the Muslim faithful.

Nonetheless, the Islamic pedigree of my paternal ancestors, and their consequently superior bearing, no doubt, granted them good stead in the local communities to which they gravitated. They married into Malay families and eventually settled in Taiping. There, they easily adopted Malay customs and manners and began attaining enduring reputations as teachers and healers; men of learning. They, and their sons and daughters, were striking people: unusually tall and handsome in a big-boned, hefty way.

In time, there grew to be no question but that they were Perak Malays, for all their Arab-Indian stock, but within the confines of the family there was an elaborate architecture of honorifics. Each position from the patriarch to the latest infant had its appropriate term of reference, a tradition that always seemed to me, as a child, uniquely ours. Many years later, however, when reporting on the peripheries of the Afghan War, I would feel curiously at home in the Punjab or Northwest Frontier Province of Pakistan, where these same terms and titles were used. My own name was unusual in Malaya, where Allah's attribute of beneficence was invariably rendered "Rahman", but in the environs of Peshawar it was all over the place. "Rehman Spray-Paint Workshop". "Rehman Flying Bus Service". Most memorably, "Rehman Guns & Ammunition". (I believe I have a photograph of myself pointing a finger at that one.) In Malaysia, however, there were times when I'd been driven to distraction by Malays who insisted that the clerk who'd filled in my birth certificate had made a spelling mistake.

But then, these were times during which the Malays were growing more fiercely protective of their own conventions than ever before. Not that that ever lessened my umbrage at their presumptions.

My father was the eldest of Ismail Kassim Ali's seven children, most of them sons. My mother was the eldest of eight, all but one of them daughters, a fact which might have influenced the decision of my solitary maternal uncle to join the Merchant Navy at the age of nineteen.

My mother's father was Indian: his father had left their ancestral village in Tamil Nadu at the dawn of the 20th Century, coming to Malaya as one of the thousands of southern Indian labourers brought in by the British to work the burgeoning rubber plantations. Periasamy was to settle in a small town at the mouth of the Perak River. His son Ratnam, my mother's father, was born in that town: Telok Anson as it was then, Teluk Intan as it is now. Ratnam worked on the Malayan Railways with the Telecoms authority, stringing up the telegraph lines that followed the railways as they opened up the peninsular hinterland. He married a Eurasian woman—my mother's mother—whose own ancestry led via the Portuguese enclave of Goa to, it was said, Madagascar, where her grandfather had once operated an ice factory. My grandfather, Hindu to the core until love wrought its usual effects, accepted Catholicism in quest of Henrietta Rodrigues's hand, and he adopted the Christian name "Raymond". This was another reason adduced for the name I was given, which on that side of my family would always be pronounced that way, but without the "d", of course.

Somewhere on the mainland near Penang lived an old Chinese woman whom my mother called "Grandma"—she was the third wife of my great-grandfather the ice-man. And there's no forgetting Old Jaafar, an Acehnese Muslim rice-seller who used to cater to the church-goers of Penang's Pulau Tikus every Sunday morning in the 1880s. Jaafar eventually decided to become a Christian himself, adopting the name "Joachim Daniel". He married a woman named Josephine. They begat a daughter, who married a Rodrigues soon after the turn of the century and in 1912 gave birth to my grandmother Henrietta.

Ah, this tangled web; how utterly Malaysian it is! In the shelter of the twin wings of my family I have cousins surnamed Halim, Aziz, Ghani, Wee, Ratnam, Kannabhiran, Arumugam, Marshall, Rodrigues. (And Keese and Kuylaars, for good measure, who were born in Australia and Holland, respectively.)

These twin eastward streams, then, one crossing overland from the Persian Gulf, the other flowing to the south, would each in the course of centuries refract through the great lens of India to meet and mingle in 20th-Century Malaya, and be in turn joined by the welter of tributaries flowing down from China. From here they would spread even further, sometimes doubling back on themselves to inoculate Western lands with the serum of their own multi-hued futures.

A hundred years or so ago, the pioneering immigrants whose descendants would shape Malaysia's unique modern identity were not often able—or willing, for that matter—to bring their womenfolk with them. In the early stages of their Malayan lives, few immigrants believed they would stay longer than necessary to earn enough money to go home, as the Chinese saying had it, "in silken robes". But for the majority of them, dreams of success quickly faded into the more elemental struggle merely to survive. Brothels, then as now, provided but fleeting relief. Intermarriage soon became the norm, and today there can be few Malaysians whose family trees do not resemble a banyan, the single tree that looks like a self-contained forest, with its superabundance of roots, each indistinguishable from a trunk.

Mine is not an unusual genealogy, and I outline it here to underscore a point I hope the Malaysian reader will recognize: that of our homeland being a confluence of destinies; history's intertidal zone. Here, catalyzed by the millennial ebbing and flowing of empires from the Hindu to the European, the great Indian and Chinese spheres coalesced, giving rise in time to a Malay culture so identifiably the progeny of both.

Which is not to say that such thoughts were uppermost in the minds of the young man and woman who would be my parents, as they courted each other against the backdrop of a country readying itself for nationhood. My father would regularly drive the hundred kilometres north from Taiping to Bukit Mertajam, where my mother's family lived in humble quarters by the railway lines, to woo her with his poetry and charm (not to mention his open-topped Austin Seven cabriolet). A Malay, Muslim youth and an Indian, Christian girl: but their disparate ancestries had become intertwined in a common language, which was English, and united by what their generation was convinced had to be a common future, which was Malayan.

Perhaps I make it sound easy; it was not. My parents' generation, as with probably each generation before and certainly since, did not share all the values of *their* parents. On both sides of what was to become my family, there were misgivings over the cross-cultural liaison my parents intended;

neither set of parents were, to begin with, very happy with the idea of their first-born children marrying out of their respective cultures. But love once again did its legendary thing, and triumphed.

So Rita Lucy Rukumani Ratnam, the eldest daughter of Raymond Periasamy Ratnam and Henrietta Rodrigues, converted to Islam, adopting the name Rosna binti Abdullah, and married Abdul Rashid bin Ismail, eldest son of Ismail bin Kassim Ali and Mariam binti Sharif, in January 1955. I was born, on cue, that October. About the first thing that happened was that both families ceased bellyaching about the sundering of traditions. I was the first of the next generation for both sides, and with my apparently insistent existence, as advertised by what was by all accounts an impressively healthy set of lungs, both the Ratnams and Ismails took due notice of the *fait accompli* of their continued participation in the ethno-cultural *mélange* their nation was destined to be. They got used to it quickly enough, which was just as well: attention to cultural stability hadn't exactly been high on either of their agendas for the preceding couple of centuries. ❑

The Matriarch

MARIAM BINTI SHARIF was saying her prayers, but I was welcome to come in and wait for her. I was Rashid's son? Fancy that. My, how I had grown. Tok Yam would surely be happy to see me. Would I care for something to drink?

No, thanks. I would wait for Dadee.

The woman—a distant relative I could not quite recognize—padded back into the kitchen. The lounge was cool and deep in shadow. Rugs and carpets covered the marble floor. Religious inscriptions decorated a wall or two. The furniture was comfortable—fabric-covered sofas and armchairs—but it felt hardly used. The lounge looked out on a wide and well-tended lawn, out of which grew a few small fruit trees too young to bear fruit. Viewed from the gloom inside the house, the evening light outside seemed bright—but it was dimensionless and flat as a blank canvas. A sparrow lit upon a hibiscus bush; a blossom bent beneath its tiny weight. Schoolgirls in white head-scarves and turquoise skirts cycled past like sailing ships. Overhead, dark clouds gathered; in the smell of the air was a promise of Taiping's famous rain.

People speak of houses as "lived-in", and other people know exactly what they mean. Something indefinable but easily recognized characterizes a "lived-in" house. What? Books and newspapers and magazines on side tables? Dust in ashtrays? Circles of damp where drinks recently stood uncoastered? Whatever: a house is "lived-in" when there is even the faintest musk of occupation about it. The ruffle of an antimacassar; indentations on the seats of settees; an arrangement of furniture that betrays its use for conversation or conviviality or even a communal watching of television.

My grandmother's house was not such a house. The furniture was immaculate. Not a speck of dust clouded the humblest surface. Porcelain flowers stood frozen in a china bowl. No motion stirred the enclosed air. All was silence and stillness. And why should it have been otherwise? My grandmother was eighty-two years old. She had already outlived her husband by forty years and her eldest child by twenty-four. She had outlived all her siblings. Her youngest child was nearly fifty; her eldest grandchild thirty-seven.

The house on Hale Lane had been a-shriek with children and thunderous with their parents warning them to be quiet or risk the unspeakable. There had been chatter in the kitchen, a constant counterpoint to the sounds of constant cooking. There had been songs in the bathrooms and music from the wireless. There had always been the tremor of footsteps on wooden floors and staircases. Even in the depths of night, the house had whispered and creaked and snored; always and at the very least, the sound of breathing, of gentle sleep. As a child, I had never known the house with fewer than half-a-dozen people in it at any one time. My happiest, and therefore clearest, memories—of festive times—involved at least that many sleeping cheek-by-jowl on the living room floor.

But my grandmother no longer lived in the house on Hale Lane, and in this bungalow on its half-acre of land there were no stairs. (Indeed, that had been one of the main reasons for her moving here: as a courtesy to octogenarian knees.)

Ah, but why do I skirt the issue so? My grandmother was preparing for death, and the house reflected this, in its shadows and silence and stillness, in its pristine and almost unnatural cleanliness. Just as the house on Hale Lane had reflected the youthfulness and joy of a large family reaching its time of greatest vitality—marriages, births, the advent of the next generation—so did my grandmother's new house mirror the closing of a long life; the gentle, insistent, imminence of death.

"Ha, who's this?"

I stood up and turned to face her. She stood framed in the open door to her bedroom, silhouetted by the yellow spill of light from within. I noticed a prayer mat on the floor; her white prayer robes neatly draped upon her bed. She seemed tiny. (I remembered a monumental woman, great cliffs of motherhood in the shelter of which I would huddle safe and snug and six years old, lying beside her as she slept, vaguely aware of great peril should she roll over in her sleep—but of course she never did.) She wore a woollen head covering, like a beret, bright yellow, and a homely cotton blouse and floral *sarong.* Her face was soft as a cloud, and her eyes danced with light. I stepped forward so that the light would reach my face. "Dadee," I said, "it's Rehman."

"La-illaha-illallah ..." She reached up and cupped my faced in both hands—they felt as fragile as a sparrow's wings. I grasped her fingers and bent forward to kiss them. She touched the top of my head. "So at last you've come to see your old grandmother ... come and sit down, my grandson, let me look at you." We sat in the lounge. The sofa hardly registered her weight. "You're darker than ever," she said, with a chuckle that shook her entire body. "You've been walking around in the sun, perhaps. Still wandering?"

"Still. It's something I have to do. I'm writing a book on Malaysia."

"Writing a book! You are your father's son all right. You're still young. When you reach forty you won't have the energy. But when are you going to have a family?"

"I don't know. It doesn't seem fated just yet."

She grimaced. "Well if it's not fated it's not fated. Why am I so old? I'm waiting for death. Why am I waiting so long? Waiting for you to have a child, perhaps. I tell you, you're keeping me alive. I won't go until you make me a great-grandmother!"

"But Dadee, you already are," I laughed. Two of my cousins had given her a total of four great-grandchildren between them, and more were on the way.

"I know, but it's yours I want to see. I want to see Rashid's grandchild before I go. So don't dilly-dally. I'm sure your mother would agree. How is she? She came to see me not long ago. She's gone very grey, but she seems healthy enough. It was nice of her to come. She stayed here for a few nights. We talked about old times." And she fell silent for a long moment, gazing ruminantly out at the rain-threatened twilight that had begun to settle upon the garden.

I believed I could sense the profundity of that silence. When my father died, there had been an attempt by his family to gain custody of his three young sons; there had been fears that my mother, born a Christian and a convert to Islam, would not raise us as Muslims. But my mother would have bested battalions to keep us, and she staunchly fended off these misguided initiatives. It was not a trauma easily forgotten, however, and for several years we were estranged from my father's family. It took that long for my brothers and me to grow up and prove those fears to have been unfounded. It also took that long for my uncles and aunts—and Dadee herself—to grow old, to mellow, to be soothed into acceptance, then respect, by the blessed anaesthesia of time.

"Have you eaten?" asked Dadee, stirring out of her reverie. I shook my head. "There's food here,"—but there was always food in Dadee's house—"I can cook you something. I'll get Kak Bee to set the table. You put your bag in the front room." There was no question, of course, but that I would stay a night or two in my grandmother's house.

But no longer. The past is a different country; strangers live there. I felt an interloper in that sepulchrally silent house, desperately seeking evidence of my right to be there. There were pictures of a certain small boy in my grandmother's photo album ... that small boy was the only legitimacy I had there, and he was gone, long gone, never to return. To believe that he remained somewhere within this large, steadily ageing, clumsy body was an act of faith no different from the soft mumbles and chants that emanated from my grandmother's room all day and half the night.

But my grandmother knew what she was doing, which was more than I could truthfully admit of myself. Her mind had lost none of its edge, nor her tongue its acid. Religion was an intensely private affair, she saw now. Those so-called priests—and where were there "priests" in Islam?—were like corralled buffaloes (how slashingly euphonious her Malay: *kerbau dalam kandang!*) chewing the grass under their noses, slurping water from a trough, then flopping over, BOOM!, to stare at the stars and say "ah yes, there is a God".

And the politicians, "HAH! Your grandfather, after the war, he and his buddies went around collecting money and clothes to give to the needy, and did he care whether they were brown or yellow or even white? Food, he collected. Clothes, cash. He and his friends were doing the real work, while all those others—oh, such big people now—were talking politics. That's why when he retired he wanted nothing more to do with the world. He just sat at home and talked religion and philosophy with his friends until 3:00 a.m."

I said: "If we had to choose between the mind and the heart, perhaps we should choose the heart."

"No," she said. "Choose both. We need both. Otherwise what the heart chooses, the mind rejects. What the mind chooses, the heart rejects. Bring your heart and your mind together. Sit them down in chairs together. Let them discuss!" She chortled, amused by her imagery.

When the time came for me to leave, early on the third morning after my return to Taiping, she walked me to the front gate. The driveway was puddled with water from the previous night's rain; the morning air was soft and sweet. I kissed her hands again. "Don't stay away so long this time." she said. I promised her I would not; I hoped never to have to leave Malaysia again. "I don't know how much longer I have," she said.

"Dadee," I said, "you've been saying that as long as I can remember."

"But it's true. Every new day is a bonus. Not just when you're old like me. Who knows how long anyone has? Your father didn't." She unlatched the gate, swung it open for me. "You know, I dreamed of your father last night," she said. "He was wearing a crown. He was being served. Like a king. I dream of him quite often these days." A tear appeared at the corner of her eye; she paid it no heed. ❑

4

INDEPENDENCE came. Preparations had been avid. In Kuala Lumpur, Tunku Abdul Rahman (henceforth, to accord with the respectful affection traditionally afforded him: "The Tunku") had spied a likely hilltop upon which to build a big football stadium. He had been a keen sportsman as a youth, and he not unreasonably surmised that sport would be a splendid unifying force for his beloved new nation. What finer symbol of Independence, therefore, than a spanking new stadium? That and an equally fine new mosque for the capital, to symbolize the elevation of Islam to the exalted temporal rank of official state religion, as decreed in Malaya's Independence Constitution. So the summit of this hill in Kuala Lumpur was levelled for the National Stadium, and the earth removed from the hill was used to fill in a valley below, and on this site was built the National Mosque.

At midnight on August 30, 1957, British Malaya ceased to exist. One second into August 31, the Independent Federation of Malaya came into being. The Union Jack was ceremoniously lowered, and the crescent-star and stripes was raised in its place. This happened all over the country, but the pre-eminent locus for this marvellous moment was the cricket field of Kuala Lumpur's Selangor Club, that supreme bastion of colonial privilege. The club, its field and the grand clock-towered building that would eventually be the seat of the nation's judiciary would attain an iconic significance forever after. They remain Malaysia's most familiar landmarks.

The formal handing-over ceremony, with its documents, dignitaries and feathered caps, took place the following afternoon in the National Stadium, which would thenceforth be known as Stadium Merdeka—Independence Stadium—for it was here that the Tunku led a rousing chorus of the word that had come to mean the world to Malaya. "MERDEKA!" he shouted, again and again, seven times in all, his frail 53-year-old voice charged with more energy than anyone could remember having heard in it before, and the crowds exultantly echoed him.

One may hear a tape-recording of this event at the National Museum in Kuala Lumpur: the Tunku's voice calling out the Word, and the people's response like surf on a seashore, washing out again and again, billowing out of Merdeka Stadium up to the heavens and into history. Many a time have I listened to that sound, and many a time have I wished that I might have been there. Oh, to have joined in that magnificent open-throated shout! Never again would anything in this nation seem so right, so true, and so good. It was the best of all possible delusions, and gladly would I have surrendered to its glorious seduction.

But I was less than two years old when the Tunku's life reached its apogee. He would live to be a very old man, dying in 1990 at the age of eighty-seven, but his longevity was in many ways a curse. He would live to see his dream usurped and distorted ... but perhaps it wasn't all that realistic a dream to begin with.

The Tunku had been a link-man; accepted by the British as the best possible leader of the fractured and disparate Malaya they had done so much to create and were now leaving behind. If anyone could clean up this mess and make something of it, the Tunku could. Consider: He was a bona fide blue-blooded prince, scion of the Kedah royal family. (That took care of the sultanates.) He enjoyed horse-racing. (The Chinese could relate to that.) He was from the north of the peninsula, historically the arrival-point of the Indian community, and he was fond of the Indians, in a distantly paternal way. (Which was all they could really ask.) And he was an Anglophile through-and-through, having spent much of his youth as a law student in Britain, where he had led a dilettante lifestyle and developed what would be an abiding nostalgia for open-topped sports cars and English university towns in autumn. Who better to bid goodbye to Empire?

The Tunku's would be a gracious farewell to the old order, and a promising welcome to the new. Indeed—and this was the irony, and the tragedy—if there was one Malayan community that held reservations over the choice of Tunku Abdul Rahman as their nation's first prime minister, it was his own.

To many of the Malays who had fuelled the post-war nationalist movement, the Tunku was a little *too* "Malayan", in the overtones of the term preferred by the British. A little too tolerant of the Chinese, a little too fond of the Indians, and a whole lot too English for their tastes. But in the eleven years since the founding of Umno, other leaders had come and gone with their various manifestos and blueprints. The Malays recognized the Tunku as the best choice they had, and there was no ignoring the willingness, even the eagerness, of the Chinese and Indian political leaders to work with him in their Alliance government. They were as English-educated as the Tunku, and could speak on equal terms with him. It made for the necessary consociations demanded by Independence.

So, for the time being, the Malays of Umno would abide by the Tunku. But in his enthusiasm for a "Malayan Malaya", they hoped he wouldn't forget which Malayan community had been there the longest; and whom the country had been named after; and who'd started the political ball rolling before anyone else, at which time the Chinese had been still sending millions of dollars back to China; and which community was pound-for-pound still the poorest in the land.

But it remained a day of celebration. There were beauty contests, parties and parades. Nationalists who had sworn not to cut their hair until this day went in search of barbers, only to find that most of them were enjoying Malaya's first National Day holiday. Kuala Lumpur's movie-houses were thronged, and the Cathay cinema claimed the honour of being the first to play the new national anthem, *Negara Ku,* "My Nation". It was mostly foreigners who respectfully stood up, however, as most Malayans had yet to recognize the tune. Well, not exactly: the tune itself may have been familiar to some, because it had been lifted note-for-note from an old Indonesian folksong titled "Light of the Moon", but this was its first use in its new guise, with its new lyrics. ("Light of the Moon" was never to be performed in Malaya again, on pain of treason.)

In the north, a bedraggled Chinese youth named Siew Fong stepped out of the jungle and surrendered himself to the nearest police station. "With Independence," he told startled constables, "we are already free." But he was untypical of his Communist brethren, and in Penang, police had to remove from certain quarters the flags of Red China that had mysteriously sprouted overnight.

But it was, nonetheless, a happy day.

The Alliance government set to work immediately. In the new Parliament, all but one of the fifty-two seats belonged to the Alliance. The lone Oppositionist was from the Pan-Malayan Islamic Party, which had contested Malaya's first elections as advocates of an Islamic republic in Malaya. They had been clearly rejected by the populace as a whole, but their pockets of support, focused in the state of Kelantan in the northeast of the peninsula, would prove durable indeed. Still, with but one parliamentarian to their cause, the fundamentalists could be ignored for the time being.

Not so with the Chinese. Malaya greeted Independence with a population of some 10 million, only half of which was Malay. The Indian community made up less than a tenth, and a sorely afflicted 10% at that. During the War, the Japanese had rounded up Indians by the thousand and sent them off to build their Burma railway—the Death Railway, as it would be known later. My grandfather had been among them, and was one of the few to live through the experience. One correspondent of the time described the survivors as "crawling skeletons". By the end of the war, Malaya's Indian community had been decimated. It was one of the reasons the Malayan Indian Congress was the last of the three major ethnic political parties to join the Alliance. Their community was still only fitfully recovering by the time of Independence.

Which left the Chinese in serious competition with the Malays for the right, in numbers, to call the place their own.

The fear of becoming a minority in their homeland had been central to the nascence of Malay politics in the immediate aftermath of the Second World War. That fear had been compounded by the peculiar fact of the war having been fought in, essentially, two countries: a bifurcated Malaya. The Chinese had suffered far more than the Malays at the hands of the Japanese, who had visited upon them all the furies they had stoked since the Manchurian invasion. While the Malays had largely stood by and watched, hundreds of Chinese had fled into the jungles to mount an armed resistance of their own. They had fashioned themselves into the Malayan People's Anti-Japanese Army, and they were ferocious foes of the invader.

The MPAJA fought a guerrilla war of liberation, and they were ideologically fuelled by the similar struggle taking place in their great ancestral homeland to the north. Out of this jungle army would evolve the military wing of the Malayan Communist Party. The end of the war in the Pacific meant little to these presumptive communist liberationists. In 1948, when it had become clear that post-war Malaya would have no truck with their ambitions, they launched the campaign of assassinations that marked the beginning of the Emergency.

The Emergency was to last a dozen years. It was declared officially ended in 1960, when the new nation was three years old. This victory, such as it was, had not come cheap. It had taken a career army officer, General Sir Gerald Templer, to give full rein to the military's perception that the communists were drawing their lifeblood from Malaya's civilian communities, and that the control of these communities was the key to defanging the terrorists. When he was appointed High Commissioner of Malaya in 1952, following the assassination of his predecessor, Sir Henry Gurney, Templer dismissed politics as a luxury for peacetime. He accelerated the "Briggs Plan", launched two years before by General Sir Harold Briggs, the Emergency's first Director of Operations.

The Briggs Plan sought to sever the communists' civilian lifelines. Entire hamlets were transplanted to hastily built "New Villages" and encircled with barbed wire, sentry towers and checkpoints. Identity cards were introduced. Communist-infested areas were branded "black", and their residents were subject to strict curfews and restricted in their movements.

It was an extraordinary effort, and it reached its apotheosis in the town of Tanjong Malim, which straddled the border of Selangor and Perak. In March 1952, there was a particularly brutal ambush of government engineers sent to repair the town's sabotaged water pipeline. Templer demanded that the people of Tanjong Malim reveal what they knew of communist activities in their area. Nothing happened, and Templer ordered that Tanjong Malim be kept under a 22-hour curfew until something did. No one was allowed to leave the town, the schools were closed and every resident's rice ration was halved. Templer effectively took an entire town prisoner for fourteen days. And got the information he'd sought.

The Tanjong Malim experience was a turning-point in the campaign. If the New Villages resembled concentration camps, the similarity was not accidental. Templer had demonstrated a steely resolve to deal with the enemy's suppliers as harshly as if they were the enemy themselves. With their supply founts dwindling and the sources of their succour and recruitment sealed, the communist battalions were driven further and further upcountry, their ragged remnants eventually melting into the deep forests of the Thai border. One after another, "black" areas were redesignated "white", life returned to normal for their inhabitants, and the threat of communist attack retreated to a distant periphery of the national consciousness.

But there was a subtext to the anti-communist campaign that would long haunt Malaysia, for the communists, and their supporters in the civilian population, were predominantly Chinese. For decades thereafter, Templer's New Villages, some of which would grow into bustling towns, but all of which would remain resolutely Chinese, with their schools and basketball courts and temples and pig-farms and market-gardens and their graveyards on their hills, would remain a visible reminder that the Enemy in the Blanket had yellow skin, not brown.

It was a terrible legacy of a terrible time, all the more so because it added yet another overlay of resentment against the Chinese. By then, their community, with its merchants and middlemen, had already been portrayed as rapacious exploiters of the poor, innocent Indigene. Gone was the image of the Chinese as tireless worker, enduring an arduous life with stoic stamina, scraping by on the edge of starvation, saving every cent he could for the sake of a better life in some distant future. In its place: the predator, the vulture and, in his heart of hearts, the patriotic point-man of Red China.

So, despite the good cheer and camaraderie of Independence Day, and despite the complete parliamentary dominance of the Alliance, the Malays and Chinese of Malaya were not the closest of friends in the new nation. There was simply too much historical baggage between them to blithely set aside.

The Tunku knew this, and he knew that the first task of the new nation had to be a redressal of its discomfiting demographics. (Ho! The ingrained reflex of the Malaysian journalist: he slumps behind a thicket of jargon when plain words seem altogether too bald.) But this the Tunku was advised: The Malays had to gain a clear majority of the population of Malaya, and be assured of never losing it.

There were three ways to achieve this. One: the Malays could breed like there was no tomorrow. But that would still take too long; generational change was no answer to immediate problems. Two: Singapore could be asked to leave. The island city was very much an entity unto itself, having been a British territory held separate from Malaya since Sir Stamford Raffles appropriated it from the Johor Sultanate in 1819. With Malayan independence, however, there had been a *de facto* amalgamation of Singapore into the Federation. The association was never formally ratified, but it was nonetheless a fact of the new Malayan national identity—and a most significant one: Singapore was home to one in five of the Federation's Chinese.

Without Singapore, Malaya's ethnic mosaic would be less ambiguous, and much more identifiably Malay. But Singapore's chief minister, the youthful Lee Kuan Yew, would not hear of it. Lee could not imagine how Singapore, resourceless and vulnerable, a Chinese gnat adrift on a twig in a Malay sea, could survive on its own. (How wrong he would be is another story. But he would be fabulously wrong.)

Three: the whole concept of "Malay"ness could be redefined. If the nub of the matter was the Indigene's fear of the Immigrant's domination, then it was the Indigene's community that needed to be expanded—not necessarily the Malay's.

In 1962, a delegation was sent to Borneo to canvass opinions among the people of Sarawak and Sabah. Both had been British territories on the fringes of the Dutch East Indies: Sarawak as the private fiefdom of the Brooke family; Sabah, the former British North Borneo, as an outpost of British commercial interests. The Cobbold Commission, as it was known, returned with the news that the people of Sarawak and Sabah would be happy to federate with Malaya. This came to pass in 1963, and thus Malaysia was created.

It remains one of the murkiest chapters in Malaysian history: very little of the Cobbold Commission's work was reported in the newspapers of the time, beyond the identities of its personnel, their objective, and eventually their results. This may have been prudent enough, given what was to happen in the region when the news of Malaysia's formation got out. But to sample the memories of most, it seems that Malayans woke up one morning in September 1963 to find themselves Malaysians, with a host of new fellow countrymen on the other side of the South China Sea. And such a host they were! Melanaus, Bajaus, Dayaks, Ibans, Penans, Kadazans, Bidayuhs, Kelabits, Kenyahs, Kayans, on and on and, as of that September morn, Malaysian Indigenes the lot of them.

It was a demographic coup of the highest order. The Chinese share of Malaysia's population dropped nearly five percentage points literally overnight. Two years later, Singapore was finally persuaded to leave the Federation. The indigenous communities of the reconstituted Malaysia could now legitimately claim nearly two-thirds of the total population, and the Malays were, at least in numbers, sitting pretty.

More to the point, the Chinese proportion of the population had been knocked down from nearly half to less than a third, and without so much as a single drop of blood being spilled in the process. This the Tunku did for all his people, and it was at about this time that he declared that his ambition was "to be the happiest prime minister in the world." ❑

The Temple Keeper

THE BARBED WIRE is long gone now, of course, and the village has spilled far beyond its original perimeter.

Indeed, Ulu Yam Baru is hardly a village anymore: perhaps 10,000 people live there now. The heart of their town is a single wide street lined with typical shophouses. There are coffee-shops and restaurants with red tablecloths. There are motorcycle workshops black with oil and grease, and spice-fragrant sundry stores festooned with brooms. There are beauty parlours and karaoke lounges. There is an air-conditioned snooker hall. Young girls sail by on bicycles. Children walk to school with knapsacks slung about their shoulders. Aborigines trudge in from the foothills bearing fruits and vegetables for sale by the roadside.

Just another small Malaysian town, some miles off the main road, not far from where the borders of Selangor, Perak and Pahang intersect; settled, domestic, "old place, tens of years old," said the young shopkeeper. But he was clearly measuring the town's age against his own, and the scales are different. For this is Ulu Yam Baru, and the "Baru" or "New" in its name betrays its provenance. Ulu Yam Baru was born with the Emergency. It was one of the first New Villages set up under the Briggs Plan to cut the lifelines of Malaya's communist terrorists.

The barbed wire and the watchtowers are gone, but it is as if they were still there: the New Villages remain characterized by a peculiar compactness. No matter how wide and empty the surrounding land, a New Village seems somehow to *huddle.* Houses edge together; lanes are narrow, straight and short. There is an inorganic feel about a New Village: it seems like an ancient abandoned jungle fortress, long overgrown but still somehow outlined from the surrounding terrain.

Ulu Yam Baru is 85% Chinese. It is quite prosperous now; a new road has been built through the Selangor hinterland and it passes straight through the town, which is coming alive with new traffic. The restaurants are doing better business; a travelling market sets up business along the main street once a week. Some people moan that the new road will "destroy" the town, by which they apparently mean rob it of its "character", but it seems the townsfolk don't much mind the prospect of being, at last, on some kind of main road.

"There are some nice things about being a small out-of-the-way town," said the Temple Keeper. "The old folk like the peace and quiet. But a town must grow. A town is people, and people grow, so a town must also grow."

"But people grow up and go away, or die."

"And more people are born."

The temple was tucked away behind one of the rows of shophouses along the main street. It looked out on a parking lot, across which was a permanent stage for Chinese operas. There had been an opera performance the night before, and this morning the parking lot was strewn with litter. Much of it had been swept into small piles and set alight. The little pyres smouldered gently, lacing the late morning air with an acrid but not unpleasant counterpoint to the cloying aroma of incense around the temple.

There was a stone bench outside the temple, and here sat the Temple Keeper. He was not an old man, but neither was he young. His hair, cropped short as a soldier's, was dusted with grey. His eyes were rheumy—it must have been from the constant incense smoke—but he did not seem to need glasses. He wore a thin white cotton tee-shirt and a pair of baggy blue trousers. "Are you a priest?" I asked.

"No, I just help take care of this place. I sweep and clean. I live here,"—he waved one sinewy arm—"in the back."

"How long have you lived here?"

"Since this place was built."

"When was that?"

"I don't know. Ten years. Twenty. I never wear a watch," he said, holding up a wrist as proof. He wanted to know who I was, where I came from and why I was asking all these questions. I told him. He listened, gazing into the middle distance, gently shaking his head. "Why?" he asked.

An unexpected question. But by no means unreasonable. I fumbled for an answer. "I wanted to see how a New Village has changed since the time of the Emergency," I ventured.

"So look around you," he said. "Take a walk around. It's just a small town, like any other. All that was a long time ago. No point talking about it now. People have forgotten. It's good that they have forgotten. Before, people were saying, 'we should never forget'. But I said we should. Just forget it. Do your work. Raise your family. Remember God. That's enough. This is not our country. This is nobody's country. This is God's country."

After the Emergency, the New Villages had been consigned to a backwater of the national conscience. No department of the new nation's government wanted responsibility for them. The ministry of rural development officially regarded them as "urban areas", and as such beyond its purview. To be sure, a few of the New Villages were indeed tacked on to the rumps of the larger towns, and could therefore tap into the urban economy. But most, like Ulu Yam, were miles from anywhere. And there were nearly 600 New Villages by the end of the Emergency, with an average population of a thousand each.

The truth was: nobody wanted to know about the New Villages. They were an embarrassment; reminders of an unsavoury time. General Sir Gerald Templer had been roundly criticized in London for his heavy-handed tactics against the Communist insurrection; his resolute advocacy of the Briggs Plan was inconsonant with decent governance. After Independence, "rural development" had quickly come to mean "Malay development"—the necessarily neat categorization of Malayans could no more countenance the existence of rural Chinese than it could urban Malays: these terms were oxymorons to the new blueprints being drawn for national development.

Moreover, it would have been politically ... *insensitive* ... to have spent government funds on upgrading the New Villages, when so much money, more than $100 million—and this is in the Fifties—had been spent on setting them up in the first place.

So the New Villagers had been left to fend for themselves, and they did. They planted tapioca and other marketable vegetables, groundnuts and fruit trees. They grew rubber, or set up cottage industries as tinsmiths or joss-stick makers. They worked as wage-earners in tin mines or rubber plantations. They worked hard, they survived, they began to thrive. The Malayan Chinese Association and other Chinese parties took them in hand; helped them organize themselves along the new nation's political lines.

But the New Villagers had to learn independence the hard way: alone. Independent they would remain. Ultimately, the New Villages created themselves. They owed nothing to any administration; they were beholden to no one. They would participate in national development on their own terms. They asked only to be left undisturbed, unhindered.

At the time of their establishment, one of the criticisms directed against Templer was that the harsh conditions of the New Villages would play to the advantage of the very parties they were meant to stymie: people would turn Communist in protest. There was a headline in a Chinese newspaper of the time: DON'T DRIVE THEM TO THE HILLS! Such wholesale defections did not happen, but an undercurrent of oppositionism did indeed bestir in the New Villages, and the government's legitimate parliamentary opponents found—and continue to find—support in those quietly self-contained little communities created by the Emergency.

"Leave it be," said the Temple Keeper. "All is well now. We have nothing to complain about. Why don't you come back tonight, and watch the opera?"

I told him that sounded like a very good idea. I thanked him for his time, apologized if I'd offended him, and took my leave. On the road out of town I paused a moment to rest my eyes on the happy activity of a school playground, where children in blue and white uniforms shrieked and laughed and chased each other about. It was a humble little primary school, its buildings of plank and zinc. It was called the Gurney National-Type Primary School (Chinese).

Not far away, on the road to Fraser's Hill, on Saturday, October 7, 1951, Henry Gurney had been shot dead in the ambush that was to result in Sir Gerald Templer's appointment to Malaya as High Commissioner. Sir Henry is commemorated in a prominent signboard on the spot where he died, and in a somewhat less obvious signboard in the forecourt of a small primary school, in a small Chinese town no one much notices, down in a valley below. ❑

5

THE CREATION OF MALAYSIA nearly led to war. The Philippines had long felt proprietary towards Sabah, which they regarded as an extension of their Sulu Sea kingdoms. Kuala Lumpur's action, Manila felt, was at the very least peremptory. Indonesia, however, blew its top.

For "Indonesia", read "Sukarno". By 1963, the one-time *Ratu Adil* had become very much the Great Dictator. Sukarno, the embodiment of a hundred million people, the grand designer of Indonesia, Sukarno the Monolithic, Sukarno the Magnificent ... Sukarno went ballistic. Sabah and Sarawak were part of Borneo, and Borneo was Kalimantan, and Kalimantan was Indonesia, and who did Malaya think it was? Sukarno depicted the formation of Malaysia as a neo-colonialist plot orchestrated by the British to undermine Greater Indonesia's hegemony over the Southeast Asian seas.

The irony was that he had a point. Sukarno's vision was merely a diseased recognition of the fact that there was, indeed, a distinct commonality among the peoples of this region. Indonesians, Malays and Filipinos could melt with perfect ease into each other's populations; but for the effects of their differing colonial histories, they were the same people, the same products of millennial miscegenation. They looked the same, thought and feared and acted the same, spoke languages so similar as to be virtually dialects of one another.

What set the Philippines apart was the Christian religion—yet, the spiritual role played by Catholicism in the Philippines, in its syncretic mysticism, its rites and rituals, its seamless blending with pre-existent animism and pagan beliefs, was identical to that played by Islam in Indonesia and Malaya. Christianity and Islam were both imported religions; they had arrived in force within 150 years or so of each other, in the 14th and 15th Centuries, by which time the Malay culture of these regions was well advanced along the Hindu and Buddhist lines laid down nearly a thousand years earlier.

It would strike me forcefully, again and again, as I roamed about the Indonesian and Philippine islands: we were one people. "There but for the grace of God and our colonial masters ...". Any one of the post-war nations of the vast Southeast Asian archipelago might have developed into any of the others, given the same outside forces. Malaya would have been the Philippines, if the Spaniards had gotten there first, if on leaving port Magellan had turned one way and not the other. We would have been Indonesia, had we had to fight for our Independence with arms and not laws. (And had we been ruled by the Dutch instead of the British, that would have been the *only* way.)

A quarter-century after the formation of Malaysia I would meet in Jakarta a man named Sutan Takdir Alisjahbana. He was eighty years old at the time, but still Rector of Indonesia's National University. In the darkness of his silent, shadowed, walled home on Jalan Duren Bangka, Alisjahbana spoke about his dream of "Bumantara"—the "Common World"; the great enfolding Malay cultural consciousness that might be formed of our united nations, if only we could recognize our common stock, our single root. "Can you imagine it?" asked Professor Alisjahbana, in a voice grown whispery and tremulous with age. "How rich and creative it would be? There would be peace for everyone, even the Chinese, everyone, because the Malays would never be in fear of destruction. We would be safe. We would be happy. We would be a great people."

But the post-war elixir of nationalism had drowned the professor's dreams in its intoxicant embrace. Sukarno would have agreed with Alisjahbana's philosophy entirely, with the one embellishment of himself at the supreme apex of this "Bumantara". Malaya had been an embarrassment to Sukarno; he had regarded our Malays as a degenerate stock, bowing and scraping before our colonial masters in hope of their benediction, assiduously learning their language and their laws. We had not won Independence honourably, with heroism and sacrifice; we had accepted the trappings in exchange for our souls, which now belonged to the British, who could do with us as they pleased. And the British had always hated the Dutch, and now they wanted to usurp the territory that had been Dutch.

Sukarno launched what was called a "confrontation" against Malaysia. Indonesian troops harried the Sarawak border. Some were even parachuted into the Peninsula, where they were quickly scooped up and sent home. Indonesian fighter jets swooped menacingly across Malaysian airspace. A foreign journalist asked the Tunku: shouldn't he do something? "What for?" was the Tunku's famous reply. "By the time our boys get into the air the Indonesians will all be home and in bed."

Indeed, the "Konfrontasi" would turn out to be something of a historic non-event. As a child in primary school, I was vaguely aware of a certain tension in the air. But it seemed the Tunku's airy dismissals of the Indonesian threat were infectious and reassuring to most, and the citizen's vigilante squads set up in certain "vulnerable" areas to guard against Indonesian paratroopers were regarded as more of an inconvenient joke than anything else.

Malaysia was scornful of the Confrontation. For one thing, Sukarno hadn't been entirely mistaken in his depiction of Malaysia's British nexus. Experienced British border scouts led an admirable policing of the Sarawak frontier, and were more than a match for Indonesian infiltrators. (There were also apocryphal accounts of Malaysia's new Iban citizens rediscovering their traditional prowess as head hunters against hapless Indonesian soldiers, but these were probably scare tactics.) For another, Sukarno himself was rapidly losing control. In 1965, there was an attempted coup in Indonesia. It failed, but Sukarno's authority was fatally undermined. Suharto began his rise to power, and ended the Confrontation.

It seems unconscionably cavalier to sum up Indonesia's defining moment in three sentences: it was so profound a change of destiny for that great nation, and its cost in human suffering would be so unspeakably high. But this is a Malaysian story, and in Malaysia 1965 was a heartening year. We had stood up to the Indonesians, and we had prevailed. Singapore left the Federation the same year, and Malaysia's name no longer seemed so much of a sick joke to the Malays.

This, then, was the Tunku's approach to nation-building. The nation he inherited had been externally created, and he would seek to define its Independent identity externally, too. Sarawak and Sabah would come into the fold. (The Tunku had hoped for Brunei too, but Brunei's oil-fields had made it rich enough, and valuable enough to the Western powers, to say no, thanks.) Singapore would leave to chart its own, insular, 75%-Chinese, destiny. A hostile Indonesia would be stared down. Malaysia would define itself, under the Tunku, by its impact on and image in the surrounding world.

It made sense, in a way, and for a while. During the Confrontation Malaysians had another external foe to unite against, now that the communists had been reduced to a ragtag band of malcontents in the jungles of the Thai border, and soon afterward there was another external cause to cheer: the formation of the Association of South-East Asian Nations. Asean was established in 1967, the most credible incarnation yet of the regional association first tried with Seato and Maphilindo, impelled perhaps by a faint echo of Professor Alisjahbana's dream. It would, in time, turn out to be one of the more enduring successes of the period, if not in its achievements, certainly in its ideals.

As I write this, I find myself thinking that the Tunku should not be blamed too strenuously for the disaster that was to occur in Malaysia. His achievement was undoubtedly impressive. For all his avuncular affability, he set in motion movements that would endure far longer than anything achieved by such posturing, larger-than-life demagogues as Sukarno. Malaysia's place in the world was first defined by the Tunku.

The pride we felt at the ending of Confrontation, with the new Malaysia intact and apparently poised for greatness, was something even a ten-year-old schoolboy could sense. The loss of Singapore was strange, to be sure, but then, to hear my parents tell of it, Singapore had always *felt* like a different country anyway—an extreme sort of colonial Chinatown, wonderful for shopping, a nice place to visit, but we wouldn't want to *live* there. Besides, there was a lot more to this new "Malaysia" of ours than the old Malaya had ever had. Our nation felt so much bigger; so much stronger and surer of itself.

This the Tunku gave us; how much more could we have expected of him? It might have been beyond human ability for him to have paid full attention to the domestic agenda as well.

The Tunku was a happy man, a successful international statesman, and in his happiness he did not seem to notice the growing disaffection of the Malays and the widening alienation of the Chinese. When he finally did, in the outcome and horrendous aftermath of the 1969 general elections, it was far too late. ❑

Tamalia

A DOLPHIN leaps free of the ocean, frozen in mid-flight, a crystal arc of water streaming off its tail.

An island rises from the sea beyond, a feather of cloud upon its forested crest. All is a glassy-blue, sun-scorched silence. Tamalia traces her fingers, fine-boned and fragile, along the edges of the photograph. Her smile widens, her eyes shine, she is there again. "Ceram," she breathes, a radiance rendering translucent the skin of her face. A strand of hair slips free of the clasp above her ear and drifts before her eyes. She sweeps it back, carelessly. She turns the page. More photographs: islands in still waters, pale blue skies, grasses that must rustle in the clove-scented wind.

And a ruined colonial house of colonnades and verandah: the roof has fallen in, murals of mould fleck the crumbling plaster, but what remains seems braced against time—this house will decay so much, it seems, and no more. "This will be my house," says Tamalia, turning her head to one side, like a fawn listening. "All I have to do is pop a roof on it. It will be beautiful." The strand of hair falls free again.

The album of photographs lies on the plastic-sheeted dining table in her father's house. Outside, beyond high walls, Jalan Duren Bangka slumbers fitfully in the heavy darkness of a Jakarta night. Droplets of sweat bead Tamalia's lip; moisture catches in the fine down at the corners of her mouth. She wipes it away with a pass of her wrist. The house is empty and silent, and the dead white glow of a single fluorescent lamp throws thick shadows into the corners.

The dolphin vaults in the sightless light.

Tamalia wears a green floral dress. Her lipstick is faded; she'd swallowed most of it with the meal we had shared hours before. She had come to my room at the Intercontinental. We had not seen each other for twenty years, since we had shared a desk in primary school. I had never forgotten that silent girl with the soft brown hair and melancholy eyes, and when I arrived in Jakarta to begin another of my journeys I sought her out. It wasn't difficult. Her surname is well-known; her father a man of substance and fame. The strange, lilting voice on the telephone remembered me. "Oh yes," she said, "you're the one who liked South Africa. How could anyone like South Africa. I've never forgotten that." I had. South Africa? It came back to me: in geography book I'd cherished as a child, there was a photograph of the Table Mountain. It looked spectacular; I must once have told her so. She asked me what I was doing now. "I'm a journalist," I said.

"How wonderful!" she exclaimed.

"I'm glad you think so. And you?"

"I'm a lawyer."

"Also wonderful. I would much like to see you."

"Yes. What time is it now?"

"Just gone six."

"I'll be there at seven."

She knocked on the door, a slender young woman in a floral dress, smiling at me through bright red lipstick. Her hair was tied back in a bun. I would not have recognized her but for her eyes, which held the same distant light I remembered from our childhood. We went to the hotel cafe for dinner. We talked. I asked her how Indonesians viewed Malaysians. She thought for a moment, then said: "Much the same way the French regard the Belgians, I suppose. Essentially the same people, but a few rungs lower down." I had to laugh at that. "That's funny," I said. "We feel the same way about you."

Our conversation floated on random tangents. She seemed ethereal, ghostly, to me. I began to regret the impulse to call her. What was there to say? We were twelve years old when we had last seen each other. We had no points of contact; no relevance to each other. This was curiosity, no more: I had wanted to see what the child had grown into. I felt ashamed, sheepish, a voyeur of time and change. But Tamalia showed no trace of such discomfort. She smiled and chattered as easily as if we had never stopped knowing each other.

"How old are you?" she asked, suddenly.

"Think," I said.

She laughed. "Oh yes. Silly of me."

And there was the link: we had lived the same length of time, even if in two entirely different worlds. (Yet, what had made them so different? There were causes, and effects: we had both gone to university in the same year, 1975, but I had gone to Britain and she to Holland.) But we had known each other once, long before, and since then we had moved in parallel through time, far apart, but measuring apace the passage of the years. And despite all those years, we had not forgotten each other's names.

"Will you come to my house?" asked Tamalia. "I want to show you something. My island."

Tamalia puts away her photo album, each image carefully mounted on the stiff black pages, each neatly annotated in precise, elegant prose. We sit in the shadows of the lounge. A guard silently patrols the grounds outside. Tamalia talks of Indonesia, the richness, the beauty, the grandeur. She recalls Kartini, the Javanese princess who died, immortal at twenty-six, in 1905. "My father says she was the finest intellectual Indonesia has ever produced," says Tamalia. "A woman!"

I try to speak of Pramoedya Ananta Toer, the writer whom I think is the finest ever to have emerged from the Malay lands, but Tamalia is disdainful. "He is a communist," she says, airily dismissive. I wonder, astonished: how could she be so naive? Or is it fear? There was an edge in her voice that sounded like a warning. It must be fear, or fear's enduring residue: her father, too, must have known that fear. He had fled to Malaysia in 1965, the year Indonesia unleashed the beast within to stalk the heartlands in a savage ecstasy of redemption.

That was why Tamalia and I had shared a desk in primary school. While her family took refuge in Malaysia, half a million Indonesians died as traitors. On their graves a new nation would be erected. Into the spaces they left behind a new order would flow. The bloodstained fabric of Indonesia would be revered as exactly that: *Sang Saka Merah Putih,* the national flag, red above for sacrifice, white below for sanctity. Death would be intrinsic to the identity of this nation, the twin of heroism. A bitter wind fills Garuda's mythic wings.

Pramoedya was not killed: he was banished to Buru Island in the Banda Sea, a prison colony within sight of Tamalia's Ceram. There, denied pen and paper, he composed four great novels in his head. He would recite them to his fellow prisoners, some of whom had been pubescent children when arrested as "Communists" in 1965. In 1973, when Pramoedya was released from Buru into house imprisonment in Jakarta, he wrote down his stories. It was an astounding feat of the intellect. His manuscripts were smuggled away by an Australian diplomat, who would never again see Indonesia, and published in the West. They remain banned in Indonesia, because Pramoedya remains "a Communist".

Tamalia does not wish to talk about Pramoedya. She does not wish to talk about Buru. In the moist heat of the night, she talks about the other islands in the Banda Sea. At times she seems light as a child, at times unutterably old. She brings out a book on batik, telling me I must buy a copy, everything is there, history, art, culture, everything. She shows me her collection of antique porcelain plates, with their delicate etchings of fruits and foliage beneath the cracked glaze.

It grows late. Tamalia telephones for a taxi. It arrives presently, and Tamalia bids me goodbye. I am driven away through the empty boulevards of Jakarta to my hotel. Tamalia's walled house is swallowed into the dark and foetid labyrinth behind me, within it the girl I had bridged a gulf of twenty years to touch, only to have my fingers pass through a wisp of smoke. Not even a trace remains, neither stain nor fragrance. But perhaps I shall choose to remember her in the frozen leap of a dolphin, trailing diamonds from the surface of a distant sea. ❑

6

MY NARRATIVE has now reached 1969, and perhaps it would not be inappropriate to pause here for a while, and restore to the scene the infant we last saw in 1955, squalling at the fates that had made him so ineluctably Malaysian.

I had had an uneventful childhood; I had been a quiet, bookish child. My father had led a peripatetic career as a teacher (which was why he hadn't been present at my birth), and he had taken his young family with him to successive postings across the length and breadth of the Malayan Peninsula. And it was a growing family; my two brothers were born, at three-year intervals, in Johor Baru at the peninsula's southern tip, and in Kuala Krai in the interior of Kelantan, where my mother's equally mobile family had come to a temporary rest. Eventually my father had received what would be the last posting of his abbreviated life, as a senior lecturer at the Language Institute in Kuala Lumpur.

It was in our house in Kuala Lumpur, on a dark and rainy night in 1967, that my father first spoke to me about my future. I was twelve years old then, in Standard Six of primary school; the next year, I would be moving on to secondary school. My father had always been a fairly remote figure to his three young sons; stern and affectionate in equal measure, but still remote. Much, much later, I would console myself with the thought that he had been saving himself for later in our lives, when we were out of our infancy and could understand more of his strong and complex personality.

That night, my father said to me: "The Malay College is not just any school. It is *the* school." That's about all I remember, although there must have been more. I do remember not being sure what he was on about. I knew that I would be sitting for the Malay College entrance examinations very soon, and I was vaguely aware that this was a place, a big boarding school way up in Kuala Kangsar, spoken of with much respect by my teachers. But merely sitting for the exams was no big deal; practically every Standard Six Malay boy in the country did so, and I had by no means excelled in school so far. I usually made the top class, but I was also usually at the bottom of that class. But here was my father talking about the Malay College in a way that made me feel, for the first time in my young life, that he actually had hopes for me. And he went on: "You must take the Sciences. There is no future in the Arts." What was this? "Sciences"? "Arts"? I couldn't even *draw!* And I was certainly no whiz at arithmetic.

The day of the entrance exam came, and the four of us who were the only four Malay boys in our primary school's top class went to take it. Ghani and Azizi were deadly serious about it; Muslini and I larked about. The other two were always in the top five of our class; Muslini and I were usually in the bottom five. Ghani and Azizi were the great hopes of our school, which would apparently be honoured to send off a ward or two to the Malay College; Muslini and I were there to make up the numbers.

So of course, when the results came out a month or two later, Muslini and I made the cut and the other two didn't. Nobody could believe it, least of all Muslini and me. I think Azizi cried. I went home a very happy kid that Friday. My father was at home when I got there, reading the newspaper. "Papa," I said, struggling to keep the excitement from my voice. "I've got the results. I passed. I have to report to Malay College on January seventh." He didn't even lower the paper. "Good," he said. Years later, my mother would tell me that was one of the proudest moments of his life. He certainly fooled me then.

Five days into 1968, my father bundled his wife and sons into the car and set off on the 200-kilometre drive north to Kuala Kangsar, a small, sleepy town dozing by a bend of the Perak River not far south of Taiping. For all its somnolent torpor, Kuala Kangsar had a distinguished air about it: it was the royal town of Perak, site of the Sultan's Palace, and of the esteemed Malay College. The school was grand indeed: great sprawling colonnaded buildings gazing serenely out upon vast green playing fields. Even the College's Prep School, the traditional clearing-house for the school's youngest charges, was a stately edifice, tucked away on its own corner of the campus. The Malay College looked for all the world like an upper-crust English public school, transplanted brick for brick for corinthian column from the vicinity of Eton or Harrow, and that impression was indeed quite deliberate.

The Malay College had been founded by the British in 1905 as a place in which the sons of the Malay sultans could acquire the rudiments of a sound British education before moving on to tertiary institutions in Britain itself. Early in its history, its portals were opened to the sons of commoners as well, provided they could make the entrance grade. (I might be charitable here, and mention only in passing the possibility that not all of Malaya's royal princes were always keen on a Western education, and the stern discipline considered an indispensable part of it at the time.)

From the grooming of princelings the College had turned to the creation of an "administrative elite" for Malaya. It was intrinsic to the British scheme of things in Malaya that the Malays would administer the country on their behalf. This is not to say that the other races were denied educational attention—other, even more venerable, schools were already functioning in Kuala Lumpur (the Victoria Institution, founded in 1890) and Penang (the Penang Free School). But none were expressly reserved for the Malays alone, and consequently there were relatively few Malays in any of them.

This was not due to a lack of ability, as the Malay College was to be instrumental in proving, but of opportunity. Until well into the 20th Century, to be a Malay in higher education was to be a royal Malay. The peasantry (and of course, this was long before the development of anything like a Malay middle class) was virtually immobile.

The Malay College changed that, and by the 1930s and 1940s had begun turning out the country's first Malay lawyers and men of letters. They would come to play a crucial role in the genesis of Malay, and Malayan, nationalism, and many of them would be intimately involved in the courtly dance of legalities that would eventually result in the blueprint for Malayan Independence. And more: Malaysia's second prime minister, Abdul Razak Hussein, the Tunku's successor, of whom there will be more to tell, would be an alumnus of the Malay College.

It was indeed a grand old school, and its reputation was well deserved. My first impression, however, was of bedlam: a horde of twelve-year-olds and what seemed to be their entire extended families, seeking out their allotted bed-spaces in the dormitories, being endlessly hugged by weeping mothers, grandmothers and aunts. I was happy to find Muslini amidst the chaos, although he seemed altogether too dazed to be coherent.

The day drew to an end; the families were waved a tearful goodbye. We had our first mass meal in the dining hall, in which were hung framed group photographs of the College's previous First-Form intakes, and were sent to our beds at nine. There were ninety-two beds in the four dormitories of Prep School. Within the soft white drapes of their brand-new mosquito nets, ninety-two young boys fell asleep on their first night away from their homes and families. From that day on, home would be a place we would only visit on holidays. It was all for the best that we were utterly exhausted.

I awoke the next morning in the Malay world, and it felt as if I had never so much as seen it before in my life. I had never heard Malay spoken so naturally and easily before.

Mine had been an English-speaking upbringing, my father had insisted on it, as that was the language that would "give us the world". But here was the Malay world, and in all its diversity of regional tones; Kelantanese in particular was a delight to the ear, but virtually incomprehensible. This being North Perak, however, most of us from the rest of the country would soon shade into the particular patois of Northern Malay in our speech, adopting with ease its rotund simplicities.

English remained, thankfully for me, the medium of our instruction, as it had been throughout our education so far. But soon after I went home for the first term holidays, I overheard my father tell my mother, his voice thick with disgust, "You hear the boy? He sounds like a Sayong Malay!" (Sayong being a decrepit little village buried amidst banana groves across the river from Kuala Kangsar.)

I think he meant for me to overhear the exchange, rather than address the point directly to me. I think he understood that the damage done to my speech was the result of a young boy's effort to fit in with his peers in an alien environment. My first months at Malay College had indeed been difficult. I had never realized how un-Malay I looked. I was one of the tallest among us, even at that age, my shoe size matched most of their fathers', and my various Indian bloodlines had unmistakably manifested themselves in my facial features and complexion. Coupled with my limited command of the Malay language, I was the butt of taunts and sarcasm.

Once, at a meal-time, one particularly vicious lad had gleefully emptied out half my cup of black coffee and topped it up to the brim with soy sauce. Downing the noxious concoction with unknowing gusto, I reacted in the expectedly spectacular manner, spraying the walls with coffee, soy sauce and spit. "There!" chortled that scum-sucking little baboon, " Now you'll be even blacker!"

I wasn't the only one mocked by the juvenile racists among us; this may have been the Malay College, but this was also Malaysia, and more than a few of us betrayed on our faces the Chinese or Indian elements of our ancestries.

But I was nonetheless one of the least "culturally Malay" of all. For there was something else that set me apart from the others, and this only the most irredeemable joked about: I didn't know how to pray.

I knew I was Muslim, and I had taken some pride of identity in being so. But my instruction in the faith of my forefathers had been largely left to an irregular succession of mumbling religious teachers in primary school, and what little I gathered from their lessons seemed mostly to do with ancient Arabian history. They had instructed us in the Arabic script, and I had earnestly traced the slithery curlicues and spirals into my copybook—it was greatly more akin to drawing than writing. My father had seemed pleased with those efforts, but he himself never played much of a role in imparting to me the details of ritual and prayer, beyond an annual trip to the mosque at the celebratory culmination of the holy month of Ramadhan. Was he derelict in his duties as a Muslim father? Enduring the humiliations of Prep School, I thought so. But later I was to think not. I believe my father was again holding himself in check until such time as I was old enough to understand a glimmering of his own profound, numinous, almost mystical faith in Islam. The ritual observances, with their mumbles and chants and prostrations, were merely a mechanical underlay to the true transcendence of the religion. He would leave it to the mechanics to drill me in the *alif-ba-ta* of it all, and come in to apply the vital finishing touches when I was older.

But perhaps my father underestimated my growing capacity for discernment. Even as a child of eight or ten, I had found it well-nigh impossible to attend to instructions delivered with a disregard for what all these arcane sounds, these *"ashaduillah"*s and *"bismillah"*s, *meant.* This was Islam? *Sounds?* Snaky script and goateed gurus? After the first few teachers had rebuffed my first curious questions, I had simply ceased to pay attention to any of them.

And then it was all too late. Six months after I'd gone to Malay College, in July 1968, eleven days short of his thirty-ninth birthday, my father died.

My mother was widowed at thirty-two. After a compassionate interval, she had to leave our quarters at the Language Institute and make do as best she could for herself and my two brothers, who were ten and seven respectively. She managed with such energy and, ultimately, success, as to reveal the true depth and power of a personality that had been hitherto held in abeyance to her husband's. But my father had lived long enough to have seen me to the Malay College, and I had a new family, of sorts; certainly, a new scaffolding within which to brace myself against loss.

When I returned to Kuala Kangsar after the funeral, it was to find a quiet gift of sympathy waiting for me. My father's death had been reported in the newspapers, and it had emerged to my schoolmates that he had been a man of Malay letters, a lecturer and librarian, who would be remembered with affection and respect by those who had known him. If I remember rightly (and if not then let me be thankful for the gloss of memory), even the scum-sucking baboon of the soy sauce incident offered me his condolences. I was glad to receive them.

But he would revert to form soon enough, and later that year I would be begging my mother, through streaming tears, to get me the hell out of that awful place, so full was it of vicious racists.

The despair would pass, however, for at the core of it the Malay College was still a school of the elite, the cream of Malay youth, intelligent, inquisitive, alert young men, and once I discovered my niche there the unpleasantness of the first year would fade. The friends I made there would remain as close to me as brothers for the rest of our lives. And there was no question but that we had the ministrations of some of the best teachers we would ever have.

It was engaging to watch the new patterns of friendship emerge and develop among us. We were divided into the College's four "Houses", named after the first rulers of the four Federated States of colonial Malaya: Idris of Perak, Ahmad of Pahang, Sulaiman of Selangor, Mohamad Shah of Negri Sembilan. This was a daily framework of association—

Prep School's house divisions were arranged according to the four dormitories—and it swiftly supplanted the more natural tendency among us to aggregate according to home states. Few of us had know any of the others prior to coming to Kuala Kangsar (Muslini and I were an exception proving the rule), and our first year at the Malay College was a safari through an exotic terrain of new friendships.

Some would form tight little cliques: there was, for example, the cabal that for two years called itself "FANS" and daubed the title everywhere in chalk. This was an acronym formed of the initials of Fauzi Omar of Kedah, Amin Ariff and Salman Ahmad of Perlis and Nik Mohamad Nassim of Kelantan—a quartet of prideful bosom buddies, flamboyant and loyal to the core, and one which demonstrated the growing irrelevance of home-town loyalties to Malay College boys.

It was one of the most important benefits of the Malay College, once the school had been shed of its royal pretensions. The College brought home to its charges the truth that intelligence and potential had nothing to do with birth or breeding, and that there was indeed a unity of Malaysian states. The College trained us to see ourselves as part of a national Malay identity, and to take pride in that. Some sons of sultans were indeed among us, but there was nothing to set them apart from or above the rest. (The Sultan of Perak's son, for example, afflicted with a slight malocclusion of his upper jaw, was universally known by the sobriquet: "Bugs". As in a certain well-known Hollywood hare.)

My niche was, what had seemed such a liability and embarrassment when I first got there, the English language. I became a school debator and a fixture in the College magazine. English, for our generation, was an effortless alternative language, yet there was still considerable respect for those of us most fluent in it. It set a certain seal on the Malay College's quality, that our English debating team could hold its own against those of the nation's other great schools, notwithstanding their more expansive resource of Chinese and Indian youth. For a mere Malay to stand up and strut the oratorical boards, his arguments prevailing, his eloquence and arrogance more than match for those of his Worthy Opponents. ... there was some pride in that.

I made the debating platform my personal bailiwick in the five years I would spend at Malay College, and although I would still rather have been a sporting superstar or a scholastic wunderkind, I held my own, helped my school satisfy its addiction for winning, and was as a result largely forgiven for my cultural deficiencies as a Malay. Rehman (what kind of name is that? "Raymond"? You sure it's not a spelling mistake?) might not have been able to extricate himself from the slightest literary tangle in Malay, but in *English,* ho, you should have heard him! That guy could *talk!*

OUR SECOND YEAR at the Malay College was the Malaysian election year of 1969. Did we know? Of course. Did we care? Enough to decorate our lockers and classrooms with the political bunting of our choice, filched from lamp-posts and billboards in town. Seriously? Good God no, and we sheepishly took them down when the Headmaster told us to stop all this foolishness, we didn't know what we were doing, politics wasn't our affair and we should leave it aside until we were older, when we could devote our entire lives to politics for all he cared. Indeed, politics meant about as much to us as religion: we dutifully followed the preferences of our parents, which meant, temporarily though it would be, an almost total preponderance in Prep School of the blue-and-white sailboat posters of the Alliance.

The Kelantanese among us, predictably, would extol the virtues of the Islamic party (Pas, after its Malay initials), not so much out of belief in a fundamentalist credo as in their pride at being Kelantanese. It was a standing joke among us: if the Kelantanese had their way, the rest of us would need passports to visit them. But the rest of us were indeed a fully Malaysian crew, and we had long stopped making fun of the peculiar accents of our Sarawakian and Sabahan classmates. (Especially since so many of them were sensational athletes.)

So the shock, when it came, left us numb and disbelieving. Our youthful generation had grown up utterly unaware that our country had been heading for racial disaster. At the 1969 parliamentary elections, held over the weekend of May 11, the Chinese and Malays alike demonstrated their divergent dissatisfactions with the way the country had been steered since Independence. The Alliance, although still the overall victor, lost the two-thirds parliamentary majority that had granted it the clout to amend the Federal Constitution without the support of the Opposition. This had been an ability deemed crucial for the steady governance of Malaysia, and the Alliance victory was fatally hollow.

The Chinese electorate had deserted the Malaysian Chinese Association, their voice in the Alliance. The accusation was that the MCA had failed to speak strongly enough for their community, had acquiesced in the relegation of Chinese interests, and had too willingly allowed the demographic adjustments of the mid-Sixties to erode their standing in the population.

It speaks to the gulf between Chinese and Malay perceptions, then, that the Malays didn't seem at all concerned with or grateful for the factors that had so incensed their nemeses. No: the Malays' anger with Umno was even more elemental. All this talk of a multi-ethnic future, this precious myth of a "Malaysian Malaysia", had done nothing to improve their lot. The Malays may have been assured of their pre-eminence in government and a clear majority in the population, but what did such platitudes mean when they held only 2% of the nation's wealth?

And what were the Chinese complaining about, when they had all the choicest cuts of the Malaysian economy? Their business interests extended from the village sundry store into every corner of the Malaysian economy: primary commodities, property development, banking, retail. Malaysia's Chinese businesses had a virtual lock on the economy in association with foreign interests and, most grievously of all, at their highest levels with the highest strata of the Malays themselves: the royal families. Theirs was, moreover, a closed system; still the familial and clan-based operations they had been in the beginning. The Malays could only look on helplessly as the Chinese made fortunes out of their helplessness.

The Alliance strength in Parliament was cut by nearly a third: the coalition won only sixty-six seats of the 103 contested. Pas, the only Malay Opposition party, won twelve. The MCA was the hardest hit of all, losing half of its twenty-seven seats; most of them to the Democratic Action Party, the principal Chinese Opposition, which went from one seat to thirteen.

On paper, the Alliance had still won the right to continue in government. On the streets, it felt very different. On May 13, the DAP staged a "victory" march through the streets of Kuala Lumpur. Many years later, DAP Secretary-General Lim Kit Siang would speak of this event with grief and regret. "We were as stunned by the election results as anyone else," he told me. "We were euphoric, but in our euphoria we lost control." To hear the DAP's version of things, their parade was swollen by numbers of Chinese trouble-makers. When skirting the fringes of Malay areas, they threw taunts and jeers at the ominously silent houses within. "Go back up the rivers and plant corn!" they yelled. "Kuala Lumpur belongs to the Chinese!"

No one is sure where the first fighting broke out, but most believe it was somewhere near Kampong Baru, a very traditional, very Malay enclave that had once been on the outskirts of Kuala Lumpur but was now in its very heart, the city having grown up around it. These scuffles ignited the closest thing Malaysia would ever see of the full-blown racial conflagration that had always been a possibility in this country, but which no one had really believed would ever happen. The riots and burnings went on through the night and into the next day. At dawn on May 14, from the balcony of his Kuala Lumpur home, Tunku Abdul Rahman watched the pillars of smoke curl into the morning sky, his heart breaking.

By the time the fires burned themselves out, leaving a stunned nation to contemplate the ashes of what had seemed so fine a dream, the official death count was 196. This was initially greeted with disbelief—witnesses had described bodies piled like cordwood near the scenes of the worst fighting—but in time it would be accepted as the least unpalatable truth of the carnage of May 13.

Not so with the Tunku's initial insistence that the riots had been instigated by communist *agents provocateurs*. Agents there may have been, but "communists" they were not. No: Malaysians had known all along who they were; had known and dared not accept the darkly malevolent suspicions and hostilities they carried within themselves. Now, Malaysians saw the truth of themselves that had underlain the fiction of their harmony, and the nation huddled to itself in curfewed silence in the long, awful months that followed.

My own memory of May 13 is a very simple one, and it has retained a vivid clarity ever since: a coffee-shop along Kuala Kangsar's main street; three bottles of Anchor beer on a marble-topped table, around which sit two Indian men, their faces drawn and troubled, one of whom refills the glass of the shop's Chinese proprietor, who's staring into a newspaper and shaking his head and mumbling over and over: *"Apa sudah jadi, apa sudah jadi?"*

What has happened? What has happened?

The Malay College was hushed in mourning. Those whose homes were near the scenes of fighting were granted rare permission to telephone their families. At dinner in Prep School, we offered prayers for our nation. But no one I knew seemed directly affected by the riots in any way. Reports from home spoke of the inconvenience of curfew more than anything else; that and a distinct effort on the part of people to be extra friendly to each other. In Kuala Kangsar, life was normal. The shops didn't shut before time, there was no knife-edge in the air. The fact of the riots seemed distant, surreal, scarcely credible.

So would it be simply too pollyannish of me to mine this dark seam for a nugget of value? Fine: Let me attend to my mother's principal memory of that weekend, which was of being handed a carton of oranges over her fence by her next-door neighbour, who was Chinese, who ran a fruit-stall at the local market, who took it upon himself to alleviate his neighbours' deprivations under the curfew that had blanketed Malaysia immediately after the night of bloodshed.

The point is this: for all the darkness and tension that had erupted, this was still Malaysia, there was still that "working concord" to which I referred earlier in this story, and the great mass of Malaysians had wanted no part in the madness of May 13. The deepest anguish of the time, then, was in the certain knowledge that the entire nation would be made to pay for the unrestrained furies of a few sections of the population, and there was nothing anyone could do but wait for the axe to fall, and know that nothing would ever be the same again. ❑

Friends

AH, KAMIL, you great gruff bluff bear of a man, what's with you these days? If only life were a rugby match, eh? We could make something of it then, no joke, hey, we could charge across the touchline like avenging giants, they'd be blowing in our slipstream like rags ... well, *you* could, anyway ... I'd just be cheering you on from the sidelines, shredding my throat in exultant praise of your heroism ...

Sure, we know the truth here: you made the First Fifteen, while my College rugby career lasted ten minutes. (Joe Baker, lah, the bastard, made me run two laps of the field for turning up late for our first rugby practice, remember? Prep School? 1968? Wrecked my rugby career before it even started ...) But you had some good times on that field, didn't you? I've remembered that one moment from that one game ever since, not that I give a shit which poor school we destroyed that afternoon on the Big School field—no, there was just that one try you scored, mate, that was sheer brutal poetry. You charged the last ten yards to the line with three of their players streaming from your torso like banners in the wind. It looked like your jersey was in tatters, but no, the tatters were your opponents. There was no stopping you that day, Kamil, you were magnificent.

Yeah well, we're not there anymore; we're here now, late thirties already. Marriages and families ... maybe the less said about them the better. I didn't go to yours, you didn't come to mine, and see what happened? But what the hell. We're still young. Young as we'll always be. Sure, it's a bit disconcerting going back to Kuala Kangsar for the Old Boys' Weekend and having the present boys call us "Uncle". Kinda focuses the mind, that, doesn't it? First it was "Abang", which was cool, really; made one feel quite grown up. But "Pak Cik"? O unkind cut!

Do you get the impression they're not like we were? Sure you do. Hell, we were *unique!* Last of the pre-69ers, that was us. And the first batch to score 100% passes at Form Five AND win the national schools rugby championship in the same year—now *there's* something to be remembered for! But the changes came thick and fast after 1969. "Elitism out." "Malay College no different from other schools." But the school remained true to its founding ethic even then: it was still reflecting the Malay ideal. First it was for the royals. Then for the "Malay Administrative Elite". Then the new nationalism. And then, during the years of uncertainty and drift, the College was drifty and uncertain. And we were there to watch it happen. Headmasters came and went every couple of years, and after Ryan and Aziz they all seemed to get progressively smaller, didn't they? What kind of weird culmination was Charlie Tot, for instance? Flailing around like a dervish with his cane—you got it once, didn't you? For some stupid macho stunt like smoking, or something. But I never did. I was an angel. I didn't smoke my first cigarette until I was twenty, the same year I lost my virginity. (Come to think of it, it may have been the same *night,* so much for the evils of smoking.)

But you weren't afraid of being a rebel. Perhaps we expected it of you. After all, we kept electing you President of our year all the way up to Fifth Form. You did all right, though. Remember the Great Food Revolt? We were in Form Three or Four. There was schoolwide unrest over the slop they were serving us to eat every day. There was a call for a food boycott on a particular night. Some of the Fifth Formers were saying we should overturn our plates and walk out. This was *serious*—there was something deeply offensive, even immoral, about doing that to a plate of rice. The night arrived. We milled about the dining hall, uncertain of how far this should go. Everyone waited for someone to tip the balance one way or the other: would we sit down and eat, or would we walk out? And you did it. You said, "Ah, enough!", and you picked up your plate of rice, banged it upside down on the table, and walked out. And we followed you, feeling positively revolutionary.

Yes, and maybe *that's* why you got caned ... but hey, it may have been stupid and juvenile, but you acted like a leader, Kamil. And we made our point; the food wasn't quite so bad after that. I know you enjoy this memory too—after all, it's one of the reasons Aji and Mae and even Lan still call you Our Leader when you turn up at one of our bashes at MCOBA.

Not that you turn up at the Old Boy's Association all that often. Neither do I. We have our reasons, I suppose. I so much respect Wan Katak for all the work he does for MCOBA. Meli, too. But Wan's the One, isn't he? The Main Man, the Lynch-pin. There's one guy with his life in order. CEO of a finance company, penthouse office, Mercedes Benz in the parking lot, gorgeous wife, lovely kids, always on the blower talking megabucks ... and still the least pretentious dude in the world, happily keeping in touch with the rest of us. Katak's a credit to everything MC stood for.

But it seems most of us are doing okay these days. Aji's still sharp as ever. (His was the most memorable criticism I ever received as a writer. Many were telling me to lighten up on the bombast, but Aji put it this way: *"Kalau budak Kolej pun tak faham, apa tah lagi lesser mortals?")* Mae's going great guns in the foreign service. Mat's Assistant Editor of *The Malay Mail* and winning journalism awards hand over fist, the sod. Wano's rich, full stop, and Ali probably owns a chunk of Saudi Arabia by now.

Ah, but you know all this better than I do; at least you've been here while I've been arsing about all over the world for lack of a home to believe in. But you know, I've been back a while now, wandering around the country. I stopped by KK. I stood on Station Road and watched a football match on the Big School field. It felt strange, and strangely exhilarating, to stand with all those geeks and their bicycles on the other side of the fence where they've been since the dawn of time, watching from the cheap seats. College boys still seem to play a solid game of football. Ah, that glorious field! Those grand buildings! From that distance, I could believe nothing had changed; they might have been us in those white uniforms, in that red-black-yellow kit. They might have been us ...

... eating *paus* in Yut Loy and toast in Double Lion. Sneaking out to watch films at Kapitol. Feeding the jukebox at Pak Kassim's, annoying the girls from GEGS. (But come on, were they ever *really* annoyed? We were MC boys, we were the Best and the Brightest, and if they didn't think so it was their loss, right? The boys from Clifford School, now *they* were annoyed.)

Maybe I'll see you back there, Kamil, come the next Old Boys' Weekend. Whoever gets there first books a bed in the Pavilion for the other. Any bed will do; you know how soundly we all sleep when we're back at MC. Something in the air, I suppose.

Or something else; something in our pasts; something in our souls. Something to do with being children growing up together; meeting at the age of twelve, parting at eighteen—but never really parting at all. That's the best thing MC did for us, I think. No matter what cars we're driving these days, nor who's high and who's low, who's rich, who's not, who's "made it" and who hasn't and whatever any of it means ... none of it really matters when we're with each other. No bullshit between College boys, Kamil. We know each other too well. Maybe that's all an "Old Boys' Network" is: a mutuality of knowing.

Given the ordure we've had to swallow since we last swaggered around Kuala Kangsar on a Saturday morning town leave in our white uniforms, the constant remaking of the Malays according to models that change with the moon, that's something to be grateful for. None of us is truly alone, and when the changes come, we change together.

Fiat Sapientia Virtus, hey? Let Wisdom be Virtue. (But what does that mean, exactly?) ❑

7

THE CHANGES CAME swiftly. On May 14, 1969, a state of emergency was declared. Parliament was suspended (merely a formality, of course; it had never reconvened), and the governance of Malaysia passed to a National Operations Council, headed by Tun Abdul Razak Hussein, the deputy prime minister. The Tunku remained nominally the head of government, but his day was done. With the NOC providing an alternative power structure, those elements within the Malay body politic that had criticized the Tunku as a betrayer of Malay interests found new avenues of advancement; an alternative power structure to employ. (They included a fiery doctor from Kedah named Mahathir Mohamad, whom we will be meeting in due course. It is appropriate, however, that his name be first mentioned here.)

The National Operations Council was composed of the principal leaders of the Alliance political parties and the chief officers of the Armed Forces and Police. Presiding over them was Tun Razak, a soft-spoken, intensely intelligent man of Bugis descent from Pahang. Tun Razak was in many ways the antithesis of Tunku Abdul Rahman. Where the Tunku was flamboyant and romantic, the Tun was dour and self-effacing to the point of drabness. Where the Tunku had dreamed a dream of Malaysia that was a symphony of ideals, the Tun had applied himself to the minutiae of the Malaysian reality. Tun Razak was, at first glance, the quintessential technocrat. He had seemed the perfect deputy, the numbers man, the go-fer, trailing in the wake of the Tunku and replacing the divots and emptying the ashtrays and generally tidying up after the great man's grand and breathless passage.

But behind the Tun's owlish spectacles there resided a gimlet mind, coupled to an iron resolve. Those who wished to continue toying with the notion of a "Malaysian Malaysia" could do so; the Tun would not trammel their ideals. But he was more concerned with hard realities, the most pressing of which was the economic debility of the Malays. The Tun saw this as the Achilles' Heel of the nation. The Malays had to have a greater share of things: opportunities to begin with, then wealth.

But how? The riots had not been an attack by one community on another; they had been a total clash, the Tiger and the Dragon both lunging for each other's throats. The Tun could not possibly agree to the suggestion, from the wilding fringes of Umno, that Chinese businesses be "nationalized" outright and delivered lock, stock and barrel to the Malays. That way madness lay, and a virtual guarantee that those Chinese who could not flee would fight. Besides, who among the Malays had the expertise to run these widespread, deep-rooted, fiscally intricate operations? No, the answer had to be a gradual but determined heightening of the Malays' abilities, coupled by the widening of their horizons. The Tun had to pave the road to prosperity for them, then lead them along it to the Promised Land. And he had to promise them the land.

If it worked as planned, the necessarily increased Malay share of the national economy would be part of an overall economic expansion that would see *everyone* do better, including the non-Malays. It should not be seen so much as the Malays being given a bigger slice of the pie, but more as Malaysia becoming a much bigger pie from which to cut that slice.

It made sense, it sounded good, and heaven knew it seemed more rational than anyone had a right to expect in the circumstances. The blueprint for this "New Economic Policy" was duly drawn up. Its essence was this: Within twenty years of its inception, the New Economic Policy would seek to attain for the Malays and other indigenous races of Malaysia a 30% share of their nation's corporate assets. Non-Malays would be entitled to 40% and foreign interests 30%.

The NEP's statistical targets were themselves subsumed within a twin objective: the eradication of poverty and the cessation of all identification of race with "economic function". In short, to hell with these stereotypes of "Malay farmer", "Chinese merchant", and "Indian labourer". They were the country's most enervating shibboleths, certainly for those afflicted with the less economically mobile identities. As for the rest, the resentment of their countrymen was a fatal corollary to their upward mobility.

The NEP would have taken off no matter how "un-Constitutional" it may have been; after the riots and under NOC rule, Malaysia was a blank slate for policy. But the Federal Constitution had all along contained provisions safeguarding the position of the Malays and their sultanates, their language and religion. It had never been envisioned that Malaysia would cease to be an identifiably "Malay" nation, and it was no great philosophical leap to depict the NEP as a more sensible mechanism to achieve this than the natural interplay of socio-economic forces; what Adam Smith called the "Invisible Hand".

And so, in January 1971, the New Economic Policy assumed its overall stewardship of Malaysia. The NOC was dissolved in February, and parliament reconvened. There were new rules: forbidden, even in parliament, was any and all discussion of Malay rights and privileges, the position of the monarchy and all matters thought likely to incite communal passions. The pre-eminent guardian against such insensitivities would be the awesomely powerful Internal Security Act, which had its genesis in the Emergency Ordinances promulgated by the British at the outbreak of the Emergency, and which provided for the indefinite detention without trial anyone deemed to have behaved in a manner prejudicial to national security.

Tunku Abdul Rahman formally stepped down in September, and Tun Abdul Razak became prime minister.

Solidifying its parliamentary standing, the Alliance roped into its fold most of the minor Opposition parties that had picked up the odd seat here and there in previous elections, with the promise that their members of parliament would get to play a much more significant role on the government benches than otherwise. In early 1973 the greatly expanded Alliance retired the name and symbol it had borne since Independence. The Tunku's blue-and-white sailboat drifted off into history, and in its place was a set of scales, the symbol of the new, "corporatized" government of the Barisan Nasional. The National Front.

Malaysia was back in business. This time, so were the Malays. Indeed, they had become more than mere Malays, the majority components of a multiracial, multilingual nation. Henceforth, their language would be known as "Bahasa Malaysia", the Malaysian Language, and they themselves were now *Bumiputras.*

This was the term, derived from the Sanskrit for "Sons of the Earth", that had been coined to embrace all the indigenous communities of Malaysia. It was more than a name, it was a statement, a title which by its very nature set those Malaysians so honoured with it above the rest, granting them the preferential treatment of the NEP.

Ironies? Consider the Sarawakian tribesman who had not even been a Malaysian until 1963—he was a Bumiputra now, a Son of Malaysian Soil, and any questioning of the privileges of his position would be, by legal definition, an act of sedition. Then consider the Chinese and Indian whose ancestors had arrived here a century or more ago, or even the *Baba,* descended from the Chinese settlers who arrived at the time of the Melaka Sultanate some five centuries ago—they were now, to be polite, "non-Bumiputras". Otherwise to be known, in their Malaysia of the late 20th Century, as *Pendatang.* Immigrant.

I DID VERY WELL out of the New Economic Policy, without even really knowing what I was doing.

While Tun Razak's economic advisers were helping him lash together the massive new state machinery that would pour initiatives and money at the Malays, in the hope that their "lot" would be "uplifted", as if it were a stranded *sampan* needing only a good high tide of cash to send it bobbing back out onto the seas of opportunity, his propagandists were out selling the dream to the nation.

But let me not be too cynical here: the Tun's PR men did a good job, and much of their initial work was well received. In 1971 there was designed a new five-point Code of Conduct called the *Rukunegara*, the "National Credo", which was patterned after Indonesia's *Pancasila*, or Five Principles. Belief in God, Loyalty to King and Country, Good Behaviour and Morality, that sort of thing. There was a nation-wide school essay competition to popularize the concept, and I won first prize in my age-group. A reporter came to take my picture, and soon I received a cheque for $250 and the reporter came again to take a picture of the Headmaster giving it to me, the pair of us surrounded by applauding prefects. Later, I was brought down to Kuala Lumpur with the other prize-winners for the award ceremony. We were given certificates. The sixth-formers received engraved platters. I was glad I was only a fourth-former at the time, because they spelt my name wrongly on my certificate. Then we were taken on a tour of the *New Straits Times* building, which had sponsored the competition and published the winning essays. They made a fuss over us, calling us "fine young Malaysians" and the like.

It was winning the Rukunegara Essay Competition that made me first think that under this New Economic Policy, no Bumiputra could ever really be sure that such "victories" as came his way were fully deserved. Certainly, I hadn't thought my essay, tossed off in two hours in response to a teacher's demand that I submit an entry, was markedly better than those that received the lesser prizes. And the second-prize winner had been Chinese, and the third-prize winner Indian! Happenstance? I didn't think so. Indeed, it escaped no one's notice that all three first-prize winners in the English-language competition were Malays, and that one of the winners in the Bahasa Malaysia section was Chinese. Wasn't this wonderful? So Malaysian were we, and we Malays weren't so dumb after all.

But I took the money anyway, and stashed away the misspelled certificate, because this was one of those things the Malay College relished: national prominence for its students. I would have been damned, however, to have gone to the award ceremony in school uniform. I wore my grey Nehru suit instead. (They were fashionable at the time.)

While all this fuss was going on over such pious fripperies as the Rukunegara, which would eventually be all but forgotten, the truly important moves were being made in the government and corporate sectors. Within months of the 1969 riots, the *Perbadanan Nasional* ("National Corporation") was established. Among the earliest tasks of Pernas was the setting up of a distribution system for Malay businesses, thereby providing them an alternative to the networks long run by Chinese middlemen and wholesalers. Pernas would grow at a sensational clip, within two years branching out into construction, properties, trading, securities and insurance; in the process opening up unprecedented opportunities for Malay entrepreneurs seeking dealerships, franchises and subcontract work.

There was also a vigorous dusting-off of such Malay economic agencies as had existed languorously under the Tunku's administration. RIDA, the Rural and Industrial Development Authority, had been resurrected in 1966 as the *Majlis Amanah Rakyat,* or MARA, a catchy acronym that spelled the Malay verb for "to move forward; to progress". (The English rendition of the agency's title, alas for the language of my narrative, was "Council of Trust for the Indigenous Peoples", although the word for "Indigenous" did not feature in its Bahasa Malaysia name.)

RIDA had existed since 1953 to provide small loans to Malay farmers, having been formed as part of the Alliance understanding that the poorest Malays should not be bereft of government assistance in the new nation a-borning. RIDA had then ventured into the cities to assist Malay contractors and businessmen, and would have gone bankrupt had it been a private-sector finance company. Perhaps it had been under-capitalized. RIDA had received only $10 million or so in the last five years of its life. MARA started up in 1966 with five times that amount. By the time this agency came into my life, in 1973, its budget had quintupled again. In the Second Malaysia Plan, 1971-1975, which was the first of the nation's five-year development plans under the NEP, MARA had more than $250 million to spend. It chose to spend some on me.

I'd taken my fifth-form examinations for the MCE, the Malaysia Certificate of Education, in late 1972. As always, I was surprised to have done well. (As always, so were my teachers.) Indeed, two years earlier, I'd been surprised to have done well enough with my Lower Certificate of Education to have been able to enter the Science stream for my upper secondary years. My father would have been pleased, I thought. Thereafter burbling along, as always, near the bottom of my class, I believed I had made a terrible mistake. While I'd been gazing in wide-eyed bafflement at the splendours of chemical reactions I couldn't describe much less fathom, those guys in the Arts stream, they who "hadn't done well enough" to be in the Sciences, were reading Shakespeare and *To Kill a Mockingbird*, and apparently enjoying literature enough to make in-jokes about it among themselves. ("Harper Lee," says Ali. "Apa, Li?" "Harper Lee, la!" "Siapa Lila?" And so on.) I developed fabulous crushes on their English teachers, while ours made me look forward to Chemistry lab.

A decade or so later, when I was to quit research science for journalism, the only ones unsurprised by my decision would be my Malay College-mates.

But there I was in early 1973, with a first-grade MCE and a MARA scholarship for my A-Levels and subsequent tertiary education in Britain. It was a good year for the Malay

College; my entire year had passed the MCE, the first 100% pass-rate the College had yet achieved, and twenty-three of us won MARA scholarships to the UK. We were among the third batch of eighteen-year-old Bumiputra men and women to be sent off to get degrees in a Science discipline. Only Bumiputras, of course, for that was what MARA was all about, and only Science-stream students, in accordance with the NEP's crying need for a new breed of Bumiputra technocrat.

The MARA scholarship scheme had begun with the NEP, and I'd like to think that this was one of the least ambiguous blessings of the Policy. For among the foreign-educated Malays of the post-1969 generation would be those whose subsequent careers and lives would most closely cleave to the NEP's higher ideals—at least among those of them who would not lose sight of what they were supposed to be doing.

We left for Britain in September 1973, having bid goodbye to a Malay College that would remain forevermore a part of our identities. MARA would pay for all our tuition, and one home vacation after our third year in Britain, and give us each an initial monthly allowance of £58. It would be adequate.

Where was the money coming from? The NEP. More precisely: the political will to boost the national treasury with borrowed funds in the name of the NEP. In the five years to 1970, during the First Malaysia Plan, the government's domestic debt had been around $1.8 billion. For the five years to 1975—under the NEP-inspired Second Malaysia Plan—it would be nearly $4.7 billion, most of it gleaned, as before, from contributions to the Employees' Provident Fund. Foreign borrowing, between the same two timeframes, quintupled to $2.3 billion.

Higher taxes was one way to offset the increasing debt; that and the hope that greater levels of primary commodity exports would help Malaysia make all the money the NEP needed. But the NEP needed a *lot* of money, and planners were concerned that some of the Policy's targets might have to be revised downward to accord with prudence. At so early a stage, however, that would have been politically embarrassing.

The decision to go more deeply into debt had already been a watershed. The MCA's Tan Siew Sin, the nation's finance minister since Independence, had run his ministry with an almost Confucian level-headedness and frugality. But his portfolio had been gradually eased from his total control since 1969. (Tun Tan was to retire from politics in 1974, whereupon Tun Razak would take over the finance ministry.) Fiscal restraint would hamstring the NEP, but in the early Seventies it seemed the dream had to address the realities, and that there would be ineluctable limits to Malaysia's creditworthiness.

Then, in 1973, oil was struck in Malaysia's share of the South China Sea, and we were all off to Britain in brand-new suits. ❑

Night Ride

THE TRAIN for Kota Baru leaves Kuala Lipis at three in the morning.

"You're kidding," said Seng Keat. "WHY??"

Why what? Why anything? Why this journey? Why not take the road, that nice new road that ran from Kuala Lipis to Gua Musang and thence Kuala Krai and the coast? Why take a train that left at three in the morning from the middle of nowhere? "Because it's still there," I said, heroically.

For many years, the train had been the only way to get from Pahang to Kelantan through the hinterland. It had always been one of my more exciting childhood adventures, riding that train with my family to Kuala Krai to visit my mother's people. My father would drive us across the Main range on the Fraser's Hill road, down to Raub and up to Kuala Lipis, a gracious little town on the Pahang River. There he would leave the car in the railway station car-park, and we would board the train with its sleeping berths and its all-night buffet car with the Hakka cooks who never slept and we would rattle through the night and get to Kuala Krai in time for Christmas.

I wanted to reprise that journey. Seng Keat offered to drive me to Kuala Lipis. ("I have to do this for you, man, I just HAVE to!") So we climbed into his immaculate little Suzuki jeep and we crossed the Main Range on the Fraser's Hill road.

It is a very special road. Until it was built by British Army engineers in the early years of this century, there was no land link between the two halves of the Malay Peninsula. The West and East Coasts pursued distinct lives, separated by the Main Range, the *Banjaran Titiwangsa,* the peninsula's central spine of mountains. Sometime in the 1890s, an eccentric English tin prospector named James Louis Fraser discovered the saddle that came to be called the Gap, across which it was feasible to cut a road down into Pahang. Fraser had no interest in going to Pahang, however; he preferred to climb higher up, where he stumbled on the edenic little plateau that now bears his name and is one of the country's sweetest hill resorts. Shortly thereafter James Fraser disappeared into the forests and was never heard of again.

But the Pahang road was duly built, and in the early 1920s the two halves of the peninsula were joined by land for the first time.

On the way up we passed the signboard marking the spot where Henry Gurney had been killed by the communists. It hadn't always been there; I was glad to see it. "I'm glad they've marked the place," I said to Seng Keat. "This the most significant piece of road in the entire country. This place is why we all carry identity cards. Here is why there's an ISA." We stopped to pay our respects to the bend in the road that had made Malaysian history. There were two small shrines near the spot; one Hindu, the other Chinese. There was the sound of rushing water; the bamboo groves by the roadside stirred in a cool mountain breeze. We moved on.

We crossed the border into Pahang at the Gap, and on the way down we barrelled through the hamlet of Tras: a row of shophouses, some great raintrees, a clutch of wooden shacks in a ravine ....

After Gurney's murder, it was found that Tras had incubated his assassins. It was the principal centre of communist supply in west Pahang. The day Gurney was shot, a police cordon was erected around Tras. A man tried to break through, and was shot dead. Among his papers was a bundle of letters from the men who'd killed Gurney, asking sympathizers in Tras for food and medical supplies. The authorities invoked Emergency Regulation 17D, which permitted collective punishment of an entire community. On November 7, 1951, precisely a month after Gurney's death, Tras ceased to exist. All 2,000 inhabitants were arrested, eventually to be scattered to New Villages throughout the peninsula.

We blew through Tras in ten seconds, and continued along the road to Raub, where we struck northward for Kuala Lipis. We passed through areas that had been among the "blackest" in the country during the Emergency: Bentong, Raub ... to this day their names bear the flavour of insurrection, of suspicion, police roadblocks, danger. But it's only history now, and Raub was merely an endless sprawl of sawmills and workshops and ziggurats of scarred red earth where yet more sawmills and factories would rise.

It was late evening when we arrived in Kuala Lipis; the low sun throwing a rich golden light on the small town on a bend in the Pahang River, unfairly blazing into the eyes of one team in a football match raucously reaching its conclusion on the municipal field. We drove straight to the railway station, to which still led all roads in Kuala Lipis. There we learned that the train was due to leave at ...

"THREE A.M.??" Seng Keat was aghast. "What are we going to do for the next nine hours?" I suggested we might find a hotel room in which to dump our bags, then perhaps explore the town a little. Neither of which took very long to do. We were back in the hotel room before the sun had completely set. Seng Keat reclined on one bed and stared at the television with the sound off. I lay supine on the other bed and closed my eyes, listening to the rain on the river. "What's going on, man?" asked Seng Keat.

"Damned if I know," I mumbled. "Just spreading my wings to the winds of circumstance."

But there was more to it than that. I told him the story of a man named Azman; a chance encounter in a small town on the other side of the mountains. Azman, now in his fifties, had been a soldier, had seen action during the Indonesian Confrontation, had killed enemy soldiers, had been lionized and decorated for the killing, had been appalled that murder should be equated with heroism. He had quit the armed services and done "other things" with his life. Azman believed—and it was a most evocative belief—that we all make a promise to God before we are born. Indeed, that promise was a condition of our birth. The lesser creatures—the stones and trees and animals—did not have to make such promises, because they could not but be true to their natures. But man was the highest creature, and if he was to be granted the capacity for self-reflective consciousness, man had to declare his intentions before being granted access to a womb on the material Planet Earth.

"What was your promise?" asked Azman. "This is the task of your life. But first you must try to remember what that promise was."

Most people go through life without even thinking they'd made such a promise, observed Azman. "Now I think I know what my promise was. I promised God I'd be of service to my fellow man. Now I'm trying to find ways to be of service. Not easy, because you do something for someone, and someone else gets jealous, but that's a different story. At least I know my promise."

I liked Azman's metaphor, I told Seng Keat; I believed I too had figured out what my promise was.

"I'm glad you're doing it," he said, "whatever it is you're doing."

"Yeah, so am I, I guess. It's like, you ask yourself, what would you do if you knew you only had a year to live? It's a sensible question, when you think about it. Does anyone know how long they're going to live? I asked myself, and the answer was clear: do this. Come home. Roam around. Write my book. Try and get it right. What would *you* do?"

"Nothing!"

"Probably the best answer there is. So what do you think of this place?"

"I'm amazed people can live here. They must be bored brainless."

"It's not so bad. Destiny pushes you here, you can make something of it."

"I know, but give me the city, man, anytime."

"Advertising has ruined you, my friend."

"But what am I doing to advertising?"

"Redeeming it, I'd imagine. Why are you watching TV without the sound?'

"Who needs the sound?"

"Indeed." I dozed off.

I woke up in the small hours. Seng Keat accompanied me to the railway station, where in the ghastly light of sodium lamps the train to Kota Baru waited, engine-less, by the platform. There were only third-class carriages. I dumped my bags in one of them. Amorphous shadows stirred sleepily on a few other seats. The floor was wet, puddled with water from a lackadaisical effort at cleaning. I rejoined Seng Keat on the platform. We embraced. "You are so much a part of me," I said. "But I'll never know why you made the effort to bring me here. I can never thank you enough, mate."

"Maybe I made a promise," he laughed. "Happy trails, buddy." And he left, walking briskly through the pools of yellow light along the platform, out of the station to where his jeep was parked, there to climb into that valiant machine and begin his long drive through the night down through Raub and Bentong and Karak, back to the Klang Valley, his home in the suburbs, his advertising agency, his own and very private adventure.

The train pulled out of Kuala Lipis. Dirty water sloshed along the floor of the carriage; I stretched my legs out across the seat. I had few companions: the carriage was dominated by a pair of Malay women—a mother and an aunt—and their five young children, four of them girls between the ages of six and twelve, perhaps, in identical garments. The fifth was a boy of about four, clearly spoiled rotten. He blustered and squawked and mewled and whimpered, as his mother and aunt and sisters fussed over him. I bore as much of this as I could, but after an hour of his screeching I exploded. "ENOUGH!" I shouted, precipitating a shocked silence in the carriage. "Can't even *talk* yet, already clever enough to scream!"

Instantly ashamed of myself, I got up and stalked to the gangway for a cigarette. Uncomprehending and fearful gazes followed me out. But the boy kept quiet, and stayed that way for the rest of the journey.

That train ride was a slow and interminable journey through darkness. We ground to a halt at innumerable wayside stations that were hardly more than lean-tos. Out of the pre-dawn shadows of the deep Kelantanese hinterland a strange and atavistic people would emerge to board the train. I was fascinated by their faces and bearing; I seemed to be seeing a lost breed of Malay. One man was the ugliest human being I'd ever seen: his head was disproportionately huge, his cheekbones jutted out like stony promontories, the skin of his face was stretched and shiny over them. His purple-lipped mouth was held permanently agape by a palisade of enormous teeth sprouting from his jaws at impossible angles. His eyes were tiny and slant; his hair a thin mat on that misshapen scalp. But he spoke to his scarcely less arresting companion in the gentlest of voices, although I could not understand a word of what was being said in that purity of Kelantanese they spoke. Young boys in Muslim robes and skullcaps got on, stood in the gangway and gawked at me with guileless wonder in their faces. Youths in jeans and lurid tee-shirts elbowed imperiously on and lit clove cigarettes.

They seemed a lost and abandoned people; if there was anywhere left in the Malay Peninsula that could truly be said to be "remote", it was here, in these obscure little villages of Kelantan, with names like Renok, Kemubu, Dabong and Pahi.

No one ever seemed to get off at any of these halts, so the carriages gradually filled to capacity. I lost my seat, of course, through standing on the gangway on a cigarette break. Two old men in religious garb appropriated my place in the carriage, and that was that; I would have to stand for the remainder of the ride. It took six hours to reach Kuala Krai from Kuala Lipis, a journey of some 250 kilometres. By the time a pink and magenta dawn had begun suffusing the mist-laden morning, I knew I would flee this train in Kuala Krai rather than endure the remaining three hours of the journey to Kota Baru.

That train ride was an affront. The carriages were decrepit; Malayan Railways seemed to have reserved its worst rolling stock for Kelantan. The backwardness of Ulu Kelantan was appalling; so incongruous was it with the level and pace of development so obvious everywhere else in the country. In the last elections, Kelantan had one again chosen to reject the federal government, in favour of Kelantan's idea of an "Islamic" administration. In the atrocious railway service, I believed I could see Kuala Lumpur's umbrage. But in the narrowness and ignorance of these people, I believed I could see why they'd made the choices they had. Or had their choices made them?

It was all more than I could bear. I had survived twenty-four-hour train rides in Sumatra and India. I could not endure more than six hours of a train ride in Kelantan. But then, there was a much more personal dimension to this particular arduousness: it was a Malaysian journey. I practically leapt off that train in Kuala Krai, chartered a taxi for the last sixty kilometres to Kota Baru and slept the sleep of exhaustion all the way there. ❑

8

IN THE FULLNESS of time, my five years in Britain would come to mean surprisingly little to me.

Surprisingly, because one would have thought these would have been strongly formative years. I was not quite eighteen when I left, almost twenty-three when I returned. But I was out of Malaysia, and it seemed almost as if time stood still until the degree was duly obtained and I went home. Perhaps I am too Malaysian for the rest of the world to be more than an occasionally interesting field laboratory of the human condition and its various social and national experiments; a place to observe and contemplate, but never to be a part of.

It was certainly interesting to observe Britain in the mid-Seventies; the place held no great horrors of strangeness for me. I had the language, and, thanks to the epithets and innuendoes I had endured in my first months at Malay College, I had already become somewhat used to being a darkie. In fact, I confess to being secretly rather pleased that my not-quite-fellow Malays might now taste some of how it felt, especially since Britain's own "National Front" (HAH! the irony!) was at that time feeling its oats.

But Britain's venerable racism would not intrude upon us much beyond the hostile graffiti in London subways or the occasional hissed invective from a passer-by, and while in London the milling Malaysian faces and stifling warmth of Malaysia Hall in Bryanston Square afforded us a reasonable facsimile of home. Certainly, the food served there, the stringy meat and long-dead chicken and watery curry and lumpy rice, was easily as good as anything we'd ever eaten in the dining halls of the Malay College.

Once we arrived in the various towns of our new colleges, however, two things began to happen to the Malaysians. First, the Bumiputras would separate from the non-Bumiputras, even if there were numbers of Malaysian Chinese and Indian students in the same towns. (And there often were, because the NEP's encouragement of tertiary education for Bumiputras back home meant a reduced number of university places for non-Bumiputras.) Perhaps there was a socio-economic dimension to the phenomenon: the Bumiputras were almost all on government scholarships or loans, while the non-Bumiputras were almost invariably self-funded. (This either meant that they were as rich as they were reputed to be, or that entire families back home were working to give one child an overseas education, in the hope that he or she might then be able eventually to do the same for his or her younger siblings.)

There was never any hostility about this curious apartheid—there would be smiles and warm greetings all round whenever the twain did meet—but neither was there much effort on either side to cement any firmer friendships. In London, there were two Malaysian student unions; one for Bumiputras and one for the rest. Nothing in their rules said it had to be that way; it was just the way it was.

Second, the Bumiputra groups would themselves divide into those who were keen to explore the possibilities offered by life in Britain, and those who were intimidated by the prospect of what life in Britain might do to them. The former would soon strike out on their own, renting bedsitters and making do by themselves; the latter would pool their resources, rent an entire house and live there together. Admittedly, this also made sound financial sense, and not all the "Malaysian houses" were filled with the fearful—merely the good buddies.

Still, some of these "centres", as they would come to be thought of, would soon become the nuclei for the spread of a new identity among many of the Malay students in Britain; one which was very different from anything their sponsors back home had ever imagined might emerge.

For these were the mid-Seventies, and it was a time of great ferment in the Islamic world. The Shah of Iran was in the last, desperate throes of his benighted reign, and the south of England, to which most of us had been sent, was also the preferred locale for the young Iranian generation that drew succour and inspiration from the preachings of the Ayatollah Khomeini, then in exile in Paris.

I cannot write with any authority on how it happened, because at the first signs of a resurgent Islamism among my colleagues I simply dissociated myself from them. But it happened amazingly quickly. Within months of our arrival I was seeing my compatriots only at lectures, watching them don progressively more bizarre attire and steadily lose weight for fear of eating anything tainted by the Unclean. (This was eventually to include bread, which may have contained animal shortening. They ate cream crackers instead, and would delegate one of their number to make a weekly trip to Southampton to buy *halal* meat in bulk.)

Southampton, the largest city of England's southern coast, was indeed the principal focus of the movement that called itself *Dakwah:* Missionaries of Islam. From the South the proselytizing force spread east to Brighton in Sussex and west to Bournemouth and Poole in Dorset, where I happened to be attending A-Level college. It was the most distressing thing I had ever experienced. We had arrived there as new friends, those of us who hadn't gone to the same schools in Malaysia, and had delighted in our new camaraderie and the adventure of newness that was all around us in Britain. We'd gone bowling and to rock concerts and the cinema, and to cafes at night to sip capuccinos and talk in Malay, revelling in the strength of our bonds in an alien land.

And then, tentatively at first but with growing insistence, some of us had begun inviting the others over to their digs for "discussions". These would turn out to be prayers, followed by a meal, then a lecture on how best to cope with life in an infidel environment. I attended a few of these early sermons—the food was too good to pass up—but I soon grew weary of the arguments that would follow any suggestion on my part that there were one or two things we might learn from the West, that our British classmates might be our friends as well, given half a chance, and that Islam might not be the full and final answer to Malaysia's problems, never mind the world's.

Let me be clear on this: no coercion or overt intimidation was ever exerted by the *Dakwah* on those of us resistant to their call. They relied solely on the subliminal force of peer pressure, and the initial insecurities and loneliness of new arrivals saw to it that their rosters remained healthy, and growing. Another thing: although I have suggested a connection between the "Islamic revolution" in Iran and the genesis of Malaysian *Dakwah*, there never seemed any infiltration of Iran's Shia creed into our Sunni boys. Indeed, *Dakwah* remained a very Malay phenomenon, distinctly nationalistic and all but closed to Muslims from other lands.

In due course, those who remained outside the *Dakwah* fold had to get used either to leading isolated and solitary lives, or to being content with British friends. I wouldn't say I was happy being on my own, but it didn't kill me, or even distress me too much.

Certainly not as much as seeing one of the brightest young women among us forgo the coveted place in medical school she had longed for so dearly. Good Muslim women weren't supposed to become doctors, for some reason, possibly to do with the unclothed human body. There were girls who actually dropped out of college entirely, relinquishing their scholarships, to marry their *Dakwah* boyfriends (it being a sin, of course, to engage in pre-marital romance.)

It got to be more than a little crazy, and eventually MARA and the other sponsoring agencies revoked the scholarships of a few of these people, and brought them home. That knocked some sense into the rest—there was a diminution in the number of proposed marriages, for one thing—but not so much that they would reconsider their newfound philosophy. The *Dakwah* movement, when it went home to Malaysia (which was much sooner than it should have, thanks to those cancelled scholarships), found fertile grounds and quickly became a fixture in Malaysia's own tertiary institutions. From there, its entry into national politics was but a matter of time.

For me, fleeing Poole in 1975 with my A-Levels and heading for Wales and Swansea University, where I was reasonably sure I would be the only Malaysian student within seventy kilometres in any direction, it was the best reason yet to damn the Shahanshah Reza Pahlavi of Iran.

MY UNIVERSITY YEARS were—what? Desultory? Melancholy? Introspective? Something like that. My A-Level grades, though not brilliant, were adequate. I was admitted into the University of Wales's Swansea College, a second-rate institution of some 3,000 students, to read for a degree in Marine Biology.

That had been an impulse decision; picked out of the college handbook much as one might grab a packet of chewing gum at a supermarket checkout counter. Until well into the second year of my A-Level course I'd had no idea what I wanted to study in university. When the decision could no longer be put off, I'd settled on Marine Biology. It sounded good. There was a bit of romance about it; a dash of glamour; a hint of adventure.

It turned out to be almost unremittingly tedious, and eventually I was to stop going to lectures altogether. This, of course, would turn out to be very nearly disastrous. Right through to my final year, however, I pulled through all the necessary exams by dint of private study and cribbed lecture notes. I enjoyed the subject well enough (I discovered a natural aptitude for the Latin and Greek of scientific nomenclature); I just couldn't abide the desiccated monologues of some truly awful lecturers and the plodding ennui of the laboratory work.

But there was no doubt that the subject itself was quite fascinating, and I actually rather enjoyed reading the set textbooks on my own. Certainly, the biannual field trips were fun. We were a small group—there were only nine of us—so the College could afford to take us on trips to Galway in Ireland and the Inner Hebrides of Scotland, places I'd certainly never have seen otherwise, to explore their pristine coastlines and examine the flora and fauna thereon.

But my academic studies quickly became but a peripheral element of my university life. I spent my time learning how to scuba-dive, which I greatly enjoyed and could pass off as an intrinsic element of my degree programme, and playing my guitar and singing songs in the university folk club. I'd taught myself to play the guitar in Poole, during the time of my *Dakwah*-induced isolation, and I got to be quite good at it. In Swansea, my guitar would help me meet more people and make more friends than I'd ever have found had I stuck with the Marine Biology clique. I enjoyed my popularity, and soon became one of the more familiar figures on campus—if not in the lecture halls.

As I'd expected, I was the only Malaysian in Swansea for my first two years there. (There was one other lad who'd enrolled at the same time as me, but he only lasted the first term of his engineering course before opting out for Cardiff, where there were about fifty Malaysian students and where he wouldn't be so alone.) In my third and final year, however, the Malaysian sponsoring agencies began sending A-Level students to Swansea's three senior-secondary colleges. Suddenly, I was the "Senior Brother" to some seventy young Malaysian boys and girls.

I was soundly taken aback by their numbers; I hadn't been aware of how many young Bumiputras were now being sent off for further studies in the West. From fewer than a hundred in my year, 1973, they were now coming out at the rate of 400 or more each year. By the time I graduated in 1978, there would be as many Malaysian students overseas as there were in Malaysia's six domestic universities.

The Swansea crowd lost no time in setting up a "Malaysian Association", and they invited me, as their Senior Brother, to address their inaugural meeting. I took along my guitar and sang them three songs, one each in Malay, English and Welsh. They applauded politely. Then I congratulated them on the formation of their Malaysian Students' Association, but I also told them I didn't quite see the point of it. "If you are friends," I said, "then surely you won't need an Association to be together. And if you are *not* friends, then being members of an Association isn't going to help you *be* friends."

The applause was somewhat muted for that, but not, I think, through any disapproval. I think they simply weren't sure what I was talking about. An Association, with its duly elected office-bearers and its Minutes and Orders of Business and invited Guest Speakers and annual Hari Raya and Malaysia Day festivals, was the very first thing they had wanted for themselves in their new environment. What would life be without one? Inconceivable, apparently. That was my first and last involvement with the Malaysian Students' Association of Swansea. They understood. They were nice kids. They treated me with respect. They knew that, as a final-year student, I had more important things to do than be a dutiful Malaysian.

Two months before my final exams, I began to realize that my cavalier attitude towards my studies had just possibly been ill-conceived. I crammed like a madman, but there was the not unimportant detail of my degree project thesis, which by then was nearly a month overdue. I'd been slated to conduct studies on a certain species of sea-urchin off the coast of South Wales. The previous summer, I had indeed done a couple of dives to that end, but that had been the extent of my "research". One evening, I walked down to Swansea beach, gazed at the darkening sky of twilight, smoked a cigarette or two, then walked back to my digs, sat down at my desk with a pad of paper and started fabricating my thesis.

It was what might politely be called a "literature review", and had that been the object of the exercise it would really have been quite a decent one. But it was supposed to be much more, and I duly concocted my figures and tables, drew up their appropriate charts and graphs and carefully annotated my totally fictitious diagrams. By the following dawn, it was done. "Population Studies on *Echinus esculentus* off the Coast of South Dyfed, by Rehman Rashid, University College of Swansea, 1978." I was quite proud of it, truth be told. As a work of the creative imagination, it was unequalled by anything I'd ever written before.

My professors saw through it as if it were glass, of course, but I think they gave me a couple of sympathy points for it anyway; an "F" for Effort, so to speak. Whatever, given my somewhat less incredible performance in the written exams, they saw fit to allow me the dispensation of a Third-Class Honours degree. I was weepingly grateful for that, because the Latin words *"cum laude"* on my degree certificate would be enough to make all the difference once I was back home and looking for a job.

I left Britain in July 1978, and went home. ❑

Fireflies

A NARROW LANE led off the main road. There was a signpost by the junction: white lettering on a green background; the words DARUL ATIQ. Abode of Freedom.

It was the sort of scene that usually flashes past at the periphery of one's vision; there and gone in the time it takes a vehicle to hiss by and vanish around the next bend. I had seen similar signs many times before, in many parts of the country. This time I turned into the lane.

The lane, becoming progressively narrower, wound for a few hundred metres through lush and wild greenery. Bamboo arched overhead, and on either side I could glimpse fruit trees. The track (and that was all it was by then) crested a knoll, then dipped down into a small valley. I saw beneath me a cluster of fishponds, a stand of banana trees, a huddle of perhaps a dozen houses. They were very simple dwellings, fashioned from zinc and plank by diligent but inexpert hands. They were grouped around the largest building, which was also the only one painted with anything other than bitumen (an effective timber preservative and insect repellent). This structure was bright yellow; there was wire mesh on the windows and a tower at one corner, and from this scaffold pouted the tin mouth of a tannoy horn.

It was, of course, the village mosque. And also community centre and possibly school: I could see a gaggle of little children in voluminous turbans and ankle-length robes spilling out of the building, then standing stock-still to stare at the stranger walking down the lane towards them.

All was silent. I could sense stirrings in the houses I passed; through a few open windows I caught glimpses of women in black robes, peering curiously at me through the eye-slits of their black veils. A youth emerged from somewhere and accosted me. He, too, was wearing the *sarban* and *jubah,* the turban and robes believed to have been the garb of the Prophet Muhammad himself, May the Peace and Blessings of Allah Be Upon Him. But this young man's garments were tattered and grubby, and his slipper-shod feet beneath them were cracked and gnarled. "Peace be with you!" he said, tendering the traditional Muslim greeting with a warm smile, extending his right hand. "What brings you here?" he asked.

"I wanted to find out about this place," I said, returning the greeting.

"You are most welcome. But the Ustaz is not here. He has gone to the town. He should be back soon. Perhaps you might speak with his assistant, who is also his son."

"That is most kind of you."

"Please wait here. I shall find him."

"May I know the Ustaz's name?"

"Ghazali. His son's name is Rizam."

Rizam was a young man of fine appearance. His clothes were clean. He wore a neatly trimmed goatee. His clear eyes flashed with intelligence and good humour. Granting me an almost effusive welcome, he ushered me to a large room tacked on to the mosque. It was, like all else in the village, exceedingly simple of construction: a cement floor, plank walls surmounted by a zinc roof. Under the midday sun, the air within was stifling. But the floor was covered with linoleum, a small bookcase of religious tomes perched in a corner, prayer-rugs were neatly arranged by the walls, and the room was immaculately clean.

In the middle of the floor had been laid a plastic tablecloth, and upon it a tray of drinks and some fried cakes. Here Rizam bid me sit, and he followed suit. He poured me a cup of sweet black tea, and bid me drink. A small girl of two or three came tripping in; obviously Rizam's daughter. She was a pretty child, with a wide and soulful gaze. He dandled her on his knee, indulgently. "Now," he said, "What would you like to know about us?"

"To begin with: what are you doing here?"

He laughed an easy laugh. "What does it look like? We are trying to live as Muslims."

I liked that. *Trying to* ... there was modesty in his choice of words. I asked him to tell me the story of this place. He shooed his daughter away, and began.

His father, Ustaz Ghazali, had been for nearly thirty years a religious teacher with the government. Like all teachers, he and his family had had to lead a wandering life, being successively posted to various schools throughout the peninsula. They had come to rest in one particular village for two years, but there they wore out their welcome. The villagers accused Ghazali of deviant teachings, and told him to leave. Ghazali had gone to the education department for help, and had been told that nothing could be done for him; perhaps it would be best if he did indeed flee, they couldn't guarantee his safety if he stayed.

So Ghazali had fled, taking his family to this piece of land he'd been told about by a friend, far from any sort of organized community, where they might live unmolested. Not all of those villagers had been hostile, however, and a few of them followed the Ustaz to this place. That was ten years ago, when Rizam was thirteen years old. The Ustaz perceived his mission to be as a *Pendakwah Bebas*—a Free Missionary—so he took to journeying hither and yon, preaching to anyone who'd listen. Many did listen, and a few were so captured by his philosophy as to follow him back here to live. So the community grew—but not dramatically, for theirs was, to say the least, a spartan lifestyle. Now there were about fifty people living there; perhaps six families. But many more came to visit or stay for a while, a few weeks or months, on spiritual retreats.

In 1984, two years after founding Darul Atiq, Ghazali had been arrested under the Internal Security Act. The authorities had got wind of his preachings and deemed him a threat to national security. "My father was getting large audiences," said Rizam. "Thousands. This was what worried the authorities." Ghazali and his family had been "relocated" to a small town in Pahang, where presumably no one had ever heard of him, and told not to leave for two years.

When the two years were over they'd come back here to their little commune, which had been faithfully maintained by Ghazali's people in his absence. "My father asked the policemen, what was different in him now, that they could release him? They said, nothing that they could see. But they said they had no argument with him, they were only worried about his followers. And most of them must have forgotten him after two years, so he was no longer a threat."

But the truth was, said Rizam, his father had never been bothered about followers. "Ten thousand, or ten, or one, or none, it doesn't matter. All that matters is Allah."

From outside there came the asthmatic rattle of a car engine in dire need of a tune-up. "That's him," said Rizam. "Now you can speak with him for yourself."

Ustaz Ghazali was a nut-brown and wizened man in his mid-fifties, his head swathed in the coils of a Palestinian scarf, his slight frame draped in the folds of a yellow *jubah*. He emerged from the battered Opel Rekord like a troll from a particularly uncomfortable cave. "This car needs servicing," he said. "I think the exhaust pipe is falling off."

His son said, "There's someone here to see you." The Ustaz appraised me with a quizzical eye, then gestured me back to my place on the floor of the prayer room. "So," he said. "A seeker. But what does he seek?"

"Stories," I said.

"Well, I know a very good storybook ..."

"I believe I may have read it ..."

"Then you should know there are always new stories you can read in it."

"I understand," I said, enjoying his banter but impatient. "But what of your story? Why did those villagers drive you away?"

"They said we were dividing the community. They said we were lost. I said to them, 'show me how I am lost. Help me mend my ways.' But they could not. So I said, 'then I must be lost indeed'. And we left."

"How were you 'dividing the community'?"

"By teaching Islam! The Holy Book tells us how to live. It says, 'Cover thyself. Pray five times a day. Fast during the month of Ramadhan.' It is all very clear, very simple. There is no compromise, no deviation. But to them, we were deviants. They did not like to see their children dress the way Muslims should dress." He puffed out his cheeks in theatrical exasperation. "We who cover ourselves decently are deviants! Those they show naked on television are not deviants!" (He was apparently referring to the aquatic events of the Olympic Games, then being televised live on all three Malaysian channels.)

"That is the way of the world," I said.

"Don't follow the world! Follow the true religion. This is God's world. These are His rules. It is all so simple. Ah, how weak we are." He shook his head morosely, fingering on his chin the straggly wisps of hair that passed for a beard. "Our brains and hearts and souls are no match for television."

But he himself might well have been, given his natural flair for the dramatic. He spoke with eloquence and conviction; his view of Islam was pure and uncomplicated, and therefore possessed of a bovine sort of strength and durability.

"But what of the other religions?" I asked. "What of Christianity and Buddhism and Hinduism?"

"False paths! That's why Islam was the last revelation, Muhammad the last prophet! This is the true teaching, the last teaching. Now we have the choice. God gave us brains so we can make our own choices. The right way, the wrong way, it's up to us. But why should anyone follow the wrong way when the right way is there, so clearly before us? This I have never understood. Even those privileged to have been born into Islam! But now, in this country that calls itself Muslim, how many true Muslims are there? Six, perhaps. Maybe seven. Hah!

"But I'm not saying we should overthrow governments. No, we just advise. And only if we're asked for advice. There is no compulsion in Islam."

He took a sip of tea. "Ah, praise be to Allah. Is it the tea that takes away my thirst? No, *Allah* takes away my thirst! The tea is merely His agent. Is it rice that takes away your hunger? No, *Allah* takes away your hunger, through the rice. You realize this, you understand a little of what Allah is. And if you understand that, then why do you not follow His rules? He has prescribed everything for you! But still they deny Him. They worship a material God!"

Which accusation could never be levelled at Ustaz Ghazali and his Darul Atiq. The commune seemed to survive on fresh air and faith. Vegetables and fruit trees were cultivated, and fish were reared in the ponds. Visitors sometimes donated money. "Praise Allah, we don't starve," said the Ustaz. "Elsewhere, we were always in debt. Here we owe nothing to anyone. We charge no fees, we have no fixed income. Yet we always have enough to feed ourselves. Isn't this proof of God's greatness?"

I asked about the children. What would become of them once they were old enough to need more than elementary education? Given the way they were taught here, it would not be easy transferring them to mainstream schools. "There are other possibilities," said Ustaz Ghazali. "We can send them to Pakistan, or Indonesia. But what is education without Allah? In what they teach in the government schools, I see only ignorance."

And so on and so forth. I left them to their outrage and isolation shortly thereafter. We parted friends, almost: the Ustaz and his son waving farewell to me, Rizam cradling his infant daughter in a crook of his arm, taking holding of one of her pudgy little wrists and showing her how to wave goodbye to me too. I found no argument with them. However crude and infantile their version of Islam, I could not honestly say there was anything fundamentally amiss with it. It lacked intelligence, perhaps, or subtlety: it was the Classics Illustrated version of Islam; Islam Made Easy; the Five-Step Guide to Salvation.

So what? Did ever a society exist without some institutionalized promise of the Quick Fix, the Instant Answer? Ghazali was a Fixer; he knew what he knew, offered no more than what he believed, and there was enough of a demand for his beliefs for the authorities to have taken entirely the wrong sort of interest in his message. It occurred to me that, up a great many blind alleys in Malaysia, in quiet little enclaves by the forest fringe, men like Ghazali were attempting to live by the dictates of their private philosophies as best they could, a step or three removed from the main road.

They were like fireflies, dancing in the darkness, invisible to the great blazing beams of the headlights on the highway, the lights so bright as to blind them. ❑

9

THE FIRST DECADE of the New Economic Policy went by swimmingly. The oil flowed. The coffers swelled. The nation restructured.

Tun Razak died in office at the decade's mid-point, in 1976, and it was a tribute to the competence of his leadership that the economic mechanisms he installed had by then assumed such a momentum as to step lightly over his passing and continue barrelling forward with undiminished velocity. The Tun was succeeded as prime minister by Datuk Hussein Onn, a gentle, aristocratic man from Johore, whose father had been the founder of UMNO. (Onn Jaafar's name has not appeared in this narrative because he was to lose the leadership of UMNO very shortly thereafter to Tunku Abdul Rahman, and fade into a glum obscurity. It was a shame. Onn Jaafar was a very good man. He had envisaged a multiracial political reality for the country from the very start. He had wanted the "M" in "UMNO" to stand for "Malayan" and not just "Malay". Had he prevailed, Malaysia might have turned out very differently. But he hadn't. End of story.)

In Datuk Hussein Onn, Malaysia would have a gracious hand at the helm of government, stern when he needed to be, but otherwise content to let Tun Razak's initiatives carry on for themselves, guided by the dictates of the NEP. An occasional touch on the rudder was all Hussein would ever really need to provide. In the end, his term as premier would reveal itself to have been little more than a political interregnum—something even he must have known, when he elevated Dr Mahathir Mohamad to the deputy premiership.

Malaysian politics, through the 1970s, took a back-seat to economics. In 1974, even PAS joined the Barisan Nasional. The fundamentalists' experiment on the Barisan benches was only to last three years, but at least it made for a little more peace in parliament at a time when there was serious business to attend to outside.

The Tun's death was mourned with all due ceremony, and he received a hero's burial, but it would be nice to see in his illustrious public career the moral that a life's true worth is measured best in what it leaves behind. And what Tun Abdul Razak bin Hussein left behind was the Malay economic planner as Godzilla.

The NEP's goals were clear indeed, but there was only so much that could be done so soon. The 1969 riots were still fresh in the collective memory, and the Policy's implementors had to be careful not to do anything that smacked of unwarranted encroachment on the Chinese sectors of the economy. On the other hand, the spurring of a new breed of Malay entrepreneur had also to be done gently, for this was all very new to the prospective Bumiputra business class. They had to walk before they could run, or risk tripping over their feet. So the Indigene was a novitiate, and the Immigrant crucial to the economy. Which left the Third Man as a target everyone could be sure of. The NEP trained its sights on the Foreigner.

There was still this last affront of colonialism: the traditional mainstays of the Malaysian economy, plantations and mining, remained almost exclusively in the hands of the British. What's worse, there was still an imperial odour about their operations, with the profits from Malaysia's resources helping to prop up less healthy ventures elsewhere in what used to be the British Empire. But the NEP had decreed a 30% limit to foreign ownership of Malaysian resources, and there was no reason to wait twenty years to get moving on this. Enter Pernas.

I have already mentioned the National Corporation's rapid diversification into a multi-sectoral role in the economy. One of the ways Pernas was achieving this was by buying into foreign interests on a minority-shareholding, joint-venture basis. Why not swallow them whole? And who better to swallow than the British plantations and mining companies? This would be undoubtedly popular among Malaysians, few of whom had cause to celebrate the continued presence in their midst of the economic descendants (and in one or two cases, the real flesh-and-blood descendants) of the Colonial *Tuans* of yore.

So, in 1975, Pernas began moving in on the British. More specifically, on London Tin, the biggest tin company in the world, with perhaps $1 billion in assets, three-fourths of them in Malaysia.

Pernas went to London and signed on the advisory services of the Rothschilds Merchant Bank. Rothschilds designed an intricate architecture of deals which culminated in Pernas' acquiring London Tin through a merger with another tin company, Charter Consolidated. The new entity, of which Pernas owned 71%, was called the Malaysian Mining Corporation, which is now the biggest tin company in the world.

Next, Pernas went after Sime Darby, the plantation giant. Its tactics were a little different this time, but they were ultimately just as effective. They involved the insinuation of Pernas nominees onto the Sime Darby board, on the basis of Pernas's 25% stake in the company, coupled with the co-operation of Sime Darby's largest shareholder, the Overseas Chinese Banking Corporation of Singapore. The OCBC was happy to throw in its 46% share of Sime Darby behind Pernas upon the appointment of Malaysia's revered and recently retired ex-finance minister, Tun Tan Siew Sin, to the chairmanship of the Sime Darby board. Pernas didn't seek outright ownership of Sime Darby so much as executive control of the company's assets, which was much the same thing.

Pernas was *the* vehicle of Bumiputra capitalism in the 1970s, and did much to launch the political career of its youthful chairman, Tengku Razaleigh Hamzah. Tengku Razaleigh was a prince of the Kelantan royal family. It may have been ironic that one of Malaysia's foremost capitalists should have emerged from the state that traditionally incubated Islamic fundamentalism, but this was to work to his political advantage soon enough. It wouldn't last ... but I am getting ahead of my narrative.

In 1978, Pernas was joined by another state enterprise dedicated to the economic advancement of the Bumiputras. This was *Permodalan Nasional Berhad,* the National Equity Corporation, which would pick up where Pernas left off and eventually become one of the richest bodies in Malaysia. PNB took off on a running start, assuming control of eleven of Pernas's most profitable companies, with a collective worth of $1 billion or so. Three years later, PNB announced itself to the corporate world in a truly dramatic fashion: the Fabulous Dawn Raid on Guthrie's of London.

Guthrie was the doyen of Malaysian plantations. Pernas, after collecting Sime Darby, had gone for Guthrie and been thwarted. It now leapt to the side of the ring and tapped its tag-team partner, transferring its 25% share of Guthrie to PNB, who then went to London to see the ever-amenable Rothschilds. Silently, PNB and its British advisers assembled the equity wherewithal to pounce on Guthrie's when the venerable British firm was least expecting it, in the very early morning of one fateful day. It cost nearly $1 billion, but it was worth it. PNB's Dawn Raid in 1981 was hailed as a triumph of almost military proportions. PNB had brought Guthrie home from London to where it belonged. Malaysia exulted.

That was enough for the rest of the British-owned plantation sector. In short order, Dunlop, Harrisons & Crosfield and Barlow-Boustead all took due notice of what the NEP expected of them, and sold the bulk of their assets to Malaysia. PNB got most of them, and later in 1981 it set up the *Amanah Saham Nasional,* the National Unit Trust, to provide every Bumiputra with $10 to spare a chance to invest in some of their nation's richest and most profitable companies. Ten years later, the ASN scheme would have nearly three million subscribers (or half the Bumiputra population above the age of consent) and PNB would command an investment portfolio worth a total of $11 billion.

Amazing successes; the work of a scintillating few Malay financiers, capitalists and corporate geniuses. But for many of the Malays whose own dreams of wealth were sparked by the burgeoning fortunes of Pernas and PNB, the NEP would seem a road paved with the proverbial good intentions. The Policy had given them access to cheap loans to start up or expand their businesses, but many of them had simply taken the money and bought new cars and houses, perhaps on the premise that to be successful, one must first *look* successful. Wouldn't prospective business partners and clients be more inclined to trust one's judgement if one tooled up to meetings in a Mercedes?

Alas, not if one didn't actually *own* the Mercedes. By the early Eighties, hire-purchase companies would be regularly taking out space in newspaper classifieds to publish the names of defaulters, and these would be sorry lists of one Bumiputra name after another. It used to curl the lip of many a Chinese merchant, who would take pride in forking out cold hard cash to buy a car: the Malays would go into debt to buy the smallest thing. Never mind the TVs and hi-fis—electrical appliance stores would offer even steam-irons or rice cookers on hire-purchase; $20 down, $2.50 a month thereafter for however long it took to pay up to 20% more than the cash price, and people would accept such terms rather than save up the pittance it cost to buy such items outright.

The Malays seemed to be most damningly different from the Chinese in this one respect: where the Chinese measured success in profit, the Malay measured his in property. The legends of the Chinese rags-to-riches millionaire, stepping off the boat with nothing but the clothes on his back and ending up richer than Croesus, were paeans to the value of frugality and sheer hard graft. He would work like a dog, saving every cent he could until he had the capital to start some small business of his own, then continue working like a dog, ploughing every cent he earned back into his business, until one day he would wake up and find himself wealthy beyond the dreams of avarice.

But the Malay wanted it all, and wanted it NOW. In 1983, it was somewhat sheepishly admitted that of the 55,000 loans MARA had given to Malay businesses by then, nearly 90% had not been repaid when due. Something was wrong with that beached *sampan* that had been meant to float out on the NEP's tide of cash; it didn't appear to be all that seaworthy after all.

And what of the Chinese in all this? He fell back on the traditional bonds that had always cemented his community; he took care of his own, and was in turn taken care of. And he worked even harder: during these years when Malay shops were mushrooming as never before, with the Chinese share of Malaysia's main-street sundry stores dropping from three-quarters to two-thirds, their average turnovers remained proportionately the same. The Chinese shop kept making, on average, three times as much as the Malay's.

Above all, the Chinese *adapted,* as he always had; he rolled with the flow. In government, the MCA, though practically unable to get any measures passed to positively enhance the well-being of the Chinese community, nonetheless guarded well enough against its detriment. The argument, and it was a potent one, was that the NEP's success depended on the Chinese continuing to bolster the national economy during these formative years, while the Malays were still feeling their way. In this, the Chinese, with his expertise, experience and savvy, would actually *help* the Malay learn the ropes of business.

It might have worked, if the Malay had actually wanted to learn the ropes. But more often than not, he just wanted to be rich. The new pattern of inter-racial co-operation under the NEP all too often consisted of the Malay using his privileges to acquire licences and permits denied the non-

Malay, then accepting a fee to be the front-man while the non-Malay ran the business. One couldn't blame the Chinese for this "Ali Baba" approach, as it was called. He was merely doing what he had always done: making the best of his situation, keeping a weather eye out for the slightest opportunity that might come his way. But the "Ali" of the equation, who believed he was being smart and making money without effort, was betraying the goals of an enormous national sacrifice. For the object of the NEP, this new national religion that had divided Malaysians into first- and second-class citizens, was to enhance Malay dignity; to prove that all that had ever constrained the Malays was a lack of opportunity, and that given the opportunity the Malays could prove themselves equal to anyone.

And all this "Ali" was doing was making asses of the Malays in the eyes of their countrymen. ❑

Followers

A TAXI WAS stuck in the midday traffic, halfway across the bridge that spans the Klang River as it oozes thickly past the Masjid Jame in Kuala Lumpur. It was the hour of the Friday prayer, and the old mosque was jammed. The congregation spilled out of the mosque and rippled across the forecourt like water in a ricefield. Even that space was not enough, and many of the faithful were laying their prayer-mats down by the roadside and onto the bridge.

In their Friday best they readied themselves to commune with the Almighty, while the midday sun burned down upon their heads through the thick brown haze of the city sky, and their corporeal bodies were wreathed in the blue and black smoke from the idling exhausts of immobile traffic. Pedestrians had to step into the street to skirt them. Tourists stared in amazement; one panned a video camera across the scene.

The taxi-driver was a young Indian man, a devout Hindu. A string of jasmine flowers dangled from his rear-view mirror, swaying in the cool breeze from the car's air-conditioning vents, and full-colour images of Saraswati and Ganésha, Lakshmi and Murugan danced and smiled in benevolent godhood across the dashboard. While the traffic lights ahead stayed red, the driver and his passenger both gazed thoughtfully at the spectacle unfolding by the roadside, inches from the wheels of their vehicle.

Thought the passenger, born a Muslim himself: What must this young Hindu make of what he sees here? Surely he might be forgiven for seeing an awful obsessiveness, a faith of the brink of fanaticism. What remains of purity when the most sacred of prayers is offered by the gutter of a poisonous street in a city choking on its own toxins? Where in this scene was the sanctity of prayer; the fragrance of jasmine?

So he asked the driver: "What do you make of this, brother?"

And the driver said, quietly: "These people are followers. With good leaders, they will be good people. With bad leaders, they will be bad people."

On the bridge the faithful composed themselves in prayer, laying their foreheads on the pavement, sitting back with hooded eyes to face the littered ditch, the mud-brown river, the hawker stalls opposite, the grime-blackened buildings, the shimmering heat haze of the street and beyond all this, Mecca.

Up ahead the lights turned green, and the traffic inched forward and away. ❑

10

"YOU ARE WHAT you are because you're a Bumi," said Miss Chee Phaik Ean, M.Sc., with eminent reasonableness. She looked up at me, the whisper of a smile on her lips, defiance glittering in her intelligent eyes. A fleeting silence fell upon the busy laboratory: it was almost a physical sensation, like the settling of a light, white, diaphanous cloth. Right ON sister, the silence seemed to say, let's see how the Golden Boy responds to this.

I was struck dumb. Me? A Bumi? I hadn't been back in Malaysia long, and I hadn't quite grown used to the pejorative overtones that had come to afflict the term "Bumiputra", as in "the bloody Bumis", etc.

What could I say? She was right. It was true. Had I not been a Bumi I'd never have received a scholarship to Britain, never have gone to university, never have come home with a degree, and never have gotten a job with the Agriculture Ministry within three months of getting back. Finding that job had not been a straightforward process; "Marine Biology" seemed as exotic to Malaysian employment agencies as it had to me three years before. But there was the Agriculture Ministry, and within it the Fisheries Department, and after a visit to a senior civil servant in the ministry I was on my way to Penang and a post at the Fisheries Research Institute.

And now I was a Grade One Government Officer, no less, thanks to my Honours degree (HAH!), on salary scale A-21. I was the first Malay officer they'd been able to hire in years.

"Okay, fair enough," I said to Miss Chee. "But come on, it's not as if the UK gave a damn about whether I was a Bumi or not. Once we got there, we had to earn our degrees the same as everyone else." (Remembering how I'd earned mine, I cringed.)

"But you *got there,* lah!" she exclaimed. QED. Checkmate. Case closed. Time for tea. My treat.

This was banter. Light-hearted, friendly. I'd been welcomed warmly enough by the researchers and technicians of the FRI; as the first of their NEP graduates, I suppose I must have seemed cosmopolitan and worldly enough not to be too obviously the product of the preferential policies that had got me there. But the non-Malays—and the FRI owed the bulk of its expertise to Chinese and Indian scientists—knew I was but the vanguard of the New Order. Soon, many more young Malays would be coming in with degrees, and they would find themselves on the fast-track of career advancement, and swiftly overtake their older, more experienced, non-Bumi colleagues.

Very early in my Malaysian career, then, I was feeling the cut of the NEP as the double-edged sword it was. It would help the Malays move faster and better, but it would never win them the respect of their fellow countrymen. Advancement they'd be given; respect they'd still have to *earn.* Malaysia had turned resolutely away from the meritocratic norms of upward mobility, but deep down, where it counted, in the hearts of all Malaysians, the meritocracy would remain. No matter how high a Malay might climb on the back of the NEP, his countrymen would always judge him personally by his own performance—which meant he had to excel, or be damned as a privileged stooge.

I tried to excel. But this was the government service, and excellence didn't seem all that high on its agenda. Many of the researchers at the FRI were much more than competent, but it was administered as a bureaucracy rather than a scientific establishment, and there was a tacit sense that only fools did more than they had to. One's salary would come anyway at the end of each month, and the progress of one's career depended little on how hard one worked, but more on how long one could stay quietly in place without ruffling feathers or rocking boats.

I was actually told as much by the institute's Director, on my first day there: "Don't rock the boat. Don't make waves." This to an eager young marine biologist who was wild with impatience to leap off boats and plunge through waves? It was not a promising augury.

So the three years I was to spend at the Fisheries Research Institute would be devoted as much to clock-watching, tea-breaking and newspaper-reading as to doing things for the fishermen, of for marine research in general. Fortunately, there was enough of the latter to make my time there interesting and educational. During the inter-monsoon seasons we would go out on the FRI's research ships—converted trawlers, crewed by an engaging assortment of ex-fishermen—to survey coral reefs or trap fish for the FRI's big public aquarium, or build artificial reefs of old tyres, the better to replenish fish stocks in depleted areas.

This was, politically, one of the more important projects of the Fisheries Department, and quite a lot of effort was devoted to setting up these structures around the Malaysian peninsula. The artificial reefs were touted as part of the government's effort to help poor fishermen, as indeed they did.

But perhaps our publicity machinery worked a little too well, because one day we received word that the Minister of Agriculture himself was coming to Penang, and that he wanted to give the press a photo-opportunity of himself fishing on one of our famous artificial reefs. This sent the Director into a frenzy. Even the stoutest of efforts hadn't made our experimental reefs around Penang productive, because these structures depended on there being at least the remnants of a natural reef system somewhere nearby, from which to draw their seed-stocks. Penang's waters were nearly dead, opaque with effluent and sewage from the big beach hotels that had sprung up along the northern coast of the "Pearl of the Orient". Within a couple of years, the FRI aquarium would have to shut down because it drew its water from the Penang strait, and its fish were dying of horrible diseases.

The best artificial reef for the Minister to fish, where he'd be practically assured of catching something that would make him look suitably heroic, was a six-hour boat-ride to the north and out of the question.

So the Director called me into his office, bid me shut the door, and gave me urgent instructions. I was to go to the nearby Jelutong fish-farm and purchase a nice, big, fat, *live* grouper. (A petty-cash voucher would be made available to me for this purpose, or perhaps I'd better use my own money first, and he'd personally reimburse me later, yes, that would be a good idea, we had best be discreet about this.)

Then I was to smuggle the fish in a gunny sack aboard the Minister's boat before he got there, along with myself and my diving equipment, and hide somewhere. When the boat had moored on the reef and the Minister had cast his line, I was to don my scuba gear, slip quietly over the side with my fish and *hook it onto the Minister's line.* Got that?

I looked at him. He seemed deadly serious. I considered my options. "I don't think I can keep the fish alive long enough, sir," I said. "We'd need to keep it in a salt-water tank with an air dispenser. It would be hard to hide that. It would make noise."

He pondered the problem, nodding slowly. Then he brightened. "It wouldn't have to be *very* alive," he said.

"Then the minute I got it in the water it would revive and want to swim away," I said. "It would not be easy to hold onto a big fish like a grouper under water. They're slippery."

He gave in. "Okay, use a dead fish."

"A *dead* fish, sir?" I said. "What will the Minister say when he sees he's hooked a dead fish?"

"Don't worry about that," said the Director. "We can always say it died on the way up."

"Yes sir," I said. "Anything you say, sir."

I didn't do anything of the sort, of course, although my colleague Edward Wong and I did go along with our scuba gear and jump into the water for the benefit of the media-men accompanying the Minister. The Director's scheme would have been rendered pointless anyway, thank the stars, because a heaven-sent passing fisherman happened to have a big red snapper in his *sampan*, and the Minister was duly photographed pointing proudly at this fish while its captor held it aloft. The Director was pleased as punch, and gave Edward and me the afternoon off.

I've *always* wanted to tell this story, and I recount it here only to underscore the point I made earlier about what it took to advance in the government service.

I made the most of my stint with the FRI, vigorously trying to atone for my lacklustre degree by writing and publishing research papers in local scientific journals, but I hated government service. Its inertia and inefficiency were bad enough, but there was also the matter of the fishermen. The more I grew to know the fishing communities of Malaysia—and I would get to know them quite well in my three years with the Fisheries Department—the more misguided and ineffectual I felt we were.

The villages were crumbling. Time and again, on both coasts of the Peninsula, we would come across fishing villages inhabited only by women, infants and the very old. On Pulau Redang, off the East Coast state of Trengganu, I learned how it was almost a stigma for the son of a fisherman to remain a fisherman himself, and not go to the mainland in search of a "real" job. I was astonished. My city-boy sensibilities would have had me gladly trade places with these people, for the sake of Redang's fine reefs and the protein they contained, for the sweet air of these clean skies. But no, these youths wanted more, and I would often see them, or those very like them, in Kuala Trengganu, the state capital, lounging around by the cinema at night in their sneakers and jeans and rugby shirts, sullenly smoking cigarettes and seeking opportunities, no doubt.

Elsewhere, entire fishing villages had simply ceased to exist. Their inhabitants had uprooted *en masse* and left for the new agricultural schemes opening in the hinterland, to tend rubber trees or plant oil palm seedlings, and live in the neat little wooden houses built for them by the government. The Federal Land Development Authority, FELDA, had been founded with the nation and grown to be Malaysia's biggest land bank and resettlement scheme. It had opened up more than a million acres of land for industrial agriculture and relocated to these vast tracts some 10% of the nation's population. Traditional farmers and fishermen had been encouraged to avail themselves of these new opportunities, and many had answered the call. The fishing industry had been increasingly left to large trawler fleets, most of them Chinese-owned, while the Malay fisherman had gone off to try his luck as a planter.

Had no one suggested to the small fisherman that his poverty might be alleviated without his ever having to stop being a fisherman? Pool your resources. Get ten fishermen together with $1,000 each, and you'll have enough for a down-payment on a trawler of your own. If you don't have even that much money to your names, go get some from the NEP, that's what it's there for. This had indeed been done on Pangkor Island, in the Straits of Malacca off Perak, and with considerable success. But it had been done—and without any help from the NEP—by a group of Indians.

It must have seemed a lot simpler for our small fisherman to accept the government's offer of a plot of FELDA land and start life over as a sharecropper. Especially since he would be much more that a mere tenant farmer: he would be part of his nation's crusade to bring development to the hinterland; part of Malaysia's progress; part of the living NEP.

And his beached *sampan* would slowly rot away on a deserted shore.

Within a year of taking up my post at the Fisheries Research Institute I was writing to oil companies and diving firms, shamelessly embellishing my curriculum vitae and pleading for a job. None was forthcoming, and I consoled myself with the pleasant diversions of life in Penang.

Penang was, despite the frustrations of my job, a very nice place to live. I enjoyed driving around the island or going up the Hill, or simply losing myself in Georgetown's colourful warren of Chinese streets. Penang was a user-friendly place. I shared a small house in Minden Heights with a Chinese teacher, Chu Chin Koo, who would remain a dear friend for life, and Phil Crane, also an avid diver and an American Peace Corps Volunteer attached to USM—"Universiti Sains Malaysia," the National Science University.

I hooked myself informally into the university's School of Biological Sciences, which had a credible marine programme and was looking for diving instructors for some of its students. The Underwater Research Group, Universiti Sains Malaysia ("URGUSM", in a word) would be a great success, and Phil and I would have our work cut out for us during our twice-weekly training sessions at the university's swimming pool.

Perhaps by virtue of its location in Penang, USM was the last Malaysian university to succumb to the ethnic polarization of its student body. The phenomenon was already making itself apparent in other colleges, with the Malays and non-Malays drifting further and further apart, and the *Dakwah* movement visibly growing in prominence.

But at least while I was there, in the cusp of the decades, USM was still a funky, lively place. Despite its name, the university housed energetic faculties in Humanities and the Performing Arts. I was glad of that; glad that a Malaysian campus didn't feel as alien to me as I had feared it would. ❑

Dream Women

IT IS NOT generally advisable to walk into a place calling itself "Singles Pub" with one's fly open.

Chu Chin Koo had suggested this place, a converted bungalow along the Tanjong Tokong road, as somewhere we might sample a bit of what Penang's nightlife had become. It sounded good to me. Very Penang. There are not too many other cities in the world where entertainment venues declare their predilections quite as boldly. Hong Kong has its Bottoms Up bar in Wan Chai. In Bangkok there's Pussy Galore in Patpong; in Manila's Ermita district, the legendary Brown Sugar. In Amsterdam, I once came upon a charming canal-side hotel catering exclusively to the gay community. It was called Hotel Come-Back, so I never did.

But here was Penang in the Nineteen-Nineties: the lean years were assuredly over, giant condominiums vied with new hotels for dominance of the fabled Ferringhi ("Foreigner") coastline, the tourist dollar was back in force, and more than a few of the gracious old mansions of sometime millionaires had tarted themselves up as gaudy watering holes, to make the most of the new prosperity. Penang's value was only partly due to the foreign tourist. For ages it had also been the breakaway haven for Peninsular Malaysians. Now the travelling salesmen were back on the road, and their needs were being met in arc-lit mansions of green neon, a-screech with Chinese songstresses in slinky red *cheongsams.*

I was glad to see the renaissance of this class of entertainment (if not to hear it). I had thought it was extinct. But it wasn't for me. My ear is not fine enough to appreciate the tonal subtlety of Chinese pop songs, however svelte and comely their purveyor, and I have never been able to consume brandy by the glass without consigning to eternal oblivion what should otherwise have been a memorable experience.

Chu assured me the Singles Pub was not that loud and inaccessible. "An interesting crowd" was often to be found there, he told me. So we went. Perhaps I should have minded my attire—but then there would have been an entirely different story.

It was quite spartan inside: a linoleum dance-floor, deserted at that relatively early hour of the evening; gantries of coloured lights; nests of tables at which sat a motley crowd of youngsters. The music—a distressing assortment of oldies, including Trini Lopez, for heaven's sake—was provided by one of the lesser Filipino bands. There was a long horseshoe bar, at which Chu and I found a perch. We ordered beers. I leaned against the bar, hooking my heels around the barstool legs. I fished out a pack of Winstons from my shirt pocket and delved into my jeans for my Zippo. I lit my cigarette with a flourish, inhaled, exhaled and surveyed my surroundings. In a nearby corner sat a young couple. He was nondescript; she was pretty. Soft straight hair cut in a stylish page-boy bob, a loose red blouse, blue jeans, red socks in patent-leather pumps. She was smiling at me. I smiled back, I hoped with just the right touch of interest. I felt undeniably an ageing roue, but I hoped it did not show.

Her smile widened. She flicked her eyes downward to my crotch. Chu was right. An interesting crowd, indeed. Involuntarily, I glanced down. My fly gaped vacantly at me like a roadside cretin. The steel teeth of my parted zipper gleamed red and yellow in the lights. "Chu?" I said.

"Huh?"

"My fly's open."

"You got a problem."

"What should I do?"

"I have no idea."

"I suppose I should zip it up."

"That may be wise."

"But I don't want to attract attention."

"Too late."

There was nothing for it. I reached down and manfully zipped myself shut. The girl broke into a happy laugh. I smiled gamely back at her. I shrugged self-deprecatingly, as if to say, "Hey, it happens, but I'm cool." I felt a complete fool. The next thing I knew she'd abandoned her companion and flit over to sit on the barstool next to me.

"You must have had some fun before coming in," she said. "Hi. I'm Sunny."

"I can see that," I said. "At least, now I can. I thought you were a girl."

"Thanks," he said, warmly.

"This is my friend Chu."

"Hi. I'm Sunny."

"Glad to hear it," said Chu.

Sunny worked in a travel agency by day. Sunny knew most of Penang's nightspots, but frequented only a few of them. Sunny liked the Singles Pub, because of the interesting crowd. Before I quite knew what I was saying, I told Sunny I'd love to see him dolled up. He squared his slight shoulders and said: "Tomorrow night. We're doing a show. Why don't you come?"

It emerged that Sunny was a founding member of Penang's Very Own Drag Troupe, the Mannequins. "Clever name, right? People who can't pronounce it say 'Man-Queens', and that's what we are!" I asked him what kind of show it was.

"Oh very dramatic! Very theatrical! Like Paris."

"The Folies Bergere," I said.

"The Moulin Rouge," he said.

"The Crazy Horse Revue," I said.

Sunny began to get excited. "We'll have head-dresses, with feather boas and swimsuits. The two most beautiful of us ... you should see them, they're so beautiful, twenty-four-inch waists, you'd never know they're not women. I'm the shortest," he said, a little ruefully. "Of the ten of us, I'd say I was number six or seven."

"That doesn't say much for numbers eight, nine and ten."

He laughed. "Well, maybe six through ten are the same. But wait till you see one and two! We have a closing number set like in a jailblock, we're all in convict costumes with chains and everything. We're all women in prison for killing their husbands for infidelity."

"A theatrical experience," I said.

"Dramatic!" said Sunny.

And so it came to pass that, soon after sundown the following evening, Chu and I found ourselves in Room 742 of Penang's plush new Equatorial Hotel, watching a group of young men transform themselves into women. And not just any women, no! Harlow! Garbo! Monroe! Madonna Mia!

Had we edited out the metamorphoses taking place before our astounded eyes (but why would we want to?), the room would have been a total mess. Piled on an elegant coffee table was a pungent heap of styrofoam boxes of pork and rice. Strewn among them were half-drunk packets of chrysanthemum tea. Garment bags lay slumped like dead animals in every corner. But at the dressing table Sunny, sheathed in a blue silk dressing gown, hair held back with a chiffon bandeau, was applying the final touches of make-up to her eyes—and she was assuredly "she" by then. The wrist, the fingers, the precisely wielded eyebrow pencil, the tilt of the jaw ... Sunny was Marlene Dietrich, and downstairs in the ballroom her audience awaited.

There were voices in the bathroom, where CB and Boo Ket were tussling over mirror rights. (But they would not be CB and Boo Ket for long: Michelle and Martha were a-borning.) On the thickly carpeted floor between the twin beds, Kim was showing Jasmine how to do her eyes. Jasmine was the Star. The Number One. Eighteen years old, discovered just a fortnight before, walking along Penang Road. "She wasn't in drag," recalled Sunny, reverently, "but even as a boy she was the prettiest girl in town. This is going to be her first show. She's going to kill them."

If looks alone could kill, there would be no doubt. Jasmine had the body of a fawn and the face of an angel. Her skin was the colour of honey; her hair was thick and lustrous. "That's her real hair?" I asked, wonderingly.

"Of course," riposted Sunny. "Everything you see here is real. Everything. *Everything."*

Jasmine tossed her head—Kim reproved her—but said nothing. She spoke no English or Malay, only Hokkien. Jasmine had never left Penang. She had not been beyond primary school. Kim said, "Yes, she's beautiful. But she's so awkward. Looks alone aren't enough. She has to learn how to move."

Kim applied one last flick of a mascara wand to Jasmine's eyelashes, cupped Jasmine's chin in three fingers, tilted her head this way, then that. "Aiya, okay lah. Go get dressed." Jasmine unfolded her legs and coiled upward. She vaulted over the bed, graceful as a ballerina, and into her high-heeled shoes. She snatched up a bag and sashayed towards the bathroom, her hair dancing about the nape of her neck. Kim watched her. "It's the shoes," she murmured in a voice low and husky. "She lives for those shoes." Then Kim began to put on her own face.

Kim was the group's "auntie". The Grande Dame, the Diva, Madame Butterfly. She would have been in her mid-thirties. To say she was beautiful would be to miss the point. Kim was one of the first Pretty Boys of Penang to have saved up enough from whoring to go to Europe for the sex-change. For ten years he had worked the bars of Tanjong Tokong. Then, ten years ago, he had gone to Holland. She had lived there ever since, in Rotterdam, coming home for a couple of months every year to see her family and friends.

Kim had a full and trembling bosom. Her hair cascaded in soft waves down to her waist. Her face was oval, her complexion clear to the threshold of radiance, her lips bee-stung. Meticulously, in absolute silence, holding a compact mirror before her, she worked her artistry on that face. The creature that began to emerge was stunning; unearthly. To watch her was almost like participating in a religious ritual. "You are very beautiful, Kim," I said, not bothering to keep the amazement from my voice. "Thank you," she breathed, almost inaudibly.

CB came bustling out of the bathroom, wearing a floral bathrobe. "Hi, I'm CB," he chirped. "Actually, this is just a well-paid hobby. Some people collect stamps. Where are my stockings?"

Sunny explained, "We have to wear nine pairs of stockings, with padding for our hips and thighs. We have to reshape our legs. It's a trade secret."

"NINE PAIRS?!" I blurted. "Isn't it hot?"

"If it makes us beautiful, why not?" said Sunny.

"Ya lah," said CB. "But when you want to piss it's hell."

Boo Ket yelled from the bathroom: "Eh Sunny ah? Lu eyebrow pencil?"

Sunny called back: "Brown or black?"

Eyebrows are the dead giveaway, apparently. Men's are thick, straight and low; women's are thin and upwardly curving. So: elaborate disguises with shadow and liner. Chu and I watched, fascinated and peculiarly disturbed, as the layers went on one after another. Each successive external layer seemed to root itself successively deeper within, reflecting outward in their voices, their movements, their personalities.

Then it was done. Five minutes to curtain rise. They were ready. Jasmine darted out the door and almost sprinted for the lift. "Aiya, so eager that one," said CB.

"You look lovely, CB," I said.

She gazed steadily at me through eyes like Liza Minelli's. "I'm not CB anymore," she said. "Call me Michelle."

It was a good show, I thought. The troupe performed nine numbers. The routines were well chosen; each one was slickly choreographed. The costumes were quite spectacular. Jasmine proved not to be the show-stopper her mentors had expected; she was nervous and stiff onstage. But she would improve rapidly, they were sure, as soon as she got used to the thrill of having all those eyes on her.

Ah, but those eyes ... it was an audience of office workers. Some corporation or other was having its annual company feast, and the Mannequins strutted their occasionally outrageous stuff before a crowd of catcalling clerks. The head table, with perforce the best view, was obese with company eminences in orchid corsages and their religiously hooded and corpulent wives, who stared sternly at their dinner plates throughout the Mannequin's performance. I nudged Chu. "Check out the guests of honour," I said. He chuckled knowingly. "Only in Malaysia," he said.

Onstage the lights shone in the Mannequins' eyes as they danced and twirled on clouds of dry ice, borne on the music of their pre-recorded soundtrack. They pouted and flounced and jiggled their foam-padded brassieres. They made phallic symbols of their feather boas and kicked high their four-inch stilettos. They flirted and preened and at one stage in that infamous closing number they all turned around and bent over and presented their black-pantied foam-padded nylon-smooth backsides to the audience. And then the music exploded in a crescendo, of sorts, and they were back with their bows and curtseys, blowing kisses into the lights, beaming into the cosmos with radiant smiles, waving to the darkling heavens. The curtain fell. The deejay called for Another Big Hand for Penang's Very Own Man-Queens, and when the spatter of applause died away he said it would soon be time for the Lucky Draw. A scattering of sequins glittered on the stage; a single white feather drifted slowly in the eddies of air above.

Upstairs in their dressing room, the Mannequins were jubilant. The show had gone very well, they thought. Kim summed up: "The men enjoyed it, the women were jealous, what to do, you can't please everybody." The dancers were swiftly shedding themselves of their costumes, but enough of the make-up stayed on to carry the illusion on into the night. Most were adjourning to a disco in Batu Ferringhi. But Sunny was quietly at work by himself in front of the dressing table, removing every last trace of make-up. He would go home and sleep; he had a job to go to the next morning. Jasmine, no; Jasmine was on her way out to destroy this night. She slid into tight jeans, fashionably ripped at the knees, and levered her slender torso into a white lace bustier. A glance at the mirror, a toss of the hair, and Jasmine was out the door and away. Which midnight disco Lothario was destined to be shocked out of his wits tonight?

Chu and I waited for Sunny to clean up, and for Kim to change into her street clothes of chiffon blouse and bermuda shorts. The four of us were the last to leave, "So did you enjoy the show?" asked Sunny. We surely did, we assured him. "So maybe we'll see you again," he said. Chu said he'd keep an eye out for all their future shows. I said I wouldn't come back to Penang without looking them up. We crossed the marble floor of the now-deserted lobby. The night clerks acknowledged our passage with polite nods. Our footsteps echoed about the high-ceilinged atrium. The automatic doors swished apart to let us out into the warm blanket of night. Chu and I turned for the car park; Sunny and Kim headed for the driveway.

The last I saw of them was the white flash of Kim's calves, and the glow of the hotel lights flaring briefly in her hair, as they melted into the night. ❑

11

ULTIMATELY, my connections at Universiti Sains Malaysia gave me a way out of government service. One of the Bio School's lecturers, who had become a good friend of mine, transferred to the Agricultural University ("Universiti Pertanian Malaysia"; UPM) in Selangor. A new Marine Science faculty was being opened there, and he persuaded the dean to offer me a position as a research associate while I worked towards a masters' degree and, eventually, a doctorate. There'd be hardly any money involved; I'd be given a stipend of $200 a month. Who cared? I quit government service and hared off down to Selangor and UPM.

And quickly regretted the move. The faculty was a big, new, gloomy building, almost devoid of human occupation. I supplemented my allowance by grading undergraduate papers, and soon fell foul of the students. It happened like this:

The group in question was a mixed bag of Bumiputras and non-Bumiputras. They were asked to pass their project reports and assignment essays to me for preliminary grading. I would receive the neatest manuscripts from Chinese students, several of whom seemed to take pride in handing in typewritten reports. On the other hand, the scruffiest pieces of work—a few paper-clipped sheets of longhand—would invariably come from Malay students. At first glance, I saw this as evidence of the economic gulf between them:

the Chinese could afford fancy electric typewriters, while the Malays could not. All the more reason not to be overly impressed by the neatness of the Chinese work, I thought. But then, upon reading the papers, I'd see an equal gulf in the diligence that had gone into them. One or two of the Malays were so obviously lackadaisical that I thought they must have handed in their rough drafts by mistake. But no: this was indeed all they thought necessary for their coursework. I was enraged. Didn't they know what they were up against? Couldn't they *see* how earnest their non-Malay colleagues were, and the standard they were setting?

And then it occurred to me that, no, they probably couldn't. I recalled lab sessions and lectures in which the Malays and non-Malays always sat and worked on opposite sides of the room, arriving and leaving together in communal groups. They didn't eat together in the cafeterias, they didn't share sports and games. It was as if there were an impermeable perspex barrier between them, and it was always there. This, I thought, is no way for a university to be.

I graded the papers according to their content. In no time, I heard from the dean's office that there had been complaints lodged against me, to the effect that I was showing favouritism towards the non-Malays; that I was, indeed, "anti-Malay". I explained my position to the dean. He listened, his delicate Malay features sombre and thoughtful. He sighed. He shook his head. He understood completely, he said, he knew exactly how I felt, he'd had an overseas education too, this attitude of theirs distressed him as well.

But he told me to be less strict in my grading. "You have to understand," he said, and left unspoken exactly what it was I had to understand. I understood perfectly. The Malays needed help; we had to help them.

About three months after this came my first personal encounter with Malaysian journalism. A friend of my mother's who worked for Bernama, the national news agency, was having a little get-together at his flat in Kuala Lumpur. My mother wanted to go, would I drive her? Of course I would.

At Musa Scully's Brickfields apartment I met Halinah Todd, who was the features editor of the *New Straits Times* at that time. She was a good-looking woman, with wavy blonde hair and sharp blue eyes. I asked her if the *NST* accepted free-lance work. "Sure," she said airily. "Send something in. If it's good we might publish it."

That was all the encouragement I needed. I'd already had one article published in the mass media—it was about the reefs of Redang, and the *Asia Magazine* had paid me US$100 for it about six months before. (The money had come just in time for one blowout party to say goodbye to my friends in Penang.) So I figured I knew what would sell.

And I could certainly do with a bit of extra money, given what I was earning at UPM. I'd been told I could apply for a university scholarship, but I didn't want to. For one thing, scholarships meant contracts, and I was sure I wouldn't want to make a career of UPM. For another, there was the matter of my B.Sc. To get a Masters' grant with nothing but a Third-Class Honours basic degree, three years with the Fisheries Department and a couple of research papers to my name, I'd have had to invoke the NEP. At that stage, I'd rather have busked on street corners than thrown myself on the largesse of the state.

Besides: I *liked* writing.

Later that same night I wrote a story on what it's like to go scuba diving on a Malaysian coral reef, and the next day I delivered it, garnished with a few of my underwater photographs, to Halinah Todd at the *NST*'s offices in Bangsar. They liked it, they published it, and they actually wanted more. This time, Halinah said, they'd like to see how I handled an assignment on a subject I didn't know so intimately. She asked me to do a story on home security. I bought myself a reporter's notebook and went off to play reporter. I enjoyed myself, had a little fun with the writing of the story, and delivered it three days later. They liked that one, too, and began to take some serious interest in me. Now, said Halinah, so much for the leisure and lifestyle pages. Could I handle a "hard" subject; something for the leader page? You bet I'd like to try, I told her, without asking her what a "leader page" was. She asked me what subject I wanted to try. The fishermen, I said. The small fishermen of the East Coast. She told me to go for it.

I sped off for a week on the East Coast, shuttling between Kuala Trengganu and Kuantan, dropping in on every fishing village I came across and talking to anyone who d give me the time of day. Back in Kuala Lumpur, I wrote up the story and handed it in. Halinah played a little with it, to my horror, but I had to admit she made it more dramatic, a little racier in the introduction. And it got a big play on the editorial page.

Halinah took me to meet Dr Noordin Sopiee, Group Editor of the *NST*. He was a melon-faced man, younger and Chineser than I'd expected. (But then I was probably Indianer than he'd expected, assuming he'd expected me at all.) He sat distractedly champing on an unlit pipe behind an overflowing desk. As he talked, bits and pieces of paper would slide off the mountains on his desk and tumble to the floor in soft trickles. I watched them, fascinated, waiting for the avalanche. Dr Noordin talked without saying very much, I thought. He said something about trying me out on "leaders", which I didn't know was the journo-jargon term for editorials. "A couple of chunky paragraphs," he said. "On this football-fixing thing." At least, that's what I think he said. He clearly had other things on his mind. After our meeting I left the building and thought no more of it, or him, or the *New Straits Times*.

A few weeks later, Halinah called to ask what had happened with the leader I was supposed to have tried to write. I confessed I didn't know what a leader was. Nobody had told me. She asked me to lunch. She took me to the restaurant of the Majestic Hotel, and over soup asked that I consider joining the *New Straits Times* as a daily stringer. I confessed I didn't know what a "stringer" was. She explained in words of less than three syllables, which I would later discover was one of Halinah Todd's special talents: "You come in every day. You write. You're paid by the piece. Ninety dollars for a first leader, seventy for a second. You try it for a month, and then you decide what you want to do with the rest of your life." Then she told me what a leader was.

So I tried it for a month, at the end of which I had to admit I'd had a lot of fun, learned more than I'd ever thought I could learn in so short a time, met a host of fascinating characters, including a disproportionate number of attractive women, and made more money than I'd ever imagined I'd see written on a cheque with my name on it as well. It also seemed I was one white-hot leader writer, who could dash off a perfectly adequate editorial in under four hours including lunch.

So when the time came to make a decision, there was hardly a decision to be made. I became a full-time journalist with the *New Straits Times* in October 1981. I didn't even bother going back to UPM to collect whatever stuff I still had there.

UPM's Faculty of Fisheries and Marine Science would drag along for a while longer before finally getting itself together. It took a nasty shock to jolt it into action, though. One day, some months after I'd left, the dean didn't show up for work. When he didn't come in the following day either, they went looking for him. They found his car parked by a remote disused mining pool, where he had carefully removed his clothes and left them neatly folded, then walked into the water.

It was just one of those things, they said sadly. He just couldn't take the pressure. ❑

A Fisherman

"ZAK, you're still going strong, I see!"

"Strong? Hah! I'm an old man now. Old Zakaria, that's me. They call me Pak Ya now. Indeed! But the tourists still call me Zak. Hey, I'm famous you know. These people come from Australia and Canada, they know me, they've heard of me. But why shouldn't they? I've been in this business for twelve years now."

"So how is your business? Looks pretty good to me. This place is looking good. Last time I saw you, this place was a little ..."

"Don't say it. It was a mess. I was just starting out then. The old boat still smelled of fish. The tourists were different, too. Real adventurers. Germans and Japs, mostly. Scuba divers. Spearguns. Or you'd get these romantic types, couples, wanting to go out to Kapas and stay there all by themselves all day and night and swim naked and make love. Kapas was not developed then. Just an empty beach. Not like it is now."

"I know. I heard about Redang ..."

"Ah, you don't want to go to Redang. I know you used to love the place. But it's not like it was when I first took you there. They've cut half the island away. They want to build a golf course, I hear. Condominiums. Madmen. Why should people want to go to Redang to play golf? Madmen build, madmen go. Ah, but never mind. Madmen are good for my business."

"Is the village still there?"

"A few of the families. One or two, maybe. The rest are all on land now. I hear they got paid well to move out. Don't know how much. But some of the old folks are pissed off and won't move."

"'Pissed off'? Where'd you learn English, Zak?"

"Come on, I can speak white people's talk, you know that. Good for business. *Giddaymate. Spreken zee doish. Don piss me off.*"

"Still the same old Zak!"

"But even older. You remember my son, Mat?"

"Sure. He was twelve. Followed you everywhere. Good little boatman, as I recall."

"He's a father now!"

"What!"

"The truth. Got married last year, became a father last month. I'm a grandfather, would you believe it?"

"Congratulations."

"Nothing to do with me. He did all the work. Lives in Kuala Trengganu now. Gone to be a city boy."

"Sorry to hear that."

"Ah, don't be stupid. You always had this romantic idea about fishermen. You think it's such a great life? You only think that because you're a city boy. It's hard. Always was hard, always will be. That's why I quit. I was one of the first to quit fishing for a living, start taking tourists. Now look, so many are doing it. But they're not as famous as me. I've got the best boats, the biggest name. No, I'm glad Mat's doing what he's doing. He'll have an easier life than me."

"But you're doing okay now, Zak."

"Praise Allah. I was lucky. The tourists liked me. I could speak their language. I did very well during Visit Malaysia Year."

"Where do you take them?"

"The same old places. Kapas. Redang. Tenggol. They all seem to have a good time. But every year you get new people who've never seen these places before. It's better if you don't compare with the past. I mean it. Everything always looks better when you look back. That's because you yourself were better then. Younger. Stronger. More handsome."

"Trengganu's looking stronger and more handsome today."

"That's the truth. There's money here now, boy. Oil money. Tourist money. Beautiful roads. New houses. Just look at this place! You saw the new mosque they're building down the road? No more wooden mosques for us! Cannot compare with before. Compare it with Kelantan, and see what money can do. Ah, but Kelantan people are holy and pious, so they don't need money."

"Trengganu people used to be like that too."

"Still are. But we don't think money is evil! Depends on what you do with it, right? These roads are good. These houses are good. Give people like my son a chance for a better life."

"But tearing down half of Redang for a golf course is not good."

"No, because how many people really benefit? Not many. Just a few rich folk. The cost is too high, you understand what I'm saying?"

"Zak, I can't believe I'm hearing you. You used to say every fisherman who wanted to stay a fisherman was a fool."

"Not *just* a fisherman. He should branch out, do business, take tourists. But this is still his place, he knows these seas. I never meant that people from Kuala Lumpur and Singapore and Hong Kong should come here and take over our place! That's too much."

"So is it too late?"

"Nah. Never too late. So we lose Redang, okay, but we won't lose the others. We learn from our mistakes. Soon nobody will go to Redang to go fishing or diving on the reefs, only to play golf. So in the long run, the reefs will repair themselves, and the place will be beautiful again."

"Sure, in about fifty years."

"Not that long. But even if so, what's the difference? Maybe my grandson's kids will get to see Redang's reefs the way my grandfather did. Maybe everything moves in a circle, you know, only our lives are in a straight line, because we are born, we grow old and we die. Ah, enough of this rubbish!

Old man's talk. You wanna boat ride somewhere? You gotta see my new boat. Two engines! I'll give you a discount. We'll take a ride. You still dive? You can go diving. Or maybe we'll go fishing."

"So you're still a fisherman?"

"What's the matter with you? I never stopped being a fisherman. But not *just* a fisherman." ❑

12

MAHATHIR BIN MOHAMAD became prime minister a few months before I became a journalist. The events were unrelated, although within less than a year people were thinking we ourselves would be. (In commercial parlance, I suppose this is what might be called a "teaser".)

Mahathir's ascent to the nation's top office was a quiet triumph. This was a man who had once been expelled from Umno, the party he had been a member of since its formation. In the pivotal year of 1969, Mahathir's vociferous Malay chauvinism and unrelenting criticism of Tunku Abdul Rahman was deemed to have gone too far, and the Tunku banished him. Mahathir had gone home to Alor Star in Kedah and resumed the private medical practice he had forsaken for politics.

But you can't keep a good man down, and Mahathir spent his free time in exile writing a book that was published in 1970 and which was promptly banned. It was titled *The Malay Dilemma,* and it was one of the strangest—and strongest—pieces of writing ever to have emerged from the Malaysian body politic. The ban on the book was lifted not long after Mahathir's rehabilitation to Umno in 1972 under Tun Razak, who gave him the ministerial portfolio for Education, and by now every Malaysian has either read *The Malay Dilemma* or heard about it from those who have. Certainly, every foreign journalist who's ever written two lines on Malaysia has found ample fodder for sensation in Mahathir's slim volume. It was, unarguably and to say the least, sensational; even more brutally honest than I have tried to be with this narrative.

Leaving aside the book's subtexts of socio-genetic theory, other than to mention the notion that the economic superiority of the Chinese was ultimately due to the physical geography of their homeland, the "Dilemma" of the book's title was essentially this: Should the Malays remain true to their cherished traditions of courtly accommodation, and allow the immigrants and foreigners to walk away with their country, or should they stop being so "Malay", and start forcefully claiming what was rightly theirs? Mahathir excoriated the Malays for their idleness and apathy, and railed against those traits of their character that had once moved the British to regard them as "Nature's Gentlemen".

Had the book been allowed free circulation at the time it was published, it would have been interesting to have seen its effect on Malaysians. I would hazard the guess that non-Malays might not have been alarmed as much as Malays would have been incensed. (Which is not to say that non-Malays would not have been alarmed at all; they would undoubtedly have been relieved that this feller wasn't running the country.)

The book was not aimed at the nation as a whole, however, but very specifically at the Malays. It was a narrowly focused polemic in which the Malays were "us" and every other Malaysian—indeed, the rest of the world—was "them". As such, the often breathtakingly crude racial stereotyping of the "them"s was only to be expected. Not that the book's stereotyping of the Malays was any less crude, but at least these were caricatures quite deliberately drawn as straw men for the shooting.

In decrying the tendency of rich Chinese to regard Malays as fit only to drive their cars, for example, Mahathir wasn't slamming Chinese arrogance as much as Malay subservience. His point was that the Malays should not be content with being mere drivers, not that the Chinese should be driving the Malays' cars.

That, of course, would never happen. Neither would Malays with nothing better to do stop driving the cars of the rich; only they'd be the cars of rich *Malays.* (I remember a particularly offensive billboard advertisement for a make of luxury four-wheel drive vehicle. Outside a mansion that looks like the White House, a Malay master turns to his Malay servant, who is polishing a Rolls Royce or some such symbol, and says: "Never mind, I'll take the Trooper instead." And his faithful manservant replies: *"Baik Tuan!"* "Very Good, Master!" And this was in 1990.)

(But let me not be a loony lefty about this: the natural order of things is such that richer people will always employ poorer people to serve them. Perhaps it was progress enough that the poorer might serve the richer of their own kind, and keep their servitude all in the family, as it were.)

Remember, too, that Mahathir wrote *The Malay Dilemma* at a time when the insults that had been hurled at Kampong Baru on May 13, 1969 must still have been ringing in his ears.

In the still-volatile atmosphere of 1970, Mahathir's book was thought far too inflammatory to live. By the time it was resurrected, the nation had moved on to the point where *The Malay Dilemma* could be read not so much as a political manifesto as a guide to the intellectual provenance of the man who would be prime minister. One of my own pet theses, as utterly unprovable as some of Mahathir's but perhaps just as plausible, holds that who we become depends a lot on where and when we were born. To wit:

Mahathir was born into a humble Kedah family in 1925, when British colonialism in Malaya was approaching its zenith. Not unrelatedly, this was also the time of greatest immigrant influx into the Malay Peninsula. (In 1927, the peak year for Chinese arrivals, more than 300,000 disembarked in Singapore.) As Mahathir grew up, he would have watched the British plantations spread and the Chinese tinmines dig deeper into his native soil. He would also have seen the new elitisms emerge among the Malays, with such places as the Malay College readying the favoured few for London's Inns of Court, from where they would return, with their little white wigs and pukka accents, to privileged positions in the burgeoning Malayan Civil Service.

Mahathir himself, as everyone who knows Malaysia knows, would be the only Malaysian prime minister never to have had an overseas education, and the only one not to have studied law. He was to go to medical school in Singapore, and there he would gain his degree and meet the woman who would be his wife, Siti Hasmah Ali.

As a 22-year-old member of the fledgling Umno then, Mahathir must have wondered what his political prospects might have been, what with all these teddibly British Malays in the party's top echelons. Even Onn Jaafar, the founder himself, was advocating opening the party to the associate membership of non-Malays. Mahathir's Malaya must have seemed a precarious place indeed, with the Malays hanging on to cultural survival by the slenderest of threads. In the subsequent course of events—Malaya's political development, the Emergency, the Alliance, independence and Tunku Abdul Rahman's administration—little must have happened to have made him see things any differently.

Yet, in 1976, when Tun Razak died and Hussein Onn succeeded him, Hussein appointed Mahathir to the deputy premiership. To say that Umno was surprised would be to put it mildly.

Tun Hussein Onn died in 1990, without telling anyone why he had chosen Mahathir as his deputy. Or if he had, it must have been in an off-the-record conversation, because I don't recall seeing the reason written down anywhere. Perhaps Hussein believed the nation had reached a point in its development where it could benefit from the energies of the one-time Rebel with a Cause. Perhaps he believed Malaysia had grown big enough, and the Malays had advanced far enough, to contain Mahathir. Or perhaps he believed that the time had come for a stronger, younger man. Perhaps,

perhaps, perhaps ... it was at least recorded that Hussein said, upon his announcement of Mahathir's elevation: "I pray I have made the right choice." Much later, he would say he was sorry.

When Tun Hussein Onn retired, in June 1981, Mahathir became prime minister, and president of Umno. He was required by his party's constitution to choose his deputy from among the three party vice-presidents. He settled on Datuk Musa Hitam, who had succeeded him as education minister.

This miffed Tengku Razaleigh Hamzah, who was finance minister, and who believed he had done enough to Bumiputrize the economy to be accorded the recognition of the deputy premiership. Certainly, Tengku Razaleigh's service to the NEP had been impressive. In fact, a credible case could be made for his having been the most important individual contribution to the activation of the NEP. Tengku Razaleigh—connected, brilliant, intensely ambitious and ten years younger than Mahathir and about the same age as Musa—had enjoyed Tun Razak's confidence and had performed splendidly. He had been successively chairman of Bank Bumiputra, Pernas and Petronas, the national petroleum corporation, before being given the finance ministry by Hussein in 1976, at which time Razaleigh was barely out of his thirties.

While in charge of Petronas, Razaleigh had driven a hard bargain with the multinational oil companies drilling for Malaysian crude. Malaysia had been earning less than 13% in royalties on the output of its South China Sea oilfields. Razaleigh pushed it up to more than 83%. Exxon and Shell didn't like it much, but there it was. Razaleigh had gotten Malaysia a deal almost as favourable as Indonesia's, and for much smaller amounts of oil. In fact, it was partly because of the multinationals' fear that Razaleigh's intentions were to nationalize the oil industry that Hussein moved him out of Petronas and into the government.

Razaleigh had left his corporations as giants in the national economy, and had become something of a legend in the process. There was also his political pedigree: Razaleigh had been instrumental in the Barisan Nasional's defeat of Kelantan's Pas state government in the 1978 general elections. He declared Kelantan a personal gift of his to the then prime minister Hussein Onn. Cockiness aside, Razaleigh was indubitably a key factor in the Barisan Nasional's capture of the historically maverick state of his birth.

But Mahathir would not be swayed. As the nation's money-man, Razaleigh would continue to be pre-eminent. As an Umno man, however, he would have to remain content with his vice-presidency and his seat on the party's supreme council, and take his orders from both Mahathir and Musa Hitam.

Musa was suave, urbane, and a political animal to the bone. He was from Johor, the nation's most politically sophisticated state, the birthplace of Umno. This imparted a geographical balance to Umno's top slate, with Mahathir from the north and Musa from the south of the Peninsula.

Mahathir and Musa made an attractive team; there was a nice yin-yang equilibrium about them. Mahathir would provide the impulse, while Musa smoothed the waters. Mahathir was the drive-shaft, Musa the hydroplanes. Those who knew both men maintained that together they would be much more effective in leadership, both national and party-political, than either might be on his own.

It was Noordin Sopiee, my boss, group editor of the *New Straits Times*, who first used the phrase "the 2M Administration" in print. It caught on immediately. Mahathir didn't like it from the start, although Musa did. Musa could never think of himself as subordinate to Mahathir. He preferred to regard himself as heir apparent, and the equal partnership implied in the phrase was much to his taste.

Mahathir put up with it for a while, but soon began grumbling that if people were so taken by the "2M" cliche, they should really understand it to stand for "Mahathir" and "Mohamad". That admonition should have alerted us to the possibility of a rift between Mahathir and Musa, but I don't recall anyone noting anything of the sort at that time. Let's face it: we didn't *want* them to fall apart; we *enjoyed* the

2Ms. They were sexy. Stylish. Fun. They had gracious wives and trendy children. They were mediagenic, and a good deal more visible than any of their predecessors had ever been. Musa, in particular, knew how to party.

During the first two years, the Mahathir administration was exciting, innovative and very popular—at least with the masses. Mahathir shook a stiff broom at the public sector, insisting that punch-cards be introduced to get government workers to work on time. He started them wearing name tags, with himself and his ministers setting the example, so that the public would know whom they were dealing with and be able to report the rude or indolent by name.

And Mahathir set a new direction in foreign and economic policy, urging the nation to shed its traditional bias towards the West, specifically Britain, and "Look East" instead. It was a matter of the "work ethic", in which Japan, Taiwan and South Korea could clearly teach the rest of the world a thing or two, and Malaysia volumes. In the other direction, Mahathir was scathing in his condemnation of the patronizing attitudes of the West, specifically Britain, towards Malaysia. If the "Look East" policy was a positive effort to impart the ostensibly Japanese traits of cohesiveness, loyalty, efficiency and diligence to the Malaysian workforce, it was at least as much the turning of a cold shoulder to Britain. Either way, we cheered. The Anglophiles among us repented, and Japanese investment soared.

Did we like it? I'd say we *loved* it. One of the first overtly political pieces I wrote for the *New Straits Times* was an analysis of the Barisan Nasional's election prospects for 1982. "It would be difficult to believe," I wrote, "that Dr Mahathir will not receive the firm support of first-time voters." After the greyness of Hussein, here was an electrifying personality; as much of a visionary as Razak but with infinitely more popular appeal. What's more, it was an appeal that seemed to cut across racial divisions with ease. Mahathir read popular sentiment like an open book—we cheered his criticisms of bureaucratic inertia and his campaign to get the public sector shaken up and cleaned out. In his first months as prime minister, Mahathir was clearly, completely, a man in his moment.

In my first months as a leader writer with the *New Straits Times*, Mahathir Mohamad was a daily fixture in my life. I bowed to the compulsive power of his popularity, but that didn't mean I was altogether comfortable with it. Under Noordin Sopiee, the *NST*'s coverage at this time verged on hagiography. Mahathir was never off the front page. There was one week in particular when I'd been asked to write three or four consecutive editorials on things he'd said. Emerging from the editor's room after yet another such assignment, I vented my disgust at this, to my mind, overweening attention. "Mahathir Mahathir Mahathir!" I expostulated. "Mahathir *farts* and we write an editorial!" A fashionably dressed young woman chatting to her friends at the features desk turned around. "What was that about my father?" she said. I looked up and saw Marina Mahathir, whom I knew worked with the magazine publishing wing of the New Straits Times Group. She seemed vivacious and attractive, and I already knew her to be an effervescent writer. "Oh-oh," said Thor Kah Hoong, a fellow leader writer with something of a flair for the dramatic overstatement. "You're in trouble now!" He was right, I suppose. Marina was smiling.

A relationship developed, as these things do. It wouldn't last, as these things don't. But in the course of it I would have occasion to meet Marina's mother and father, and that personal knowledge of them would inform my impressions of Mahathir ever after. Datin Seri Siti Hasmah would always seem the quintessence of gentleness and grace to me. Once, when Marina was unwell, her mother showed me a logbook she was keeping of her daughter's condition; every medication, every temperature reading, minutely noted in neatly ruled columns. Siti Hasmah was still, after all, a doctor. And a mother. "We worry about Marina," she sighed, carefully putting away the notebook. "She's really quite frail, you know. But she's so independent-minded. So stubborn. Such a free spirit." That she was. My being there was proof enough of that.

And in the harsh years to come, I would remember having seen Mahathir come home after a routinely long day at the office, wearily trudging up the stairs of Sri Perdana, the prime minister's Kuala Lumpur residence, to the family lounge, there to grunt a not unfriendly greeting at me, slot a video-cassette into the VCR, unbutton his bush jacket and flop into an armchair to watch a re-run of *Eight is Enough,* his favourite television programme. And the harshness would attenuate a little. And then I would think of his wife, and find myself unable to believe that such a woman would countenance the sort of man Mahathir's bitterest enemies were convinced he was. I could not believe she could stand for such corruption as Mahathir was being accused of. They would say I was ridiculously naive. I would shrug and say maybe.

In the 1982 elections, the Barisan Nasional won 103 of the 114 seats it contested, garnering 61% of the popular vote and halving the parliamentary Opposition. It was one of the most emphatic electoral mandates Malaysia had ever granted. Mahathir's campaign slogan had been: *"Bersih, Cekap, Amanah".*

Clean, Efficient, Trustworthy. ❑

An Artist

NIZAMUDDIN AMBIA lives in a very quiet part of the country: a village nestled in the folds of low hills not far from the old palace of Negri Sembilan.

The village called Kampung Gajah has been there for a very long time; the house in which Nizam lives is one of the more recent additions to the village, and it was built the year his mother was born. Nizam's mother, Puan Zainab, is more than sixty years old now. She is a formidable lady, a widow, sharp of wit, quick of tongue, and built like a meat-safe. Puan Zainab does honour to the matrilineal Minangkabau tradition; every nuance of her carriage bears the weightily maternal stamp of the matriarch.

In poetic contrast, Nizamuddin, her eldest son, is slender, delicate, graceful, and soft-spoken almost to inaudibility. He wields his *tjanting,* the batik artist's wax pen, with the dexterity of a seamstress doing needlepoint, or a surgeon splicing nerves. Nizam is a quiet and melancholy creature, a gently troubled man with a soft, sad smile. He is thirty-five years old, and he knows not what he is doing, nor why he exists—at least, such does he profess. Very soon after graduating in "communication arts" from the Mara Institute of Technology in Shah Alam, Nizam gave up all pretence of an aptitude for commerce and the metropolitan life of the Klang Valley. Many who knew him said this was a shame, for Nizam had a rare talent for graphic design, a sureness of line that translates well into the sort of art that tourists and advertising agencies seem to enjoy the most. Nizam's work was highly "accessible", but the trouble was, Nizam himself was not—least of all to himself.

So he left the Klang Valley and went home to Kampung Gajah, Sri Menanti, Negri Sembilan, to live with his mother and dedicate himself quietly to developing his style, whatever it may turn out to be. The truth is, he finds it easier to wrestle with the conundrum of himself in the familiar surroundings of Kampung Gajah. Here, he might at least live in fitful peace with what he cannot yet fathom. Who is he? What is he supposed to be doing? Even: Why is he so fixated on all these questions?

And the hardest question of all: Are his doubts merely an intellectual conceit?

Nizam does not know.

Things seem so much surer for his siblings. His two younger brothers, Azizan, a teacher, and Eddie, a student, home now during the school holidays, both seem to pursue lives of easy certainty. Listen to them bantering with their mother in the kitchen: "The *adat perpatih* is outdated!" blusters Eddie, referring to the matrilineal tradition of this quarter of Negri Sembilan; the custom that will see this house and everything in and around it passing in time to Puan Zainab's oldest daughter, and not Nizam. His mother responds: "Men have been saying that forever." Laughter rises above the clatter of cooking utensils; it seems this is one line of argument that's been going on forever, too.

But the *adat perpatih* is an anachronism; a 500-year-old legacy of the West Sumatran settlers of this region. Enshrined now as an element of Malay custom, it persists as an embellishment of identity quaint as a Minangkabau roof, and hardly more significant.

Nizam smiles his soft sad smile, but does not participate in this well-worn debate. He has other things on his mind. Things like: "What do you call someone who does not have a bedroom, but sleeps anywhere in the house?"

The point he wishes to make, in this obscurantist manner, refers to the breakdown of boundaries; the dissolution of private territory. Nizam senses that he is growing beyond the need for personal space; he is becoming a child of the universe. Like Socrates, his home is becoming defined purely by the boundaries of his skin. It is an evocative emotion—there is something holy about it, something that tends toward the ideal of the wandering ascetic, the *sadhu*. But Nizam's exploration of this peculiar, exhilarating, frightening impulse must begin here, in this shallow valley he knows so well; this aged little community tucked away in a fold of low hills in the heart of Negri Sembilan. If Nizam is to leave home, he must first *be* home.

So let me walk with him, this slight and troubled man, as evening settles on this little valley and the narrow sky above begins to drain of light and heat. In the blue cast of the evening light, these old houses seem ghostly. Here is a structure that must have been magnificent the day it was completed. How many two-storeyed wooden houses still exist? Here is one, seventy years old and black with age, its *tiang ibu*—its central pillar—an entire forest tree. What a marvel it must have been; what a marvel it remains. The descendants of the man who built it still live here, but no one dares climb to the upper storey now.

And there, on an acre of land overgrown with waist-high weeds, a single light glows in a single small house. Nizam tells me an old man lives there alone, shunning all human contact. Thus has it been for decades. All around in this quiet enclave are stories. In each glimmering of light through the trees, each fleeting shadow in the window of an ancient house, is a story. But I am on a journey that permits me little time to stop and listen; I curse the impulse that has me constantly moving on, moving on, towards a destination I know will be just another way-station once I get there ... but for now let me walk with Nizam down this village lane, past these silent old houses in wide grounds out of which stretch tall durian trees laden with fruit. Any moment now, the first of the season's bounty will fall, and the heavenly aroma of this magnificent fruit will fill these dales.

The village idiot sails by on an ancient bicycle, calling out Nizam's name in a voice that sounds as though it has been filtered through sludge. He is a cheerful lad, as the mentally impaired so often are, and Nizam and he pause to exchange pleasantries in the Negri patois, a dialect of Malay almost as unfathomable as Kelantanese to the uninitiated. Zul is not the only one here so afflicted; there is a distressing effect of the inbreeding, the marriage of cousins, that so often takes place in isolated rural communities. But the village embraces and cares for its deficient, so good-natured are they, and so willing to do odd jobs for anyone.

We walk on to the end of the lane, where it joins the main road. Even this is not much of a road; it is the minor spur off the Kuala Pilah road that leads to the abandoned capital of Sri Menanti, where Raja Melewar, the first of the Sumatran princes to assert some semblance of rule in these regions, built his palace in the late 18th Century. We turn and walk back, the evening now barely distinguishable from night.

"Am I a bohemian?" asks Nizam.

"I don't think so," I reply. "A bohemian is a rebel of some sort, a defier of convention. I know you feel as if that's what you are, but I think you're much closer to your heritage than you think. It's just that, these days, for a Malay to be true to his heritage is itself almost an act of rebellion." Which is as long a speech as I've given recently. But Nizam seems quietly reassured.

We reach his house. I cast a stick into the thick undergrowth across the lane, where there used to be a ricefield. A quail, startled, takes flight in a flurry of wings. Nizam's house glows with light; his mother is in the kitchen preparing dinner. In the front porch, his latest batik painting, half done, lies stretched on its wooden cradle. On the front steps his brothers sit, smoking cigarettes. They greet us warmly, but with the reserve befitting younger siblings when addressing their elders.

Nizam will sleep tonight in the space surrounding the *tiang ibu* of his house. It is a sacred little place, and he sleeps well there. I have been given the guest room in front, which used to be occupied by an elder brother who died a few years ago. It is a sweet and comfortable room, with its floor-to-ceiling windows paned in coloured glass, opening out on a riot of hibiscus bushes and a grove of bamboo.

In the morning I am awakened by Puan Zainab in the garden below those windows, yelling bellicose imprecations at a squirrel ostensibly responsible for dislodging the first durian of the season. But it turns out to be a most delicious fruit, decidedly ripe and a promising augury for the harvest to come.

It makes a good taste to hold in the mouth as I take my leave of Nizam to continue my journey. The historian Richard Winstedt once described Negri Sembilan as "that delightful little state of lost causes and incredible beliefs, breathing from clustered hamlets and sequestered ricefields the last absurdities of the matriarchal system."

"Absurd", Sir Richard? No more and no less than any other system, you must agree. And from at least one of those hamlets clustered around its sequestered ricefields might still emerge something of lasting value ... but I suppose that must depend on whether or not Nizamuddin Ambia believes his art to be a legitimate means of escape. ❑

13

SO THE BARISAN NASIONAL was returned to power in grand and sweeping style, and in the all-encompassing euphoria of the moment we dreamed grand and sweeping dreams. But there were three subtexts to the outcome of the 1982 general elections, three details, that were to have a most profound bearing on what was to come. First and obviously foremost, the authority of Mahathir Mohamad as the head of the Malaysian government was established beyond question, and the rank-and-file of Umno bowed to his leadership of the party. The Rebel had come home at last, covered in glory.

Second, a young man named Anwar Ibrahim began climbing to the stars. This is the first mention of his name in this narrative. It will not be the last.

Third, the rivalry between Musa Hitam and Tengku Razaleigh Hamzah was deemed settled, and those in the body politic who had seemed to favour Razaleigh found themselves on shaky ground.

They included *New Straits Times* group editor Dr Noordin Sopiee, who would soon be moved out of the newspaper and given charge of a new think-tank being set up to advise the Mahathir Administration on foreign policy. It was to be called the Institute of Strategic and International Studies. In due course, Noordin would raise ISIS to a position of respect in the region. At the time of this transfer, however, it was clear that the object of the exercise was to show that there could be no ambiguity over who held ultimate and total authority over the paper. The *NST* and its subsidiary publications belonged to the Fleet Group, which was the investment wing of Umno itself.

It seemed ironic that Noordin would be axed the way he was, for his direction of the *NST*'s election coverage had been almost jingoistically pro-Barisan Nasional. Had the 2Ms not been as generally popular as they were at the time, I might have been even less comfortable with the contempt we heaped on the Opposition—when we weren't ignoring them completely. But then, the Umno papers' unquestioning support of Umno and the Barisan Nasional was an absolute given, and the careers of their senior journalists and editors would hinge on more subtle things; such as who received more front-page coverage, or whose statements would appear on Pages One or Two, and whose on Pages Three and Four, and where on those pages they would appear, top, middle, or bottom. (Middle was the worst, apparently. The *NST* was a full-size broadsheet, and the bottom of its pages were more comfortably read, despite the smaller headlines down there.)

It was on this basis that Noordin had miscalculated. I choose the word carefully: he had not "misread" the Musa-Razaleigh rivalry; he had seen it more clearly than most. He had simply erred in his conclusions as to its eventual outcome. And so Noordin was out, and his deputy, Dr Munir Majid, ascended to the position of NST Group Editor.

Munir was regarded by Umno's power-brokers as more of a "Musa man" than Noordin, or at least less of Razaleigh's. He was a more "hardbitten" journalist than Noordin. Although even younger than Noordin (Munir was still in his mid-thirties at the time of his promotion), Munir matched his predecessor's impressive academic credentials, including a PhD from the London School of Economics. He was a man of penetrating intelligence. But he was also of full-blown, Penang-born Indian-Muslim descent, and with his very Western educational background he lacked the credentials for full admission to the Malay political process.

(I should mention that there was indeed a man of Indian-Muslim ancestry in Umno, and he even held a cabinet post. He was Abdul Kadir Sheikh Fadzir, deputy foreign minister at the time. The merciless ribbing he got from his cabinet colleagues made my juvenile ordeals in Malay College seem tame. Kadir would gamely join in the jesting, however, laughing along at their slurs about his colour and their mimicry of his Penang-Malay accent, doggedly proving himself a Good Sport, deputy-ministerial portfolios being not all that easy to come by. Mahathir himself also had Indian blood, but in his case only the Opposition ever made any bones about it.)

Be this as it may, Munir wanted to see a harder, sharper edge to the *New Straits Times.* He didn't share Noordin's fondness for editorial flamboyance, and was somewhat disdainful of the newspaper's role as a medium of entertainment. Munir wanted sterner stuff; "harder" news, deeper and more insightful economic analyses to circumvent the unspoken obstacles to his being a political insider. Having owed his promotion to Musa Hitam, however, whether he liked it or not, Munir was bound to give Musa the time of day—and the necessary column space. He attempted to balance the accounts, for the swiftly vanishing sake of journalistic objectivity, by continuing to use Noordin's "2M' formula—and this was what finally provoked Mahathir's testy insistence that the slogan stood for his own initials, and not those of his and Musa's.

Musa acquiesced, with his characteristic smiling grace, and the appellation dropped from use. By then, however, it had become very clear who called the shots in Malaysia. Mahathir was at the unchallenged helm of an office that, over the previous decade, had been given an enormous concentration of power by the executive needs of the NEP. Mahathir fully intended to use that power to its limit, and then push those limits even further. His political imprimatur set and sealed, Mahathir set to work on the Malaysian economy.

But he was no economist; he was a visionary. And his vision for Malaysia was for the final exorcism of the humiliations he had endured under colonialism. Mahathir wanted Malaysia to be a big, strong, developed nation, able to compete with and beat the Western world. No more little brown men at the feet of great white masters. No more faithful servants; no more obsequious puppets; and certainly no more hewers of wood and drawers of water. Malaysia had to industrialize with a vengeance. It was a matter of *pride.*

The irony of it was that Mahathir's idea of industrialization owed more to 19th-Century Britain than to 20th-Century Japan. Mahathir wanted *hardware;* the harder and bigger the better. Heavy industries. Iron and steel. Cars. In Mahathir's eyes, a nation was not "developed" until it had these Big Things, these steel mills and car plants, making such things for itself, for all the world to see and respect.

The Heavy Industries Corporation of Malaysia, HICOM, was established in 1980 with a start-up capital of $500 million. Within five years, it had invested well over $2 billion in cement, iron and steel, engineering plants and the Proton Saga car project. Economists warned that this was too much, too soon, and for far too small a consumer base. We condemned them as nay-saying merchants of doom, the "nattering nabobs of negativity", to recall Lyndon Johnson's tart exercise in alliteration. They were small-minded. They lacked imagination. They had no confidence; no *faith.*

In 1987, Perwaja Trengganu, HICOM's billion-dollar steel plant on the Peninsular East Coast, shut down after losing money hand over fist since it opened. Kedah Cement, which had been HICOM's venture to compete with the established producers of this strategic material, was the least productive plant of its kind in the country. Perwaja was eventually turned around, but to add insult to injury—at least for those who had seen in HICOM the Malays' riposte to Chinese industrial dominance—it was made to work by a Chinese millionaire industrialist.

Eric Chia had made the biggest of his many fortunes as a distributor of industrial machinery. The government asked him to do what he could for Perwaja. By the end of 1989, Chia had made a going concern of the moribund HICOM behemoth, and he did it not as a wealthy boss but as a sensitive manager.

Fully aware of the suspicions and resentment that had attended his arrival at Perwaja Trengganu, in that very Malay and Muslim state, Chia's first initiative was to build a new prayer-hall for the Muslims. Then, new canteens with better food more constantly and cheaply available. Reasoning that Perwaja's predominantly Malay workforce would respond to discipline (the Malays having always made good and loyal soldiers), he outfitted Perwaja's workers with smart new military-style uniforms complete with rank insignia. Instantly, he had a visible management structure where none had existed before. Morale rocketed, and productivity with it. Then, Chia trimmed the plant's production targets to more realistic levels. Perwaja spluttered, coughed, and throbbed into life.

Eric Chia proved that Mahathir's dreams were not unworkable, if the approach was right. But he did this at the end of a decade during which a great deal of damage had been done; much of it irreparable.

HICOM, after abandoning Kedah Cement and Perwaja Trengganu to Chinese salvors, had concentrated on its most visible project: the National Car. This had become such an article of faith with Mahathir that it could not be allowed to fail. It didn't: launched in 1985 with the fanfare of a moonshot, the Proton Saga is today ubiquitous on Malaysia's roads. It has 60% or more of the market share for cars in its class. It has been successfully exported to Britain. (Despite the initial protests of Japan's Mitsubishi Corporation, who had designed the Saga, provided the technology and management for its plant and supplied 40% of the car's components, partly on the understanding that Proton would not compete in Mitsubishi's other markets.) The Proton Saga has been a success, but it didn't start making money for its manufacturers until 1990. When it was introduced, it was priced so cheaply in order to secure its market that it was instantly tagged the *"Potong Harga"*. The "Cut Price".

We had a good laugh at that. But we couldn't laugh at the Great Tin Fiasco. In fact, we couldn't even mention it; hardly in polite conversation and certainly not in print. This was an effort to replicate the spectacular corporate raids and takeovers of the Seventies, but it was famously ill-advised. Simply put, it was an attempt to corner the world tin market.

Sometime in 1981 or 1982, Malaysia began quietly buying up tin on the world market, in the hope of pushing up prices and forcing traders on the London Metals Exchange to either default on their forward contracts—that is, their commitments to future purchases—or meet them with tin bought from Malaysia at higher prices. It didn't work. The demand for tin was not that great. Other producers stepped into the breach. The United States released tin from its stockpile. And the London Metals Exchange changed its rules to allow traders to pay fines instead of defaulting.

When it became clear that the scheme was not working, Malaysia abandoned it. With all that extra tin out on the market, by 1984 the price of the commodity had fallen to half what it had been before the exercise. Malaysia was aggrieved with the United States and the London Metals Exchange for underhandedly derailing the scheme (they changed the rules, the cads!), but could do little except count the losses. Which were never revealed, but which by some estimates may have run as high as $500 million.

Never mind. Malaysia pushed on undaunted. The West had proven itself as duplicitous as Mahathir had been saying all along. It was time to Look East. Hong Kong, say. Where better to dabble in a bit of potentially profitable property speculation? Between 1979 and 1983, Bumiputra Malaysia Finance, a subsidiary of Bank Bumiputra, the first Malay bank set up under the NEP, loaned more than $2 billion to three Hong Kong property firms. Most of the money, which represented two-thirds of BMF's entire loan portfolio, went to a company called Carrian.

Then, in 1982, Britain announced that Hong Kong would be handed over to China in 1997, and the territory's property market collapsed. BMF's first response was to throw even more money at the problem, and it too swirled down the sinkhole out of which Britain had pulled the plug. Early in 1983, Bank Bumiputra sent one of their internal auditors to Hong Kong to see what, if anything, could be salvaged. Days later, his corpse was found on a hillside with the rope that had strangled him still looped around its neck.

Malaysia lost a staggering amount of money in the Carrian Affair. Astonishingly, there would be hardly any legal retribution against the principal figures involved. BMF directors Lorrain Osman and Rais Saniman spent the next ten years socked away in London and Paris, respectively, fighting extradition to Hong Kong to stand trial. Lorrain became the longest-serving remand prisoner in British history. I saw him briefly in early 1987, while attending one of his endless extradition hearings in London. He looked an unlikely villain by then; a frail, stooped figure, what was left of his hair turned completely white. At the time I began writing this narrative, in early 1992, Lorrain and Rais were still lost in the labyrinth of extradition proceedings. Theirs was a virtual imprisonment, and I suppose there might have been some poetic justice in that.

They might have done better simply to return to Hong Kong and face the music, which played a sweet enough tune for Carrian boss George Tan. In a decision that shocked even louche Hong Kong, Justice Dennis Barker granted Tan an unconditional discharge on the grounds of "insufficient evidence". Barker was subsequently to die in a motoring accident in Malta. He was not greatly mourned in Hong Kong or Malaysia.

The ghost of BMF would never be laid to rest. In all the eighteen volumes and 6,000 pages of the BMF Inquiry Report, released in 1986, there was no hint of who should be held ultimately responsible for the loss of $2.5 billion in public funds. Well, perhaps there was: the Opposition certainly saw evidence that Mahathir and Tengku Razaleigh knew more about this business than they were letting on. But that was only to be expected of the Opposition.

It was during the BMF debacle that I began to realize how truly ridiculous it was to try to be a journalist in Malaysia. This awesome thing; this inconceivable sum, *two ... billion ... ringgit.* Gone. Just like that. How? Who were these people who had the right to play with so much of our money, and how come no one had ever heard of them? And no one so much as held to account, let alone locked up for a hundred years in atonement for the sheer magnitude of this betrayal. And how did we deal with it? By attending to the Wider View. The Malaysian Dream. The needs of the NEP in its creation of a nation in harmony; no race threatened with cultural extinction; equal opportunities for all; a school in every village, a level playing field in each.

While Petronas came in to bail out Bank Bumiputra, on Mahathir's orders taking an 87% stake in the shattered bank, we remembered the Dream, and wrote of the need to Put This Behind Us, Learn From This Lesson and Move On.

I began to see the Malaysian journalist as one of the saddest creatures in the nation. Our readers dismissed us as lapdogs of the government; the government considered us instruments of policy. But the truth was that Malaysian journalism was replete with people of intelligence and integrity, good and honourable Malaysians, who were finding that their careers demanded enormous efforts of conscience.

For the journalist *knew* things; he saw and heard things. He knew first, and he knew more than those who read his newspapers and magazines. His readership would know only what he told them, while he would know from source. The masses only saw what the journalist described, while he was there to see it for himself. To not *know* is bad enough, but at least there is this axiom of ignorance being bliss. To know and be unable to *tell* is much, much worse.

It was hardly any wonder that there were those who would collapse beneath their burdens of knowing, and that others would armour themselves in cynicism. But what is a cynic if not an idealist with bruises? Malaysia's journalists would be among those most personally damaged by the Mahathir years, and their tragedy was that it was their idealism that kept so many of them going as long as they did.

Ultimately, the survivors among Malaysia's journalists would be those who spent their entire careers gazing at the Wider View, staring devoutly at the stars as the ground rocked and rolled beneath their feet and fissures opened up and swallowed those less attentive, or less disciplined, or simply less durable. For the Great Tin Fiasco and the BMF Catastrophe were just the beginning.

What, shall this narrative of mine descend into no more than a litany of outrage? Ah, but these were outrageous years. At the end of 1983, Mahathir attempted to curb the powers of the nation's monarchy and precipitated a constitutional crisis.

Malaysia's Independence Constitution had been patterned on India's. There was one unique feature of our defining document, however, and that was its prescription of a Constitutional Monarchy for the nation. Indonesia, upon its unilateral assumption of Independence in 1946, had simply scrapped all its sultanates and declared itself a republic. But in Malaya, the defence of the sultanates had been a primary impetus behind the anti-Malayan Union movement. It would have been unthinkable, then, that the blueprint for nationhood would not make provision for the country's nine hereditary royal houses.

An appropriate model was found in the system of royal succession long practised in the state of Negri Sembilan, the "Nine Territories", sandwiched between Selangor and Johor, that had formed out of the breakup of the Kingdom of Melaka in the 15th Century. In Negri Sembilan, overall sovereignty was shared among the Chieftains of the four largest districts. At set intervals, these *Undangs* would elect their Paramount Chief from among themselves, ensuring that each one would in due course get his chance to be First Among Equals. It was a sensible system. Not only did it prevent any one fiefdom from attempting to conquer another, it also provided a safeguard against any one ruler proving incompetent. He could be voted out by the others and replaced by the next in line.

Three centuries later, this was the system adapted for the new nation. The nine sultans of the Malay states were organized into a Conference of Rulers, and every five years they would elect from among themselves the *Yang di Pertuan Agong*. "He Who Is Supreme Among the Most Prominent", to give the title its proper English rendition. Far easier to say: King.

It would be a largely ceremonial post, but for one key power: no legislation could be enacted into law without the King's seal. Thus, in theory, the Monarch would be able to express his disapproval of legislative proposals by withholding his assent, whereupon Parliament would have to reconsider such proposals. This had never happened. But Mahathir was concerned that it *might.*

In 1983, the next in line for the throne was the Sultan of Johor, a man with a famous reputation for taking his powers very seriously. Some saw Mahathir's moves to curb the monarchy as a pre-emptive strike against the possibility that the Sultan of Johor might play fast and loose with his role. But I believe there may have been a deeper text to the episode: Mahathir did not enjoy ambiguities in leadership; he did not like the notion of separated powers. And he certainly had no great love for the sultanates.

I suggest three reasons for this. One, the sultanates could be said to have been historically responsible for the subjugation of Malaya to foreign imperial forces. Theirs had been the original treaties with the British, of course, but one didn't have to go that far back to make the point. The Malayan Union proposal had been *accepted* by the sultanates when the British had put it to them immediately after the Japanese Occupation, and it was the *rakyat,* the people, who had risen to the defence of their rulers. From that point on, the traditional exaltation of the sultans as Protectors of the People had rung hollow.

Second, the sultanates were above the law. This rankled badly, because some of the sultans were deriving from this constitutional privilege benefits that had never been intended to be part of it. Many sultans had extensive business interests and were extremely wealthy. The seeking of a royal connection, if not outright patronage, had become standard operating procedure among businessmen wanting concessions of land and natural resources—which had meant the British before Independence and the Chinese since.

Third, the sultanates provided the Malays a fount of their identity and a focus for their loyalty—that, indeed, was their ultimate power. But the effect of this was to keep the Malays in thrall to a hereditary sovereignty, and this flew in the face of everything democracy was supposed to achieve. The sultanates, by their very existence as an institution, restrained the upliftment of the Malays. They bid them genuflect; they kept them humble. (I imagine this must have made Mahathir's blood boil.)

In short, the Monarchy was an anachronism, and an enervating one at that. It may have been good to have kept the trappings of so venerable an institution alive in the ceremonies of governance—after all, the sultanates gave the Malays a history of five centuries and not just a few decades. But to have such figureheads presume to wield real authority over a democratically elected government ... no, this Mahathir could not abide. In late 1983, he tried to do something about it.

The Conference of Rulers took a stern view of his presumptions, however, and after a tense few weeks Mahathir was compelled to retreat. But not completely: the monarchy retained its power to delay legislation, but not to deny it. For Mahathir, it was not a total defeat. But neither was it a total victory, and he was not one to accept such an outcome with equanimity. He would bide his time, but when the time was right, he would take on the sultans again.

The nation was on tenterhooks at the end of 1983, in the thick of all this. I watched the contest as closely as I could, and with great excitement. Part of me was rooting for Mahathir, for I shared his reservations over the role of Malaysia's monarchy—if indeed I was reading them correctly. But another part of me also cheered the sultans when they parried Mahathir's main thrust, because I was also convinced that Mahathir wasn't defending Malaysia's democracy so much as his own position as its ultimate symbol.

I had come to believe that Mahathir regarded the democratic process not as a means by which the people might rule themselves, but as a means by which they would decide who would rule them. Democracy existed so that the people might choose their own King. And the people had spoken.

But the constitutional storm blew over, and the waters had calmed by the time Sultan Mahmood of Johor ascended to the national throne in 1984. As things turned out, he would get on much better with Mahathir than anyone had expected. ❑

Jay Bee

AND SO to Johor, bastion of the south, most venerable of remaining sultanates, domain of monolithic monarchs, definer of the national language, the nation's most politically sophisticated state, birthplace of Umno ....

Being from the north, I have never been able to relate to Johor. For me, this has had much to do with the Main Range, the Peninsula's spine of mountains. North of a line drawn between Muar and Mersing, the Main Range and its associated spurs, the Bintang Range in Perak and Kedah and the Eastern Range in Kelantan, Trengganu and Pahang, form a constant backdrop to every inland view. Anywhere north of that line one can stand with one's feet in the Straits of Melaka or the South China Sea, turn around to face the shore and see in the distance that gradation of blues, familiar as a mother's face, rising to meet the sky in serrations of forest-clad peaks.

And what do these mountains mean? ("Mountains" ... let us not lose perspective here: Gunung Tahan, the tallest peak in the Peninsula, is 2,187 metres high. But still ...) They mean forests and rivers and aboriginal tribes; they orchestrate the assembly of clouds, and therefore generate a regularity of rainfall, and therefore an amelioration of climatic extremes. Most of all, they prescribe limits to the cultivability of land.

So, north of a line drawn between Muar and Mersing, the mountains exist to curb human ambition, imparting to it a certain sense of scale and proportion. Where those limits have been defied—there is no example more egregious than the concrete-and-neon excrescence of Genting Highlands on the Selangor-Pahang border—the travesty is so visible as to be its own vile mockery. The mountains themselves hold up to view the abuses inflicted upon them; theirs is an inescapable admonition, and a reminder of the utility of humility.

In Johor, the Main Range peters out; the mountains diminish into rolling hills and dales, ideal for the planter. In Johor, there have been no limits on the cultivability of land, and so the land has been most thoroughly cultivated. In Johor, there are individual oil-palm estates of nearly 40,000 hectares. No distant escarpments; no gradations of blue, only an endless sea of disciplined green. In Johor as nowhere else in Malaysia, there are far horizons for the ambitious to contemplate. Johor has long been conducive to the seductions of territory, conquest, dominion.

Oh yes, there is a mountain in Johor: Gunung Ledang, Mount Ophir, near the Melaka border. Barely a knoll, really, a thousand metres high, but such a place is this! Mentioned in the *Sejarah Melayu*, the *Malay Annals*, no less, as the haunt of a fabulous magical princess, desired by no less an eminence than Sultan Mansor Shah himself! Gunung Ledang, where Hang Tuah and his friends learned the mystic martial arts that were to render them peerless as warriors! Ah, the stories that could be told of Gunung Ledang, the blockbuster movies that could be made ....

No, there is little in Johor that tends towards humility. There should be no wonder that at the apex of this state presides the most flamboyant royal house of the Malays, headed by a sultan with a private militia and a penchant for giant American motorcycles, once profiled with rare amazement by the easily-bored Paul Theroux. Let there be no doubt that Johor Baru chafes mightily at the time it has taken the federal government to accord it bona fide city status.

And let there be even less doubt that Johor Baru is the foulest and most pestilential place in the Malaysian Peninsula. Through the heart of this sore afflicted town flows the Sungei Segget, a river by only the most extravagant leap of the imagination. To say it "flows" is to do hideous injustice to the word; the Sungei Segget is a rank, black, stagnant, noisome ditch, filling the town centre of Johor Baru with the aroma of raw sewage and rotting carcasses. At the first sight and smell of the Sungei Segget, it is no longer difficult to imagine the river that must flow through Hell.

On the east bank of this foul sump is a wide and vicious boulevard of banshees, named with lasting disrespect after Tun Abdul Razak. Perhaps only in Bangkok or Jakarta does a pedestrian feel as much of a desperately moving target. On the west bank are shops and office buildings and carparks, which at night are filled with eating stalls. (By the banks of the *Segget!* Oh, such alimentary outrage!)

At night—and the nights start early in downtown JB, and end very late indeed—these buildings shimmer in neon and flashing lights: here a disco, there a *karaoke* lounge, upstairs a cabaret, down this alleyway a bar. In the backlanes between these buildings, shadows consort in whispered deals and liaisons, cars with tinted windows purr slowly by with their headlights off, sudden ejaculations of motorcycles spurt out and scream away.

There is a psychic dimension to the Segget's stench: Johor Baru smells of spiritual ordure, of bodily secretions, improbity, tumescence and lust. Casting about for an image to capture my feeling for JB, I settled on that of the grating over a bathroom drain; that thing that traps scum and slime, down through which befouled water slops and out of which, at night, cockroaches emerge.

Of course, this is all Singapore's fault. JB is for Singapore what Bangkok is for Malaysia: the parade-ground and watering-hole of the Beast. Squeaky-clean Singapore; those who might believe you lack genitalia surely do not live in Johor Baru. And, famously, Singapore is no longer the place of Saint Jack; on festive occasions they've even taken to importing from Malaysia the transvestites for what used to be Bugis Street, there to parade and preen like starlets in the decorated and gentrified waxwork of what used to be Singapore's organic heart. Come on, Singapore, why dontcha come up and see us sometime, is that a roll of bills in your pocket or are you just glad to see us, you prideful loathsome place, you with your superciliousness and contempt, bring to us your Willy Sentosas, your Ang Mo Kio Mosquitoes and Jurong Johnny-boys, your swollen crapulent masses, yearning to burst free ....

I went to Johor Baru to meet Wahid. He said he'd meet me at eight in the lobby of the Merlin Inn; it was midnight when he got there. He apologised; it had taken him longer to dress than he'd expected. He'd wanted to look his best, and let's face it, Wahid doesn't even *begin* to look his best before midnight.

"What do you think?" he said, unfurling from the chaise-longue in the lobby like a great cat, the black velvet sheath dress slit to the black-stockinged thigh, the wrist a-dangle with costume pearls, the earlobes heavy with long ear-rings that glittered like gold, the firm-muscled shoulders bare, the hormone-induced bosom lightly dewed with sweat, the body six feet tall in three-inch stilettos, the face ... "This is my Grace Jones look," said Wahid, framing the face in both hands and pouting the plum-painted lips. "So very *Vogue,* don't you think?"

"Wahid," I said, "you look spectacular."

"Thank you," he said. "I made this dress myself. Shall we adjourn to the bar?"

Ho, Wahid, where does one begin to tell your story? There was once a fashion designer, brilliant, talented, three-point-nine grade point average in college, a face by Michelangelo, the bones and skin and eyes a precious gift of his Ambonese ancestors. But this lonely, gifted man was not a man at all, and how does such a creature play such a hand of cards? Wahid played the harlot, prowling like a dark angel the midnight streets of Kuala Lumpur. (You know the Selangor Club padang? Batu Road? The Kowloon Hotel? Wahid knew.)

"I could make sixty dollars a night, sometimes more. It was hardly ever raw sex, if you know what I mean; mostly they'd only want blow-jobs. Sometimes they'd only want to sit and talk. Once I got this guy who wanted me to perform sexy poses and slowly strip while he sat on the bed in his underpants and masturbated. It was no problem for me. But you know, only with my true lovers did I ever offer my rear. That's a very intimate and loving thing. You don't share it with everyone."

The tragedy of this was that Wahid could only love straight men; he was not gay, not homosexual. He was a woman, who wanted her men straight. But what sort of straight guy wants a drag queen for a lover? So Wahid joined that sad sorority of whores who paid gigolos to live with them and love them—the "spados", they were called, for their affections were never more than a function of the money and gifts and drugs the queens had to spade over them.

Oh yes, drugs ... or would you believe there was never a crying need for respite in this lifestyle? Any way you can get it ... Wahid was a heroin junkie for so long it's pointless trying to remember when it began. And when the lovers were coming and going in a blur of unfulfilled longing, the junk was all that ever stayed. But he is nothing if not a survivor—they all are, those who aren't dead or worse—and eventually Wahid was able to kick the habit and keep heroin out of his life. No more midnight rendezvous by the monsoon drain in Kampung Baru ....

He returned to Johor to open a boutique of his own. It did very well for a year or so, but he'd had to borrow money to get it started, and the money had come from family members, and you know how they can be, there's no repaying the interest on such loans. There was a falling out, the usual things were said, words no less wounding for their predictability, and Wahid fled to JB to stay with a sister and her family while waiting for things to sort themselves out.

Such a Muslim family! The mother in full *purdah,* the father a gruff and thuggish cove with badly dyed hair and a job as an auctioneer of bankrupts' property, the four children fat, spoiled and sullen, all living in a small terrace house somewhere in the Larkin district. And in this terribly Malay household, this amazing creature, this tall man with breasts and a fabulous wardrobe.

"Your situation, Wahid, is a little weird."

"I'm used to it," he said, draining the last of his Guinness Stout through a straw and signalling the waiter for another. "Do you like the bracelet? Chunky. Like me. It goes with this chunky build. Oh look at him!"—him being the flustered, yet clearly flattered, waiter—"Slim hips, mm, that's my type."

"Are you like this all the time?"

"Of course not! But when I dress, I have to party, you know what I mean? I have to *dance.*" And he named the disco to which he would be adjourning after our meeting. There would be other queens there; moving with practised grace on the dancefloor, feeling the lights on them, and the eyes in the shadows. Would I come? Knowing those streets, hearing their howl even through the thick glass of these three-star windows, knowing the smell of the black air outside, "I don't think so," I said. "It's past my bedtime, and this town and I don't exactly get along."

"I know what you mean, but this is JB. You have to dance. If you don't, they'll dance on your bones."

So we asked the clerk at the front desk to call a cab for Wahid, and we waited outside till it came, crawling off the flyover like a scabrous beetle, and into this vehicle did Wahid fold his velvet-clad frame, the bracelet clicking against the glass of the closed window as he waved goodbye and the taxi pulled away.

On the flyover, a pedestrian tried to cross the road and was sent leaping back to the curb by a motorcyclist flying murderously off the Causeway from Singapore and wailing up through the gears of his lethal machine. "Hoi!" shouted the pedestrian. The motorcyclist, without decelerating, turned his helmeted head, raised his left fist, middle finger extended, and roared so loudly I could hear him above the scream of his exhaust: "FUCK YOU!!"

Jay Bee.

They'll be dancing on my bones before I find anything good to say about the place. ❑

14

OH THOSE EIGHTIES; such years were these! My own career was going great guns, despite the trials and tribulations visited upon the Malaysian media in general. But then I was never to gain admission into the inner sanctums of editorial management; my place was instead a weekly column at the bottom of the leader page in each Friday's issue of the *New Straits Times*, and there I had a lot of fun.

I'd been tried out in an editor's position—Noordin Sopiee put me in charge of the *NST*'s Entertainment Desk in mid-1982—but I was hopelessly lacking in the necessary management skills. It had been a very rapid promotion, to be sure; I'd been with the paper less than a year. But there was also another contender for the post, a journalist only about a year older than me but far more experienced. Kee Thuan Chye had been Number Two on the Entertainment Desk for some time, and he resented my being put in over his head when the editor's chair fell vacant. To Kee, as I imagine to many others, the principal factor behind my appointment was my Bumiputra status.

This Bumi thing had never gone away for me, of course, nor had I expected it to. It had tainted my years with the Fisheries Research Institute and terminally undermined my stint at UPM. My Malay College contemporaries were all moving up in their chosen fields and professions, but the ambiguities of our privileged status under the NEP were lost on none of us. Our school years had been dedicated to the diligent pursuit of merit, but these prizes had now been taken from us. Some of us had grown resigned to these new realities, and were happy to screw the system for all it was worth. Some rebelled outright, and vowed to have no part of it. Others—and I included myself among them—felt that we had to move with the system, push ourselves up as high and fast as we could, then work from within to change it. We had to win the respect of the non-Malays, or everything was useless.

As a writer with the *NST*, I was sure that at least my ability would be obvious enough for people not to see my career profile purely as a matter of privilege. Either you could write, or you couldn't; and whether or not you could would be clear as words on a page, no matter what your position. There was at least that much honesty about it. And I could write.

But writing is by its very nature a solitary pursuit, and I couldn't run a desk to save my life. I could never get used to giving people orders, especially when those people had all been in the business far longer than I had. I compensated by trying to do everything myself. Kee and I fell out, loudly and acrimoniously. The Entertainment Desk became a tense and unhappy place, and after six bitter months I was taken off. Kee was made editor, and I was given a column of my own to play with all by myself.

Kee made a very good editor; the paper's entertainment pages flourished under his authority. And my column became very popular. Of course I enjoyed it; the attention was delightful. It was wonderful to receive letters from people I didn't even know, people of all ages, all races, from all over the country, telling me they liked what I was doing. But there was also this: the column's popularity granted me more and more leeway in what I could write about, and how I chose to write about it. And, sure enough, the Bumi thing began working for me. By virtue of my name, I was able to take on subjects that no non-Bumi commentator would have been allowed to treat with as much impunity.

It seemed the "work-from-within" approach was proving effective after all, and from being almost purely devoted to "lifestyle", my column became more and more political. Humour was the key, I quickly learned, and I would use it to cloak what I hoped my readers would see as pertinent political commentary. Some did, some didn't. Enough did.

I began to take it as a personal challenge to test the limits, to write about as many of the things that were happening to Malaysia as possible: the political hot potatoes, the "sensitive issues". (Once, when asked to judge a school debate, I noticed that the written rules prohibited any mention of these "sensitive issues". The definition of what was "sensitive" was a negative one: anything written in the newspapers, said the rules, was *ipso facto* not sensitive. I flattered myself with the thought that I had singlehandedly desensitized a number of these topics. But that, of course, was a conceit.)

Sometimes I'd entertain myself with the simply extreme. Once, in a particularly cheeky mood, I wrote an entire piece on the usage of the word "fuck", without actually using it, of course. That column ran, although more than a few readers thought it was in seriously bad taste. But there were other columns that didn't. A piece on BMF was the first of my serious comments to be "spiked". And when it came to the constitutional crisis over Mahathir and the Monarchs, Munir Majid told me not to even *think* about taking on the subject.

So it wasn't too long, then, before my trawling of the national interest for suitable topics started getting snagged on the rocky reefs of taboo. Out there in the real world, in the Malaysia beyond the carefully chosen phrases on the monitor screens of the *NST*'s editorial floor, the honeymoon was over.

The euphoria was gone. In the nation's highest office there resided a man who no longer seemed the repository of shining hope we had believed him to be. In the glummer quarters of the body politic, there began to be heard grumbles about "The Dictator". In the more optimistic circles, there were fervent hopes that the massive financial losses of Mahathir Mohamad's first two years as prime minister would be offset by greater commodity exports and revenue.

The basis for this optimism was Malaysia's export earnings in the latter half of the Seventies, which had been very good indeed. Extrapolating from this growth rate, planners were hoping for earnings of more than $60 billion in the first half of the Eighties. But theirs is an imprecise art at the best of times—which these most certainly weren't—and they couldn't have foreseen what would happen to oil prices in the mid-Eighties, and the consequent damage across the board of Malaysia's commodity revenues. The planners would turn out to have over-estimated export earnings by a factor of two.

In July 1984, Mahathir Mohamad removed Tengku Razaleigh Hamzah from the finance ministry and replaced him with Daim Zainuddin. Razaleigh's ouster had been expected ever since he lost his fight with Musa Hitam for the deputy premiership. But Daim's appointment was a surprise, and not a very pleasant one for most. Daim was a self-made millionaire in his own right—I remember drawing that particular parallel of Daim with Razaleigh in my column, welcoming this evidence of continuity—but there all resemblance between the two men ended. Daim was as mysterious and quiet as Razaleigh was brash and loud, and he certainly was no politician.

What Daim was, was a businessman through and through—and a childhood friend of Mahathir. By the time of his appointment as finance minister, Daim had become one of the richest Malays in the land. He had started out in property development, and moved from there into company acquisitions. Just before Mahathir pulled him into the Cabinet, Daim had bought more than 40% of the United Malayan Banking Corporation, the nation's third-largest bank. UMBC had previously been shared between Pernas and Multi-Purpose Holdings, the investment arm of the Malaysian Chinese Association. Daim had acquired his stake from MPH. The following year he increased his share of UMBC to more than 50%, and the year after that he sold the lot to Pernas for a tidy profit.

Who knew how much Daim was worth? Some said $300 million, some said $500 million, others said more. But what was important to Mahathir was that Daim harboured no political ambition. He was no Razaleigh.

Then came a diversion. In the worst possible way and at the least opportune moment, Chinese politics regained centre stage. The Malaysian Chinese Association had kept itself to itself for much of the preceding decade, quietly attending to the business of its community. At the dawn of the Mahathir years, however, there had begun a leadership struggle between party president Lee San Choon and his deputy Neo Yee Pan. Lee came out the worse for wear, and resigned in 1983. Neo became president, and was immediately challenged by a young tycoon named Tan Koon Swan.

There had never been any love lost between them. Neo was a traditional Chinese politician, having risen slowly through the ranks of the party. Tan was a parvenu, a 45-year-old millionaire businessman, whom Neo had often criticized as a leading exponent of "money politics". But Tan had evidence that Neo, in his battle with Lee San Choon, had benefited from the padding of the MCA's membership rosters with fictitious names, and Tan rode this issue to victory. In November 1985, Tan Koon Swan became the youngest-ever president of the MCA, and clearly the most popular in decades. He was young, rich, handsome and sophisticated, and he had crusaded against dirty deeds. He was seen as an exemplar of the new generation of Malaysian Chinese. And then he fell to pieces.

Multi-Purpose Holdings, mentioned above in connection with Daim Zainuddin's fortunes, had been established in 1975 as part of the Chinese community's response to the NEP. Tan, a corporate hot-shot with a Harvard MBA, had been made its managing director. The Chinese community supported MPH with high hopes and cash, boosting their corporation's paid-up capital to $450 million by 1982. In return, MPH tried to assure its shareholders a stake in corporate Malaysia against the exponential spread of the nation's Bumiputra firms.

It wasn't easy: each time MPH made a move towards acquiring available Malaysian assets, Malay politicians would cry foul and insist that such acquisitions be made by PNB or some other NEP agency. MPH was forced to seek more expensive and less lucrative foreign assets instead, and by 1984 it was deeply in debt. But it remained a precious institution to the Chinese, who seemed prepared to overlook MPH's financial problems in light of its political value to them. By the time Tan Koon Swan made his spectacular bid for the MCA presidency, however, MPH was spread thin and stretched tight. Its Hong Kong shipping company was losing money. So was its Singapore trading firm. And, alas, so was Tan Koon Swan himself.

In the months he spent battling for the MCA presidency, Tan was fatally diverted from the urgent needs of his business interests. His personal investment portfolio included a large stake in Singapore's Pan-Electric Group, which operated in the hotel, property and marine industries. But the group was not doing well, and within days of Tan's triumph with the MCA, Pan-Electric defaulted on its repayment of a syndicated loan. Tan, frantic, appropriated MPH funds to try and shore up the tottering corporation. He was too late. Pan-Electric went bankrupt, in a crash so huge as to compel the Singapore stock exchange to close down for four days in fear that the sinking ship would suck everything else down with it.

Tan was arrested in Singapore, charged with criminal breach of trust and stockmarket manipulation, and sentenced to two years' imprisonment. He emerged a born-again Christian, having found God in prison. But the MCA, membership in disarray and finances in a shambles, had lost theirs.

Perhaps, had times been better, there might have been more of a tendency among the Malays of Umno to gloat over the misfortunes of their erstwhile partners in governance and sometime economic masters. But times were now bitterly difficult. In 1986, oil prices fell to half what they had been two years previously. The value of a barrel of Malaysian crude was now only marginally higher than what it had been in 1975. Palm oil was a third of its 1984 price. Rubber, too, was down to pre-1980 levels. And we already know what happened to tin. The bottom line: in 1986, a kilogramme of tin cost $15.20. In 1980, it had been worth $36. Given the effect of the price decline on production levels, the value of Malaysia's tin exports for 1986 was a quarter of what it had been in 1980.

The year 1986 was the nadir of the Malaysian economy; the very worst of times. The NEP's momentum ground to a virtual halt. After all the sacrifices, there seemed but a snowflake's chance in hell of the NEP's targets being achieved on schedule in 1990, and the government had to bite the political bullet and admit it.

Those targets had already been readjusted. Not long before, Mahathir had called a press conference to explain the latest figures in the NEP's progress report. There was a damning indictment in that document: after thirteen years of the NEP, poverty, it seemed, had gone *up* a few percentage points. Mahathir wanted us to be aware that this was because the parameters needed adjustment. There was no "absolute" poverty in Malaysia, he noted; no one starved in this country. Hence, "poverty" was a matter of definition. The original parameters had been inadequate; they had not taken into account such things as mains electricity and piped water, for example, which undoubtedly raised the standard of living but did not figure in purely income-based assessments of household well-being.

This was eminently reasonable, I'd thought, but it begged an obvious question. No one else seemed interested in asking it, so I did. I raised my hand. The prime minister recognized my right to speak. "This being the case," I said, "we could meet the NEP's targets tomorrow, simply by adjusting the parameters accordingly." In the crystalline moment of silence that followed, I thought I heard the quiet sizzle of my goose being cooked. Mahathir said, very softly, "If you have a better idea, let me know."

But it turned out not to have been such a bad idea after all, for an appropriate statistical adjustment was indeed made and we were able to announce, within the week, that the official incidence of poverty in Malaysia was not nearly 30%, but 19%.

But this was an aside. By 1986, Mahathir had more important things to attend to. Paramount among them was the restiveness within his party. The second echelon of Umno was becoming more vocally critical of their leader's increasingly authoritarian ways. As things had turned more and more sour, so had Mahathir built progressively higher barricades between himself and his senior ministers. We heard of top-level meetings in which Mahathir made clear that he trusted no one, and that he considered loyalty to be the supreme measure of a minister's worthiness to hold a portfolio. The country had to be run his way, and only his way. Arguments meant disloyalty, disloyalty meant conflict, and conflict in governance was the last thing Malaysia could afford in this "recession". Those who were calling him names behind his back should consider themselves warned.

After one such lecture in early 1986, Musa Hitam reportedly turned to Mahathir and asked, banteringly, if he, Musa, was also under such suspicion. Mahathir said yes, and Musa quit.

It was disingenuous of Musa to have feigned surprise at Mahathir's suspicions. The two had been growing increasingly estranged. Rumours of a widening rift between them had been circulating for months, at one stage compelling Mahathir to theatrically fling his arms around Musa for the benefit of press cameras. But as Mahathir's popularity had waned, Musa had come to think of their association as a liability, and a detriment to his own career prospects.

Musa fancied himself as prime minister, and in this he was boosted by the popular sentiment that he might make a good one. But it was becoming clear that Mahathir had no intention of relinquishing office as gracefully as Hussein

Onn had done, handing over the government to his deputy while he settled into the role of elder statesman. In other circumstances—should Mahathir die, say—it was by no means assured that Umno, and Malaysia, would readily forgive and forget Musa's association with a man who seemed to be rapidly becoming the most unpopular prime minister of all time.

Finally, given Mahathir's unpopularity, Musa might have gambled on it being a popular move at that juncture to leave him. So Musa quit, and all those deemed to have been his supporters suddenly found themselves in much the same predicament that Tengku Razaleigh's people had been in four years before.

(They included Dr Munir Majid, Group Editor of the *New Straits Times* and hapless "Musa man", who was promptly reassigned out of journalism and into banking. Munir would do just as well there as Noordin Sopiee had done with ISIS, but that wasn't the point. Munir was succeeded as *NST* group editor by P.C. Shivadas, one of the kindest and gentlest of men. Some thought Shivadas's tenure would be as a caretaker until some suitable Bumiputra could be found to take over. But Shivadas would prove to be so very cautious and circumspect an editor that it would take a major catastrophe to unseat him. This, however, would not be long in coming. And again I have jumped ahead of the story.)

Now Mahathir was alone. The two men most obviously keen on succeeding him, Musa Hitam and Tengku Razaleigh Hamzah, were out of it. That left a cratered dead-man's zone immediately around the prime minister. Mahathir's choice of his new deputy only emphasized the elimination of his successor generation. Ghafar Baba was even older than Mahathir, and not in robust health. He was, however, a competent administrator whose political ambitions had long since been fulfilled. So Ghafar was no threat to Mahathir.

Which prompted all eyes to turn to Anwar Ibrahim, and see there the anointed heir apparent.

Just before the 1982 general elections, Mahathir had asked the young man to join Umno. Anwar's supporters were stunned when he accepted. Anwar (who was also an alumnus of the Malay College) had been a firebrand in his university days; a flaming orator and the leading light of the Muslim Youth Movement. ABIM (after its Malay initials) had been one of the nation's leading forums of Islamic radicalism, and many drew wry parallels between the organization's acronym and Anwar's initials. Under the Razak Administration, ABIM had been severely proscribed under the Societies Act. Anwar had actually served eighteen months in detention under the Internal Security Act for his activities as ABIM leader.

And now he was in Umno, and moving straight up at escape velocity. Mahathir appointed Anwar minister of culture in 1983, then of agriculture in 1984, then of education in 1986. That set the final seal on the prodigal's ascendance, for every prime minister since the Tunku had held the education portfolio before attaining the summit of their careers. People wondered: Why had Anwar accepted Mahathir's invitation? His subsequent career profile provided the answer. The offer must have seemed entirely too good to refuse. What could have driven Anwar Ibrahim during his firebrand years and subsequent sojourn in detention, sustaining him against the opprobrium of the Malay political elite, more than the thought of someday running the nation? This was the prospect Mahathir was laying before him.

A more interesting question would have been: Why had Mahathir made the offer? Perhaps for the same reason that Hussein had appointed Mahathir his deputy in 1976; which may have been in turn a decision prefigured in Razak's restoration of Mahathir to Umno two years earlier. Razak's biographer William Shaw presents this as evidence of Razak's political shrewdness: If the pursuit of "Malay unity" was Umno's founding myth, Razak dramatically demonstrated his commitment to it by welcoming a famous dissenter back into the fold and granting him a senior Cabinet post.

Then again, perhaps the Malay political consciousness also recognizes something enduringly compelling in the idea of the rebel.

I am not, and never have been, "Malay" enough to fully understand the complexities of Malay heroism. A few years after the episode of which I'm writing now, the director of the Police Special Branch, while interviewing me for possible subversive tendencies, would pose me the conundrum: "Who do you think was right? Hang Tuah or Hang Jebat?" It was a question that seemed to strike to the very heart of matters; the true "Malay Dilemma".

During the Golden Age of the 15th Century, Hang Tuah and Hang Jebat were the best of friends and the principal warriors of Sultan Mansor Shah, sixth ruler of what had become by then the Melakan Empire. The sultan, mistakenly believing Tuah to be guilty of treason, ordered him executed. Tuah, never deigning to contradict his ruler's orders, accepted the verdict. But Jebat, outraged by the injustice, rebelled. So the sultan ordered Tuah to kill Jebat. The two warriors were closer than brothers, but Tuah carried out his master's orders and killed the man he loved most. Their names have come down through history as the two preeminent heroes of Malay legend—but for diametrically opposed reasons. Jebat was the man of conscience; Tuah the paragon of loyalty. Both were men of equal honour, equal valour. And both were rebels, in their way. Jebat rebelled because of his conscience; Tuah rebelled against his conscience itself. Which was the greater sacrifice? Who was the greater hero? A most complex question, folding upon itself like an origami puzzle. I could not say. (Especially since the answer most obviously depended on who was asking the question.)

But perhaps, again, I romanticize too much. From a baldly political viewpoint, Mahathir's move to bring Anwar on to his side was smart enough. Anwar's entry into Umno certainly helped the Barisan Nasional win his home state of Penang in the 1982 elections, and his new prominence in the ruling party certainly seemed to plane the more jagged edges of his personality: Anwar would not seem quite so much the radical Muslim rabble-rouser once ensconced on Umno's Supreme Council. Still, rebel to rebel: the baton did pass.

But Anwar was still very young—he was not yet 40 years old when Malaysia began getting used to his sudden stardom within the Establishment—which meant that Mahathir was clearly in for the long haul.

In July 1986, I secured an opportunity for a one-on-one interview with Mahathir. He greeted me warmly enough, saying he read my column and found it "interesting". We talked for about an hour, on a variety of subjects ranging from environmental issues to allegations of high-level corruption. ("I keep saying," he kept saying, "show us the proof. If you show us the proof, we will surely take action. But no one has any proof. So what can we do?")

I asked him about leadership. Shouldn't a leader be the embodiment of his people? "Many people think they are such embodiments," he smiled. "A leader has to motivate his people. He must get them to be more than they are." I asked him about his legacy. What would he leave behind? I think he misunderstood the question; or perhaps I hadn't made it clear that I was asking him to describe the Malaysia he wanted to leave behind. But he thought I meant him personally. "Nothing much," he said, softly. "Just a gravestone."

As I wrote up the interview, what began to emerge was a portrait of a man beset by difficulties, forced to be harsher than he wanted to be in order to prevail over those who wanted his job merely for the glory of being prime minister, while he, Mahathir, needed this job because with its power he could make something great of this country. I was later told I made him sound "like a stern uncle"; a disciplinarian, yes, but an essentially benevolent one, who did not spare the rod, but only for fear of spoiling the child.

That was one of the kinder comments. In the general atmosphere of 1986, however, my credibility went down the tubes. It did me no good to insist that this was honestly the way our meeting had gone; these were his answers to my questions; and if that was the impression he'd given then perhaps there might have been an element of validity to it. No: I was pilloried. My long-gone personal connection to his family was invoked to explain my "bias"; that and the next general elections, expected for later that year. A man I respected asked if I was hoping for a ministerial position in the next Cabinet reshuffle—it was a most painful gibe. My disillusionment deepened; it seemed being a Malaysian journalist meant having to take crap from everyone. What did they expect, that I would write that Mahathir was a corrupt, dictatorial megalomaniac who was interested only in feathering his own nest to the applause of a gallery of lickspittle sycophants?

I suppose the horror of it was that yes, the salacious and the slanderous would indeed have gone down well with the Malaysian news consumer, if only as an antidote to the daily humiliations of the news media. Malaysia wanted to scream, and all we could do was to provide a daily dose of soothing bromide. It was one of the many standing jokes about the *New Straits Times:* it was an NSThetic. But I didn't feel like laughing, and neither did anyone else. The very worst of it was this: I was convinced that Mahathir himself would not have been outraged by a bit more backbone in the Umno papers; a little less slavishness. The contempt in which the *NST* was held did not reflect well on his administration. But if his editors were happy with their humility, he could live with it.

The 1986 elections were held in August. The Barisan Nasional was returned to power with its two-thirds majority intact, but with a slightly diminished share of the popular vote. Most of the Barisan Nasional's losses were due to the travails of the MCA, which lost ground to the Opposition Democratic Action Party as the Chinese electorate expressed its unhappiness over the Tan Koon Swan and MPH scandals.

The *NST* performed its usual service to the community, running grotesque editorial cartoons against the Opposition and shedding all pretence at being anything but a party political paper. I tried to do what I could, by concentrating on covering the Opposition. Tongue in cheek, yes, lip curled into a supercilious sneer—can you imagine the *gall* of these people, presuming to oppose the Barisan Nasional? Just listen to what they're saying, isn't it *outrageous?*—but at least I managed thereby to report what they were saying. It was the least we should have done, and the most I could do.

When the elections were over I tried to find a way out of the country for a breather. My career had soured beyond bearing. My column had become a burden. I had lost my sense of humour; I couldn't find all that much to laugh about in the things that were happening to Malaysia. I had been in Umno's lavish new $400 million skyscraper headquarters on election night, freezing in the severe air-conditioning all through that long night as the results came in from across the nation to be flashed up on the auditorium's giant TV screen. In the darkest hours before dawn, the Barisan Nasional attained its two-thirds majority. A victory jingle, composed with supreme confidence well in advance, was played over the PA system. Shortly thereafter, Mahathir had come down from his eyrie in the building's tower block to receive his victor's laurels. His two bodyguards chaired him, awkwardly. There was a spattering of applause; a few whistles. The reporters sloped off to write up their stories for their papers' final editions, aware more of their fatigue than anything else. Reflecting on the euphoria that had attended this moment in 1982, I saw in this gritty, tired dawn a parable of the changes that had taken place in the intervening four years.

The money lost in cackhanded fiscal adventures. The grandiose "prestige" projects—including the Umno headquarters itself. The schisms in the ruling party, and the desuetude of the other principal components of the Barisan Nasional. The general air of suspicion and hostility that had come to settle upon Malaysia like a toxic fog. Perhaps above all, the sense that the NEP had become the private instrument of the national leadership. Mahathir's Umno had become synonymous with Malay advancement; you cleaved to Umno, or you were left behind. You rode with Umno, or you missed the bus. This was not the way it was supposed to be. The NEP was supposed to be *Malaysia's* device, not Umno's. But it had become hard to tell where one ended and the other began.

My personal distress was amplified by my role with the *New Straits Times*. I emphasize again: the most galling thing about being Malaysian was being a Malaysian journalist. The way we behaved was not only a disgrace to our profession and an insult to our readers, it was a disservice to our owners. There was no escaping the fact of our ownership, but we could have done our job better nonetheless. The *NST* did not have to be sensationalist, or oppositionist, but we could have been *credible*.

Mahathir was an elected leader. With that as a basic premise, it would not have been impossible to have constructed a rationale for Malaysian affairs that would not have held us up to ridicule and mockery.

The NEP was an axiomatic good: it was fundamentally wrong that any Malaysian community should fear eclipse and jeopardy at the hands of any other. But something had gone awry; the NEP seemed to have taken a backseat to the creation of a power elite. No, worse: it had become a tool for the very creation of that elite. The government media organs should have been able to dedicate themselves to the higher ideal of national development for all Malaysians, and not lose themselves in meeting the political needs of a few. But we had not made the effort.

At dawn on the morning after Election Night in 1986 at the Umno headquarters, Mahathir and his entourage left the hall. As he passed the assembled reporters (all standing dutifully to attention), he caught my eye. I fancy a little personal connection passed between us at that moment. He inclined his head, and the ghost of a smile flitted across his features, upon which triumph was creased with deep weariness. I nodded. "Okay, Boss," I thought. "You win."

I applied for a Nieman Journalism Fellowship to Harward, and was unsuccessful. (The Fellowship's Kuala Lumpur agent warned me not to get my hopes up too high; he usually recommended journalists from *The Star*, the *NST's* MCA-owned rival, a newspaper often described by foreign observers as "feisty".) So I asked for a transfer to the *NST's* London office for a year as London Correspondent. Shivadas was happy to grant it. I closed my column, which by then had run for nearly four years, packed a bag and left for London that October.

And missed all the fun. ❑

Hang Tuah

HYSTERICALLY HISTORICAL! Grateful am I to the young man who provided me this delicious definition of what Melaka has become: the Latest Greatest Tourist Trap in a country now veritably crevassed with them. Aneel knows Melaka well enough to not care if he never sees it again; it's his ancestral home, but ancestry has come to be synonymous with pain for him. So I shall immediately draw the veil of compassion on the young man now attempting to reassemble a shattered life in the far north of the Peninsula, but not before this one last doff of my cap to his way with words. "Hysterically historical"! Perfect!

History, alas, is built in stone. In any serious attempt to understand modern Malaysia's obsession with monumental architecture, it is important to recall that wooden structures are about as long-lived as the more durable human beings. A wooden house a century old is a feeble relic indeed, frail and tottery and fragile as paper. But *stone!* Now *there's* a material to spit in the face of the aeons!

Conquerors build in stone, with single firebrands razing to the ground the grand wooden palaces of the vanquished. The Portuguese built their church and fort; the Dutch their warehouses and godowns, and these 500-year-old buildings are the oldest extant structures in Malaysia. (If one discounts the 1,000-year-old Hindu and Buddhist temples of the Bujang Valley—and in this Muslim nation one almost always does.) And what are the Stadthuys and St Paul's and the Porta de Santiago and A Famosa if not reminders of humiliation? But history is undeniably appealing to the foreign tourist, so let's make the most of these items; let's tart them up and wash them in light and sound, and try to make a point about the evils of imperialism while we're at it ....

Downtown Melaka had become a congested and unappealing warren of choked streets, souvenir shops and overpriced hotels, and its environs were raw with stripped earth and flashy new buildings: a mammoth supermarket, a monumental government office block. There was also a new state mosque, and I breathed a prayer of thanks to the long-gone geniuses who developed the three-tiered design of the traditional Melaka mosque. They created something so refined and elegant as to withstand the Brobdingnagian pretensions of modern Malaysian architects. The Melaka state mosque is a beautiful tribute to a classic design, even if it is the size of an intergalactic spaceship.

But no, otherwise Melaka was: "There's the new Jusco! There's the government office! Here's the new oil refinery!" (A massive complex indeed, set to create 30,000 new jobs and obliterate a small village by the seaside near Tanjung Kling. There was a story here: the village was putting up a fight. In the grounds of the mosque was a sign that read, "Defending Our Land Is A Holy Struggle". Every house, shop and eating-stall had a similar placard, "We Will Perish With Our Property". "The Right To Land Cannot Be Denied". "We Will Fight For Our Homes To Our Last Drop Of Blood". And so on ... but it didn't seem as if anyone was paying any attention. Construction bustled along on the petroleum complex, sprawling out behind barbed-wire fences, vast as an airport.)

So I sought history in the person of Aloysius Robless. A retired schoolmaster with silver hair and boundless energy, Aloysius may be one of the great unsung hero-historians of Malaysia. A painstaking genealogist, he has traced his Eurasian family line all the way back to 16th-Century Portugal, in the process unearthing the Robless and Rodrigues family crests. ("And they call us *gragos*. Shrimp. Hmph!")

Aloysius' fixation with Melakan history borders on obsession. Back in the mid-Seventies, he may have been the one to have discovered Hang Tuah's tomb. There again, it may not be: Hang Tuah is said to be buried in at least half-a-dozen places here and in Indonesia. But the grave Aloysius found in a dense copse of trees on the outskirts of Melaka town was that of a giant of a man, at least ten metres tall, if its length is anything to go by. The inscription on the headstone was worn into illegibility, but this didn't stop the authorities prominently signposting the site as a possible contender for the honour of being the legendary warrior's final resting place.

A quick circumambulation of the mysterious grave, and we were off in Aloysius' redoubtable Toyota to visit Hang Tuah's well. A magical place: the well had never been known to run dry, even during the worst droughts. (And Melaka had been suffering just such a drought for nearly five years, a calamity that may now result in the inundation of tracts of the Main Range through the building of dams for water storage.)

True to legend, the well was full of water. And also litter, which I dutifully fished out with the bucket provided. The surroundings of the well had been tiled, and a roof erected over it. There were signboards telling an abbreviated version of Hang Tuah's life-story. There was a large picture of this story's climactic moment: Hang Tuah lunging at Hang Jebat with his killing kris-thrust, full-stretch like a scrum-half going for the line, face twisted in a rictus of rage.

Around the well enclosure and lining the road approaching it were the inevitable souvenir stalls, festooned with identical offerings of lurid sunsets, shellcraft, key chains, carvings and Quranic inscriptions on pieces of varnished wood. I picked up a crudely carved pen holder, on which had been inked a picture of a kris and Hang Tuah's most famous words: *"Tak Melayu Hilang Di Dunia"*.

On, this fabulous line. Hang Tuah had died undepicted in art; there was no likeness of him remaining. But this was hardly appropriate to his stature as the Number One Malay hero of a newly emergent nation, so a representation of what he should have looked like was duly concocted, rendered in bronze and displayed prominently in the National Museum in Kuala Lumpur. A magnificent specimen: the physique of a weight-lifter, wild moustaches, arms akimbo, legs splayed. Upon this bas-relief was engraved those words. Such words! They have always been translated as: "The Malays Shall Not Perish From The World".

How uplifting it is to hear such fortitude and courage, such defiance and strength, from the heroic embodiment of a people held docile under foreign powers for well nigh half a millennium.

So potent is the emotion that few ever made much of Hang Tuah's peculiar grammar. *"Tak Melayu Hilang Di Dunia"* properly translates as "Not Malay Vanish From The World". Either the language of the Melaka Sultanate was a lot looser than it is today, which is saying something, or ...

"He meant exactly what he said!" insists Aloysius Robless. We are sitting in the lounge of his house by the seashore, the french windows opening to a modest sweep of lawn ending in a stand of dwarf coconut palms, and beyond them the sea. "What does "Melayu" mean?" He ferrets out from an over-crowded bookshelf an aged Indonesian dictionary. He riffles through the pages until he finds the entry he is seeking. Triumphantly, he points it out. "See what the word used to mean?" he says, finger on a line: *To flee.*

The Malays were named, it is commonly held, after a region of south Sumatra. (There is to this day a small town in the Palembang region named "Malaya".) The word may have been derived from *melayar,* the verb for "to sail". The Malays may therefore have been named for the act of migration from southern Sumatra, by which the Sri Vijayan refugee Parameswara fled to Temasik (now Singapore), and thence to Melaka at the dawn of the 15th Century.

Granting the benefit of the doubt to this derivation of "Melayu", and assuming that the word was still current as a verb a generation or two later, in the time of Hang Tuah, Aloysius is convinced that what the warrior truly meant by *"Tak Melayu Hilang Di Dunia"* was that his people had to flee their ancestral homelands in the Sumatran archipelago, or face extinction. The statement was not the pugnacious declaration of fortitude it has been read to be, but a pragmatic testament to the wisdom of strategic withdrawal. After all, the only reason Parameswara founded Melaka was that his chosen base on Temasik was being laid waste by the Thais, who were making the most of the breakup of the Sri Vijayan empire. Was the founding of Melaka therefore the result of an act of cowardice; the fleeing of a bested chief, unable to face his enemies? No. *Tak Melayu Hilang Di Dunia*. It is better to flee than perish; one might then live to start anew, to fight another day.

So the traditional translation of Hang Tuah's line still holds true: the Malays have indeed not perished from the world. But only because they knew when to run. Like all good gamblers, they knew when to fold.

"Do you think anyone will buy this?" I asked Aloysius, somewhat incredulously despite his convincing consonance of facts.

"Nope. Hang Tuah is too important to them now. For all the wrong reasons. He was a prominent historical figure in the court of Sultan Mansor Shah, that's all. He led a romantic life, and the scribes of the time were all romantics. Just read the *Sejarah Melayu* or the *Hikayat Hang Tuah*. All romances! Myths and legends, fairy tales. You have to be careful how you read all this as history. But now the legend is more important than history. So if I were to suggest that Hang Tuah was as much a strategist as a warrior, you think people would see this as a credit to him? No, all that matters is that he walloped Hang Jebat."

But the Malays have a dearth of heroes, unlike their Indonesian cousin-brothers, who paid with much blood for the ideal of nationalism. No Singgamarajah, Cut Nyak Dien, Ibu Kartini, General Sudirman. No grand benevolent monarchs, no shining religious saints, no nationalists untainted by controversy. So back we go to the Golden Age of the Melaka Sultanate, and what do we find there? The encampment of a hapless refugee, first in a line of rulers culminating in a tyrant of a sultan, deserving of none but the most contrived praise.

So whom to portray as an exemplar of the Malay ideal? The Fearless Warrior: that fabled creature otherwise so rare in Malay history. Defender of the Throne, Keeper of the Faith. Brave, belligerent, damn near invulnerable and loyal to a fault. Exalt this creature, make a political icon of his favourite kris (since 1946 the central symbol on Umno's party flag), glorify him in a history as fictionalized as Shakespeare's *Richard III* and lo! The Malays Shall Not Perish From The World.

Yes, and Hang Tuah was ten metres tall, don't you know? ❑

15

AN *NST* SUB-EDITOR held a telephone handset to the television set in the newsroom. At the other end of the line, in a small office in London's Holborn district, I listened to a Malay voice announcing the results of the Umno presidential elections. Mahathir Mohamad had retained the presidency of the party by forty-three votes of the more than 1,000 cast. "Did you get that?" asked my colleague in Kuala Lumpur.

"I'm not sure," I said, "Did he say *forty-three?*"

"Guess so." He laughed, sardonically. "One busload."

"With a seat to spare for the conductor."

In April 1987, at the biennial Umno General Assembly, Tengku Razaleigh Hamzah challenged Mahathir for the party leadership. He had been joined in his bid by Musa Hitam. In the weeks running up to the assembly, Umno had fissured into what pundits were referring to as "Team A" and "Team B". By those forty-three votes, Team A had won.

Staring out the window of the *NST*'s London office at the bustle of High Holborn below, the number kept repeating itself on a tape-loop in my head. I had to conclude that I was glad the challenge had been unsuccessful, but for only one reason: It would have been very *wrong* for the leadership of Malaysia to have changed on the miserable strength of forty-three votes. What would that have told us about democracy in Malaysia? That out of sixteen million people, one busload was all it took to decide who would presume to rule the entire nation? Yet, I realized, this was precisely what had happened. One busload. I saw an image of a Sri Jaya bus leaving Umno's headquarters in Kuala Lumpur, filled with forty-three smiling passengers waving Umno flags. The most powerful single busload of people in history.

Of course, the result was such that Razaleigh could not possibly have accepted it as a defeat. Neither could Mahathir afford even a hint of magnanimity in so equivocal a "victory". If Razaleigh's supporters had been on shaky ground before, this time the ground would be emphatically pulled out from under them. All those who had supported Razaleigh and Musa were ejected from their party and government posts. Suddenly, we in the Malaysian media found ourselves with new skin to flay, an expanded Opposition to vilify. It was disconcerting, because suddenly the Enemy included near-as-dammit half of Umno.

My sojourn in London was a quiet, therapeutic, book-laden retreat, professionally unremarkable for the most part. I checked up on our student community, to see how things had changed in the decade since I had been there as a student myself. I emerged from the experience bemused and befuddled.

The students seemed a whole lot smarter than we had been, for a start. They were stylish, confident and sophisticated. They seemed to enjoy themselves more. They delighted in holding regular dances and balls, and these would be black-tie soirees rustling with fancy gowns and tuxedos, fragrant with perfumes and gleaming with hair gel. Certainly, there was scant trace of the religious extremism that had so tainted my own student experience in Britain.

But the vaunted Malaysian student associations had become something very different. In the Seventies, as I have described, these had been polarized between Bumiputras and non-Bumiputras. Now they had evolved into outright political groups. The Malays had their "Umno Club", the Indians their "MIC Club", the Chinese their "MCA Club".

(There was also a "DAP Club" and a "Pas Club", which kept themselves to themselves.)

Were they political? Not really. Sure, their office-bearers would sometimes meet to discuss current affairs in Malaysia, and they would invite visiting Malaysian politicians to be their guest speakers, but by and large they were social clubs. Now there was no social polarization—all the races mingled happily at each other's shindigs. But they would attend those dinners and dances as members of their Mother Parties. It was so very strange. On the one hand, it was outrageous to think that Malaysia's political divisions had become a natural fact of life for the Eighties generation. On the other, wasn't it good that these divisions should not, in fact, divide them?

But surely it was *wrong* that these young Malaysians abroad should identify themselves so naturally with Malaysia's political parties. But surely it was *right* that they should subsume these political identities within themselves, and thence rise above them, as they seemed to be doing.

I couldn't work it out; the question swallowed its own tail and looped elusively around my conscience. In the Seventies, Malaysian students overseas had been thoroughly divided by race and religion. In the Eighties, they had begun to reassociate with one another, but only through the vehicles of party politics. Perhaps it was evolutionary after all; perhaps the time would yet come when young Malaysians would no longer need political security blankets to shield them from their peers of other races.

Walking back through a soft spring night to my studio flat in Little Venice after one of these dances, I found myself elated and dismayed in equal measure. Which is to say: profoundly confused.

The highlight of my year in London was Mahathir's state visit to Britain in the summer of 1987, shortly after that nail-biter of an Umno vote. He seemed to enjoy being out of Malaysia, and I could relate to that. When they weren't enjoying the lavish attention of their hosts, Mahathir and Siti Hasmah went to the opera and took long walks together, hand-in-hand through woods and gardens. We had the chance to meet, informally, at various functions. Siti Hasmah was her usual gracious and attentive self, but I was too ill-at-ease in Mahathir's company to make much more than small talk. He looked drawn and tired. He took pills from a small pillbox he carried in his coat pocket. "For my throat," he said, hoarsely.

I could understand that. In fact, for all the unhappiness that attended the mention of his name back home, I was proud to see Mahathir perform in England. It seemed, out there, he was in his true element, fielding the awkward questions of reporters with fluid ease, delivering speeches that sang with pride in what he was making of Malaysia; promoting the nation as a fine place for foreign investment and presenting to prospective investors a new and resolutely welcoming package of incentives.

After six years as prime minister of Malaysia, this was Mahathir's first official visit to Britain. It was something of a triumph, then, that the Kedah kampung boy was now in the homeland of the historical interloper as an honoured guest, red carpets under his feet, the British prime minister his confidante. It would have been churlish to have sneered at the pleasure Mahathir took in his arrival in Britain on his own terms. But I was tempted to do so nonetheless.

I returned to Malaysia that August, and plunged into a tempest of controversies and excitement. By mid-1987, the cumulative tensions of the Mahathir years had reached a head. Indeed: a great many heads.

THIS WAS THE WAY it was in August 1987:

Social reformists were criticizing the malleability of the Malaysian Constitution under the Barisan Nasional's parliamentary majority.

Mahathir was criticizing the Supreme Court for "interfering"in the business of parliament.

The sultans were criticizing the erosion of the authority of the Monarchy.

The Chinese were criticizing education minister Anwar Ibrahim for his ministry's decision to give senior positions in Chinese schools to teachers who had not been educated in Mandarin.

Everyone was criticizing the government's award of a $3 billion highway contract to a company widely believed to be closely connected with Umno, headed by a young man who had once worked for finance minister Daim Zainuddin.

Tengku Razaleigh Hamzah was suing Umno for what he claimed had been irregularities in the party elections that had denied him the presidency.

Was this fodder or what? I kicked off a new-look weekly column and plunged into the fray, delighted that Malaysians were at last learning to speak up, and not cower in silence as the fate of their homeland was decided by mere busloads of two-dollar politicians. Within weeks, however, it was clear that the thunder and lightning of these many stormfronts were awakening from their two-decade slumber those wrathful Malaysian Beasts, the Tiger and the Dragon.

No; wrong simile. The Beasts had never fallen asleep: they had been cast into separate cells buried deep within a mountain fortress on which was carved, in letters big enough for even the gods to see, the initials NEP. The fortress had been guarded by serried ranks of troops, collectively called the National Front. But the fortress required vast amounts of money and energy to contain the awesome power of its prisoners. After two years of the deepest economic recession in memory, the money for maintenance was no longer there and the necessary energy was being dissipated by the quarrels and rebellions and mutinies that had broken out among the troops that guarded the mountain.

So the fortress began to crumble, and within it the Tiger and the Dragon began to roar and fume.

Even without the Chinese-education issue, the unrest of mid-1987 was becoming shamefully racial. In protest of the highway contract being awarded to United Engineers Malaysia, Opposition politicians had rallied protestors from the Chinese suburbs of Kuala Lumpur to picket the new toll plazas that were, alas, the first tangible manifestation of these new infrastructural projects.

Why *Chinese* protestors, when *all* Malaysians would have to pay these tolls? Simply because the Opposition parties of Kuala Lumpur were Chinese. They had no other communal base; nowhere else to go. The ethnic divide in parliament had ensured that it was impossible for any political mobilization along anything other than racial lines. So Chinese youths picketed the Cheras toll-plaza, and some threw stones at the clerks in the ticket-booths. Perhaps it wouldn't have mattered who those clerks were, but the fact was that they were all Malays. That's the way it was with the NEP. And who would have begrudged these farmers' children taking jobs as toll clerks, if that was the best the NEP could do for them?

That racialism could assert itself over the highway controversy would have been bad enough, even if there hadn't been an outright racial issue doing the rounds of popular sentiment. But there was. And it had to do with Chinese education, no less; a matter at the very heart and soul of the Malaysian Chinese community. Those teachers who had been promoted were all Chinese, all fluent Mandarin speakers, but that wasn't enough: they had not gone to Mandarin schools as children. This was seen by Chinese educationists as at best a display of disrespect on the part of the Malay leadership, at worst an attempt to further undermine the foundations of their culture in Malaysia.

Would that it might never have been so. Why *should* there have been "Chinese" schools in Malaysia, or "Malay" or "Indian" schools for that matter? Because the British, in their vaunted wisdom of divide-and-rule, had set up Malayan education in just such a way. To be fair to our colonial masters, the various communities had been happy to accept this pastiche of a system at the time, given the gulfs between the races. And for those more truly "Malayan" there had been the institution of "national-type" schools in the English medium, open to children of all races, wherein their mother tongues were taught in "POL" classes—"Pupils' Own Language". No dispensation was ever made for Hindi, Urdu, Punjabi, Malayalam or Telugu; nor for Cantonese, Hokkien, Hakka or Teochew—languages as mutually unintelligible as they were all decidedly "Indian" or "Chinese". The Indians were taught Tamil; the Chinese Mandarin. Because the Malay language was essential to the curriculum for all, the Malays were taught Islam instead.

Had all schools been multiracial, however, Malaysian education might have been much more authentically Malaysian in flavour, and their wards that much more multiracial in their outlook. But the vernacular schools had persisted, because after Independence it was well-nigh impossible to suggest phasing them out without raising the ire of the Chinese and Indian communities. And so Malaysia continued to be dotted with these strange, outlandish schools, in which Malaysian children were taught in languages that severely cramped their prospects under the NEP, or indeed anywhere else in the modern world.

The Tamil schools were the sorriest of the lot; tucked away in plantation clearings, their classrooms filled with those doomed to the lowest rungs on the ladder of national opportunity. The Chinese schools were much better off, as a rule, because most of them were privately funded, or at least supplemented with private funds, by the Chinese business community.

For all that they tended well to the academic development of their charges, they did absolutely nothing for national unity. Indeed, by the fateful month of October 1987, they had become the central totems of national discord.

What horrified me, however, was the ridiculous—indeed, Chaplinesque—misunderstanding that had first stoked the flames of Chinese outrage. In reporting on the initial stages of the issue, the press had described the teachers in question as "non-Chinese educated". If ever there was a case of sheer editorial stupidity, this was it. It was an ungainly, awkward, unthinking term, what with that hyphen between the "non" and the "Chinese", and without another between "Chinese" and "educated". (Why not "non-*Mandarin* educated", for pity's sake? Why not make it clear from the very start that it was a *language* at issue here, a medium of instruction, not an entire *race?)* One glance at the description, and it was no wonder that the first impression the public had of this matter was that "non-Chinese" teachers were being made senior assistants of Chinese schools. Even in the throes of the ensuing controversy, there were people who would suddenly realize: "You mean they're *Chinese?*"

Yes, they were Chinese. And they were teachers who had taught in Chinese schools all their lives, some of them for twenty years or more. This was one issue that should never have gotten past the first few mentions in the newspapers and the swift response of the education minister, to the effect that he was sorry for the misunderstanding and would attend to the grievance. But no, by then the heat had ignited the tinder of Chinese disaffection, and smoke was billowing from the nostrils of the Dragon.

But perhaps this had little to do with those teachers. Perhaps, by then, the Chinese community had had as much as it could endure of what Malaysia had become. For nearly two decades the Chinese had suffered the indignity of secondary status under the NEP, and they had watched their political representatives in government rendered powerless to do anything but squabble among themselves over what could or could not be done. Then there had emerged a promising new leader, and within days he had self-destructed, taking their cherished Multi-Purpose Holdings with him.

The Chinese knew the Malays still regarded them with fear and loathing, because so many Malay politicians had risen to prominence through playing on those atavistic fears. The Chinese knew that as long as such attitudes were politically useful to the Malays, the Malays would continue to measure the Chinese by the ugliest and worst among them: the exploiters, the predators, the chauvinists, the Malay-haters.

In the course of these twenty years, moreover, a new Chinese generation had grown up and gone to school in a Malaysia that bore scant resemblance to anything their fathers may have dreamed about. A terrible apartheid had evolved in Malaysian education; an ever-widening chasm separated the Chinese schools from the rest of the national education system. Bahasa Malaysia had become the pre-eminent medium of instruction right up to tertiary levels, and even the Chinese schools were turning out young Malaysians fluent in the national language. Yet, for the sake of "Chinese culture", these were young Malaysians who had never interacted with their peers of other races from the mainstream schools. Worse, they seemed to have grown unwilling ever to do so. Within that mountain fortress of the NEP, the notion of Malaysia as a single, united nation must have seemed a pious, narcotic fantasy.

So, over this pathetic issue, the Chinese revolted. They called a boycott of the schools involved. And the Malays declared themselves ready to meet heat with fire. Umno's youth wing started organizing a massive rally at Kampung Baru (where else?), from which half a million Malays would march to Stadium Merdeka. Banners were drawn, lurid with the kris, the wave-bladed dagger that was the symbol of Umno and of the Malay warrior, atop slogans calling for Chinese blood. Madness was again in the air.

In his capacity as minister of home affairs, Mahathir Mohamad, like Poseidon setting free the Kraken, unleashed the Internal Security Act and bid it go tame this fractious land. On the night of October 27, 1987, operatives of the police Special Branch spread out across the nation and began arresting social activists, environmentalists, Chinese educationists, Opposition politicians and sundry radicals. In all, 115 people would be detained without the possibility of trial. The small fry among them would be released within several weeks while the more prominent would be kept behind barbed wire for eighteen months.

The day after the first arrests, three newspapers were banned, one each in the English, Malay and Chinese languages, egalitarianly enough. I wrote the next day's editorial in the *New Straits Times,* in which I adopted a mournful tone, lamenting that the government had no recourse but this, lamenting most the closure of the three newspapers. Two weeks later I was summoned for questioning by the director of the Special Branch. Here is an expurgated account of that meeting, penned in response to the many people who were consumed with curiosity over what happens behind the closed doors of Malaysia's secret police. This piece was published in full in 1990 by the Resource & Research Centre of the Selangor Chinese Assembly Hall, to whom I am grateful for permission to reproduce it here:

> VERY WELL: I shall tell you what happened on Thursday, November 12, 1987; although this story must begin a little over a fortnight earlier, on Tuesday, October 27.
>
> Maznah came to see me at the office. She is a lecturer at USM in Penang, and she had a book she wanted me to review. Nothing spectacular; a collection of papers on rural development, including some of her work. Maznah and I knew each other vaguely; we had gone to primary school together, and now we were useful, if distant, "contacts" for each other. She had come to Kuala Lumpur two days previously, to stay with friends and to see me. That Tuesday morning, she was ashen-faced. She clutched the book she'd wanted me to review, but it seemed to have become unimportant. The night before, at 2:00 a.m., Special Branch detectives had come to the house in which she'd been sleeping and arrested her friend and host, University of Malaya lecturer Tan Ka Kheng.
>
> Maznah had hidden in her room, terrified. It was coincidental that we'd had an appointment to meet the following morning, but this was the first that anyone outside the authorities—and the families of the detainees—knew of that pivotal moment in our nation's history. Tan Ka Kheng was the first of the 115 people who would be arrested under that massive invocation of the Internal Security Act.
>
> We summoned a reporter from the *NST* Crime Desk, and he made a few phone calls. This is usually a pointless

exercise when it comes to Special Branch activities under the ISA, but it made everyone feel a little less troubled to think that it might even be possible to make a few phone calls. We learned nothing about what had happened to Maznah's friend. I comforted her over lunch in the *NST* canteen. Throughout that day, however, news kept breaking of more and more arrests. The initial quizzicality turned into horror. The following day, Wednesday, October 28, *The Star* newspaper ran its now-infamous front-page display of the first dozen detainees. Its publishing permit was immediately suspended by the Home Ministry, as were those of the *Watan* and the *Sin Chew Jit Poh.*

We were in a turmoil of confusion and fear. We had not the slightest inkling that a crackdown of this magnitude was even being contemplated, much less executed. The number of detainees kept rising; each successive update compounding the astonishment and disbelief. But when, at about 3:00 p.m., the news broke about the newspaper suspensions, a limit was breached.

There are always surprising quirks in what people call "human nature". You can have the meekest and most submissive of people, people whom you would never credit with the fire of rebellion, but when something unimaginably traumatic befalls them they discover a core of steel within themselves. They turn and face the furies full-on, and they rediscover their integrity and their conscience. So was it with the *New Straits Times* that Wednesday.

A high, keen resolve arced out above the tempest of shock and horror in which we reeled. We watched the emergency broadcasts over television; first the Inspector-General of Police, then the prime minister, addressing the nation. And then I sat down and wrote the next day's editorial. It was passed by the Acting Group Editor and his Assistant (the Group Editor being at the time in Bali at the Asean Editors' Conference), and accordingly published.

The editorial was extensively quoted in the world media, generally in substantiation of a widespread denunciation of the Malaysian Government's action. It's always thrilling to see your work gaining any kind of international recognition, but I had the feeling there would be a price to pay for this.

The heat was almost immediate. By mid-morning of that Thursday, the Police and Home Ministry were demanding to know the reasons behind the composition and publication of that editorial, the identity of the writer, and if a full retraction would be published the next day. In the general turmoil of the moment, however, most of us had other things to think about.

Indeed, the editorial comment seemed to be part of a galvanizing of the *NST*. One senior executive had remarked that with the closure of *The Star*, this was a chance for the *NST* to "make a stand"—to establish from within the chaos a sense of responsibility to itself and to Malaysian journalism. "If we don't do it now," he warned, "we never will." But that "stand" was never made. The Group Editor returned from the Bali Conference on Friday; by Saturday the *NST*'s capitulation was complete. The demanded retraction was published as an editorial on Sunday.

But the heat remained. I was told it might be prudent to "lie low" for a while, although no journalists were expected to be detained. My weekly column was temporarily suspended—I didn't mind, it seemed the only way left to protest—and I took emergency leave to seek out some solitude and silence within which to reassemble a badly shaken perspective.

On Wednesday, November 11, the *NST* received a telephone call from the Special Branch,asking that I present myself for questioning at 2:30 p.m. the following afternoon. The Group Editor called me at home and informed me of the request. "They just want a chat," he said reassuringly. "If they'd really wanted you, they'd have come and got you. Don't worry. You'll be all right."

The next day, I had lunch with my mother at a favourite local Indian restaurant. She accompanied me home, where I bathed and changed into smart clothes: black trousers, a grey shirt and matching tie complete with shiny new *NST* tie-pin. I hugged my mother and brother, their face masks of apprehension, and told them exactly what my Group Editor had told me. It seemed to do them about as much good as it had done me. Then I got into my jeep and set off. "It's only an interview," I told myself. "Don't get melodramatic. "But I felt tuned to a strange clarity all the way to the Police Headquarters; I was acutely aware of the other vehicles on the highway, people waiting at bus-stops, the shades of the roadside foliage, the liquid quality of the bright afternoon sunshine.

As I passed the Railway Station and the National Mosque, changing down to take the turn-off to Police HQ, I felt two sharp twinges of pain in my chest. There is a history of heart disease in my family. "Not now!" I thought, wryly smiling to myself at the thought of a possible headline: Journalist Dies of Heart Attack En Route to Police Questioning.

I parked the jeep where they told me to, and went to get a gate pass. The two young constables on duty asked me whom I wished to see. Datuk Rahim Nor, I told them, Director of the Special Branch. The man's name carries a tangible aura among his subordinates in the Royal Malaysian Police Force. Both constables looked at me with sudden interest. One asked me where I was from. "New Straits Times," I said. Understanding looks passed between them. As they busied themselves with the requisite phone calls and forms, I gazed out at the city below. It was a completely familiar scene, and all the more poignant for that.

The constable handed me a slip of paper. "Do you know where to go?" I shook my head. "That building over there. You'll have to get another pass when you go in." Passes in hand, I located the inner sanctum of Malaysia's secret police with little difficulty. Entering, I encountered a familiar face. He was a detective-sergeant I had met in London the previous July, accompanying the prime minister on his European tour. "Hello!" I greeted him cheerily, shaking his hand. "We meet again! Different circumstances this time, though." His smile was a little wan, but genuine. We'd nearly become friends, the last time. "I'll see if Datuk's free," he said. "Wait here."

He stepped to a large yellow door and opened it a crack. He peeped gingerly in. I almost laughed aloud. Here was a man adept at the midnight capture, exhibiting a wholly incongruous timidity in the orbit of his chief officer. Datuk Rahim, I mused, must be quite a man. The sergeant turned to me. "Yes, he's free. You can go in."

It was a vast, dark, windowless office, cooled by a pair of rattling air-conditioners. Two large oil paintings of indifferent quality hung on adjacent walls. One depicted a battle-scene; the other was a portrait of a heroic Malay figure, stripped to the waist and hefting a spear. Framed certificates and memorabilia were the only other decorations, along with a pair of ornamental kris on a sideboard. Stepping forth from behind his large, glass-topped desk, Datuk Rahim Nor bid me take a seat.

He was a very big man—as tall as I am and twice as broad—and he was not fat. He wore check trousers, a striped shirt and a sport jacket. A craggy, sculpted face; prominent cheek-bones, a thick moustache. He looked to be about fifty, but his age was scarcely reflected in his powerful build. In his stern and troubled eyes, shielded not at all by the reading glasses he affected as he opened my file, I recognized something awesomely heroic. In different circumstances, it might have been comic.

In the folder he had opened before him, I saw a photocopy of my editorial. Certain passages had been emphasized in yellow highlighter. He tapped at the paper. "What is this?" he asked aloud. I wasn't sure if he was being rhetorical, so I stayed silent. "Didn't you know why we did what we did? You are not stupid. So what are you? This is what I want to know. I read this, and I am confused. I want to know: who is this fellow? How does he think? So perhaps you will tell me."

He got up, walked to the door and summoned an aide. An Assistant Superintendent, I believe, although rank is difficult to determine in the plain-clothed Special Branch. He was Chinese, middle-aged, and he carried a clipboard with sheets of blank paper. Datuk Rahim turned to me. "Would you like some coffee?" he asked. As I fumbled for an answer to the totally unexpected question, he turned to the ASP and asked him to get coffee for all of us. The drinks were brought in by a clerk and set before us. The ASP made himself comfortable and prepared to take notes. Datuk Rahim turned again to my file. I cleared my throat and started to say something. He cut me off. "I'll let you talk later," he said. "First you listen. You knew the tension was growing. You knew what was happening, or if you didn't I don't know what you're doing as a reporter. All those rallies, all that talk. People don't know when to stop. We had to act. We can't just let things build up until people start killing each other. You heard what the IGP said on TV. You heard what the prime minister said in parliament. And you still write something like this. Why?"

This I had expected; this I had rehearsed. "I couldn't say this was a good thing to happen to this country, Datuk," I said. "I had always wanted to believe we had left 1969 behind us; that we had grown and matured. I think it is a tragedy we seem to be still the same."

"But you don't understand why we had to do what we did?"

"Yes I do, but I don't think it's something we can be proud of. I think we should be sorry that we had to do it."

"Yes, I too am sorry, but you see what *The Star* did? They made it look like someone died. All the pictures on the front page—all non-Malays. We arrested Malays too, but they made it look like we were only going for the non-Malays. That was unfair. They made it look racial. I know your newspaper has been losing out to *The Star*. Don't think I don't understand. You have to worry about circulation ..."

I cut in: "It's not as simple as that, Datuk. I've never considered circulation to be the only measure of a newspaper's quality. There's a reason I've stayed with the *NST* all these years, instead of joining *The Star*. I don't condemn *The Star*, but I prefer to work within the establishment. *The Star* does its job its way; the *NST*'s job is different. I've always wanted the *NST* to do its job better, but that doesn't mean we must be like *The Star*. Our jobs are not the same."

He pointed to a bright yellow line in the editorial. "So why do you defend them?"

I thought about fabricating something elaborate, but decided it would be very foolish of me to try and delude this man. "They were fellow journalists," I shrugged. "Our colleagues. Your brother is still your brother, even if you disagree with him."

He seemed to accept that. "But how can this be published? Who makes the decision? Didn't anyone question you?"

I thought back over the events of two weeks before, testing the memory of what it had been like on the editorial floor of the *NST*. I remembered the resolve, and then replayed the way the things had gone subsequently; the way things were now, me sitting there in that office, sweaty-palmed, this dark and angry man asking me questions I didn't know how to answer .... "It was a very stressful time, Datuk. It was hard for us to understand what was happening."

"You were confused."

"Yes."

"You didn't know what you were doing."

"Yes. No."

He let my collapse hang in the air for a moment. "So will you be confused again?"

"No."

I think it was then that I knew I would be walking out of there alone and unescorted. It was then that I proved I was not a threat. I was safe. I would not go to prison, or even lose my job. Effortlessly, he had won. I understood authority, I understood power, and I knew where they lay.

"Your bosses say good things about you," said Datuk Rahim. "They say this fellow is 100% Malaysian, you cannot question his loyalty. I say that's nothing; even the communists are 100% Malaysian too. They too love this country."

I was expecting this too; he'd said the same thing to my bosses, the Chairman and Group Editor of the *NST*. They'd told me he'd said it. I had a rehearsed reply, and I was able to send it out on autopilot. "Yes, but they want to sweep aside our system and install a new one. I believe in evolution not revolution." This was no time for subtlety.

He looked penetratingly at me. "That's right," he said.

The ASP looked up from his notes and asked me where I'd gone to school and university. Had I ever been active in student politics? Who were my friends in school? What were they doing now? Did I keep in touch with them? I grew thankful that I had always been something of a loner in life; that I had spent my university years playing guitar and singing songs in rural Welsh folk- clubs rather than agitating for global reform.

Datuk Rahim resumed. "What are a hundred people," he said almost philosophically, "compared with 16.4 million? Nothing. A sacrifice. How well do you know our history? Who was right, Hang Tuah or Hang Jebat?'

I felt myself beginning to lose grip. This meeting, never less than surreal, was growing bizarre. "I'm not sure what you mean," I said.

"Who was the greater hero?" he persisted. "Hang Tuah or Hang Jebat? Hang Tuah was very faithful to the sultan, but Hang Jebat rebelled. Hang Tuah was ordered to kill Hang Jebat, and he carried out the order, even though Hang Jebat was his closest friend. That was his loyalty. Which one is the true hero?"

"I don't know."

The interview lasted two hours. Having determined that I was no threat, Datuk Rahim wanted to know what I knew of others. I was glad to be able to tell him, in all honesty, nothing. I grew grateful for those very things in my life that I had always lamented—my isolation, my ignorance, my lasting inability to belong to any group or align myself with any one community. In the end, I understood why Datuk Rahim perceived in me no threat to any socio-political order; far from being a spokesman for some misplaced ideology, I was simply another aberrant misfit of no particular consequence, whose only impact derived from a facility with a language of diminishing importance in this country. I felt like a moth, elaborate of plumage but naked and dead, pinned to the wall for the scrutiny of a faintly disgusted hobbyist.

On my part, even as I absorbed what I could of the details of the meeting, I realized that the observational skills I had developed through my career were of little use. He was impenetrable, unreadable, godlike in his remoteness; more a philosophy than a figure of authority. I wondered about his wife, their children. I pictured this man, sitting up here in this vast dark office, contemplating in furrow-browed concern the shrill little activities and small deceits of the scuttling creatures below and finally, slowly, ponderously, with heavy heart and hand, casting down the bolts of ultimate power to quell their dangerous and petty quarrels.

My coffee grew cold. Datuk Rahim chain-smoked Benson & Hedges cigarettes. I dearly wished I could light one up myself. Finally he stood up and said: "All right, you can go now."

"You mean I'm free to go?" I asked, in what must have seemed a transparent attempt to seek some reassurance. I should have known better.

"Well, I don't know about "free" ...," he said, pulling out another folder from the stack on his desk.

The ASP ushered me out. "What happens now?" I asked him, as the door to Datuk Rahim's office swung shut behind us. "I don't know," he said. I walked to the lift and rode down to the ground floor. I returned the first of my two passes and walked down the long drive to the guardhouse to return the second and retrieve my papers. I climbed into my jeep and drove out of the compound, down the access road and out into the traffic of Kuala Lumpur.

I went home, knowing my country had changed, and with it my career and my life, but not knowing how.

I cannot look back upon this episode now without the greatest shame. So feebly had I defended myself. A word for the journalistic fraternity, and then it was yes sir no sir three bags full sir. My capitulation was complete, and virtually immediate. Why?

He had said: "We arrested Malays too ..."

Yes, you arrested Malays: Oppositionists from Pas and a couple of nasty little pieces of work from the wilding fringes of Umno. But why did you not arrest the Umno Youth leaders who had planned that Kampung Baru rally; who had stood before those vicious banners and warned the Chinese not to trifle with the Malays?

He had said: "The communists are 100% Malaysians too ..."

The *communists??* This was 1987! Whatever remained of the Malayan Communist Party was either prepubescent or senile, and the party itself was within months of declaring itself defunct and coming down the mountain to resettlement shacks in the Thai lowlands. What manner of country did he believe this was?

And he'd said: "What are a hundred people in a nation of 16.4 million? Nothing. A sacrifice."

But he had not arrested merely a hundred people. I shall not forget the ashen faces of my mother and brother as I'd left for that "interview". He had arrested a hundred families, a hundred sets of friends and relatives, and friends of relatives and relatives of friends ... he had arrested everyone who read of those detentions or heard of them on the radio and TV .... He arrested an entire nation.

But I had said nothing. I sat and played with my fingers and tried to give the right answers to his questions and make the appropriate grunting sounds during his monologues. I wanted to be let go. I was *scared.* And he knew it, and believed it right and proper that I should be. I don't think I shall ever forgive myself for that fear. So effortlessly do the manipulators of fear exert their nefarious power on those so easily scared. And how self-righteous they are, the custodians of such power!

Awful, awful power; rooted in the conviction that no enemy is so great as the enemy within. The Enemy is Us.

May I never be scared again.

The changes made themselves apparent soon enough. Among the first of them was the restructuring of the national media. The MCA's *Star* newspaper would eventually reopen under Umno direction—a simple transfer of authority between Barisan Nasional partners. The *New Straits Times,* for the third time in five years, would undergo a change of editor. P.C. Shivadas was moved out (to his relief, we imagined), and his place as group editor was taken by

Abdul Kadir Jasin, a thoughtful, self-effacing Kedahan who had distinguished himself as editor of the *NST*'s business paper and then of the *Berita Harian,* the group's Malay-language daily. I liked Kadir. He was a man who could clearly see the Big Picture, and he had certainly paid his dues as a newspaperman. But I wasn't sure he would make a good editor of the *NST*. In London during Mahathir's visit there the previous year, Kadir and I had shared a breakfast over which he'd spoken of what the *NST* needed to be. An urban daily, he suggested, read by the middle-class intelligentsia; its circulation halved from nearly two hundred thousand to under a hundred thousand. Then, reasoned Kadir, the paper could be bolder and stronger, because it wouldn't have such a mass audience. I was sure I couldn't agree with him on this, but at the time it seemed an idle mind-game to play while waiting for the next stop on our subject's schedule.

After *The Star* was banned, however, the *NST*'s circulation went up to nearly half-a-million, and the company chairman, Desa Pachi, made a rare visit to the editorial floor, where he stood on a chair and used a loud-hailer to exhort us to our best efforts in making the most of this circulation windfall. It was, in the circumstances, a grotesque performance.

The nation had fallen into a fearful silence, and as 1987 shaded into 1988 Mahathir was able to devote more time to his immediate political concerns. Tengku Razaleigh's suit to get the Umno elections declared null and void was dismissed, but Justice Harun Hashim ruled that there had indeed been irregularities in some of Umno's branches at the time of the party's April 1987 assembly, and that as a consequence Umno as a whole had contravened the Societies Act and should therefore be deregistered.

That was momentarily shocking, but Mahathir swiftly re-registered the party as "Umno Baru", or "New Umno", while Razaleigh registered a new party called "Semangat 46", or "Spirit of 46", after the year of Umno's birth. Razaleigh wanted to make clear that he was dedicating himself to restoring Umno to its "founding ideals", whatever they were.

To Mahathir and his new Umno, however, it was back to business as usual. Razaleigh would have to try his luck as common Oppositionist. In due course, we received instructions to drop the "New" from Umno's title.

There remained one last matter to be settled. The judiciary had granted injunctions against United Engineers Malaysia and its highway contract, refused to uphold expulsion orders against certain foreign correspondents, granted publishing permits to human- rights gadflies, and even ordered that the New Umno had to *buy* the old Umno's assets, and not simply take them over. Mahathir's criticisms of the judiciary for "interference" mounted in intensity, and at last the Lord President of the Supreme Court was moved to write to the King and ask for a royal intercession against the depredations of the Executive. Sultan Mahmood Iskandar conferred with Mahathir, and apparently liked what he heard, because the only intercession he conceded was to suspend the Lord President and five other judges. After the due process of a tribunal, the Lord President was sacked for "judicial misconduct". Two other Supreme Court judges were also dismissed.

That was the end of the road for me. Until then, I had doggedly kept believing we might recover from the rapid-fire concatenation of calamities that had assailed us. I could see causes and effects, and I could still rationalize what had happened; fit it all into the unfolding patterns of Malaysian history, and discern ways and means by which Malaysia might emerge the stronger for these catastrophes. But when the Supreme Court got its head blown off, I gave up.

My ideal of journalism drew from a sporting metaphor: We were not a football to be kicked around by competing teams. Nor were we on either of those teams. Nor were we up there in the bleachers, cheering on our chosen teams and barracking their opponents. No: we were the Man in Black. The Referee. Always in the thick of the action, running up and down the pitch as hard and fast as the hardest and fastest player, never more than a few paces from the ball, but never touching that ball. That was our role, and who cared if we were popular? Referees rarely were, but there could be no game without them.

It was one of Malaysia's most eminent jurists, the retired Lord President Tun Suffian Hashim, who had said it best for me. "When those above think you're favouring those below," he had written, "and those below think you're favouring those above, then you're doing your job well." Tun Suffian had been speaking to jurists, of course, but he helped me realize that of Malaysia's four pillars of governance—the executive, the legislative, the judiciary and the monarchy—the press owed its philosophical provenance most to the judiciary.

And Malaysia's judiciary was decimated. Great gaping holes had been blown on the highest bench, and they would be filled by the premature promotions of the definitively inexperienced. Moreover, these jurists would know they owed their elevation to political forces, and their consciences would trouble them as much as the knowledge that they would never command the respect of Malaysia's legal fraternity. To peer over the bench and see nothing but contempt at the Bar—how would that impact upon the discharge of their duties? The Malaysian judiciary would be a beleaguered and fearful shadow of what it had been.

I tendered notice of my resignation from the *New Straits Times*. It was immediately accepted. A few weeks later, I received a telephone call from a regional newsmagazine based in Hong Kong. They asked me to join them. I accepted, and in early October 1988, seven years to the day since I had become a journalist, I embarked upon my years of exile. ❑

Journey to the East

ANGELS WERE WITH ME on that flight, dressed in cream and lavender, perfect skin and limpid eyes, delicate mouths delicious in peach lipstick. Cabin baggage by Louis Vuitton and Chanel, lotus feet shod by Ferragamo, watches by Rolex and Girard Perregaux, jewellery ... but even my Hong Kong-trained eye was not expert enough to discern the taxonomy of jewellery. There was a lot of it, though: earrings, necklaces, bracelets and brooches. Who were these unearthly creatures, and what did they mean? One was named Tracie, the other Elizabeth. These Singapore shopping sprees occurred once a month or so, more frequently if they were feeling exceptionally glum or happy. They liked Singapore. The shops! The hotels! They knew Singapore very well; at least, those quarters of the island subtending from Orchard Road. They had never been to Kuala Lumpur. "What for?" they asked, in voices that tinkled like Waterford crystal chandeliers. "Singapore has everything."

"But you're Malaysians ..." I said, somewhat feebly. Yes and so was their travelling companion that evening, that malodorous and ill-appointed fellow they found sharing their row of seats on the flight from Kuala Lumpur on its stopover in Singapore on its way to Kuching. Did I discern a pair of ever-so-slightly wrinkled noses at this reminder? Did I hope they would notice the Mont Blanc clipped in the frayed and unwashed pocket of my Cerruti denim shirt; the rusty Tag-Heuer on my grimy wrist?

"We're Sarawakians," said Tracie, and Elizabeth smiled, causing a celestial chorus to hum in harmony.

And what might that mean? The next day, over lunch in a Kuching coffee-shop, it meant considerable outrage. I was sitting with a group of men including the assistant chef-de-mission of the Sarawak contingent to the just-concluded national sports meet in Johor Baru, where Sarawak had won the overall championship by a score of gold medals but was, as usual, treated like the country cousins of the Peninsula.

"The papers!" blustered Mr Tan. "They just don't care! The fourth day, we had sixteen golds, they printed zero! ZERO!" He held up a thumb and forefinger linked in a circle. "So we complain, and the next day they get it right, but not one word of apology!"

As our group included the Kuching bureau chief of the newspaper in question, Mr Tan's umbrage had a keen edge. James Ritchie did his best to mollify him. The approach James chose was to sincerely agree with him. "Ya," said James, sombrely. "Those guys in KL just don't give a damn about us."

He was not lying. Earlier that morning I had sat in James's office as he spoke on the phone to his newspaper in Kuala Lumpur, asking what had become of this story or that feature, sent days or weeks before and neither seen nor heard of since. But there had been no one there to take his call, the editors were all out, so James had to convey his distress to a secretary and hope that something would eventually filter through to someone who might have something to do with what went on there.

James had banged the phone down—more gently than I would have, in similar circumstances—and we had gone off to meet this group for lunch. "They don't give a damn," muttered James, darkly, as we left his office. "Sarawak is just savages and jungle and rivers to them. The issues are logging and Penans." Not long before, a veteran Malaysian news editor had visited Sarawak for the first time in his life. "I said to him," said James,"'First time, ah, Pak Samad? In twenty-nine years?' He smiled and said, 'Ala, sorry, lah.' This place is so far away from them."

James loved Sarawak with all his heart. Penang-born, son of a policeman, a reporter for the past twenty of his forty-two years, James had first arrived in Sarawak as a seventeen-year-old schoolboy, and had vowed to make his career there if he could. The opportunity had come in his early thirties, by which time James had been ten years a journalist, and he had leapt at it. He had been in Sarawak ever since, developing a famous reputation for derring-do, charging up rivers and barging into the jungle to befriend the many native tribes of the interior, while striding with equally brash confidence through the incestuous labyrinth of Sarawak politics.

Now, ten years on, James Ritchie was something of an institution in Kuching. He knew everyone; everyone knew him. James was, I knew, a fine newsman: connected, energetic, informed. But five years previously, he had succumbed to the most seductive trap that ever opens before a reporter—all the more so because it only spreads its enticements before the best of them: He threw in his lot with the political leadership. James had written a slim book on Sarawak's chief minister, Taib Mahmud, and had been instantly branded a stooge. I'd read the book in KL, not long before the end of my career with the *New Straits Times*. It was not an expert biography; there was far too much adulation in it. Still smarting from the cuts and barbs that had assailed me since my sympathetic interview with Mahathir Mohamad, I remember thinking, "James Anak Ritchie, what have you done to yourself?"

After five years, James was still trying to regain some of the credibility he'd lost, but Kuching was still a small town when it came to politics, and there were those who might never forgive him. Nonetheless, James remained a personable charmer of a man, good-looking with his Malaysian-Scottish ancestry, fluent of speech and fleet of mind, and he was still, by and large, a man in his element. If only *NST* KL would treat his stories with some respect. It wouldn't even matter that after twenty years he was still only Journalist Grade B, he was as used to it as he'd ever be, if only they'd give his stories their due.

Ah, never mind. That's life. Peninsular Malaysians (James used the disparaging phrase, "Orang Malaya") had never given a damn about Sarawak, why should things start changing now? As long as the chief minister remained pally with KL and 95% of the oil and gas money could go over there, KL would let Sarawak get on in its jungle-tribe way, and keep the timber money.

("Timber money". Vuittonic angels on shopping sprees in Singapore ....)

"But this is too much!" expostulated Mr Tan, the assistant chef-de-mission. "We keep winning and winning, our kids beat their kids at everything, and they still treat us like second stringers! Just wait. Soon Malaysia's badminton champion is going to be Sarawakian. Malaysia's swimming champion. The whole national hockey team will be from Sarawak. Then maybe they'll take notice!" He sipped his coffee. "Maybe."

That night James took me to visit some young Iban friends of his. Their names were Jimon, Raden and Matilda; two brothers and their sister. They shared a room in a decrepit stilt house in a shadowy quarter of town. It was a housing estate. James made me note how there was almost a physical boundary between the zone of the "ordinary folk" and the "tribal" area. The former was neatly tended and well-lit; rows of modest terrace houses with cars in their driveways and potted plants in their yards. Then, abruptly, the streetlights grew fewer and further between, the ditches began to stink, the darkness thickened, the houses became wooden hulks in dense shadows.

James' three friends lived in such a house, one of the lesser properties of a well-known local politician. It was a rickety structure; it shook as we climbed the stairs. There were six rooms, clustered around a communal space littered with cheap shoes and rubber slippers. Each of the rooms earned eighty ringgit a month for the politician. James knocked on one of the doors, which was so flimsy it swayed on its hinges at his touch. The door swung open; a slender youth peered out. James greeted him effusively. The youth—Jimon—smiled, backed away from the door, beckoned us in.

His sister—Matilda—was frying fish at a gas burner. She was pretty, in a plump and splay-footed way. She smiled shyly at us. A small television set was making noise in a corner; watching it was a strapping young man introduced to us as Anthony, a fellow tenant of the house. Raden, we were told, was taking a bath. James and I sat down on the linoleum-covered floor. James fished out of his wallet a ten-ringgit note and bid Jimon go get us a couple bottles of beer. While the lad went out on that errand, and James engaged Anthony in conversation, I surveyed the room.

It was humble. Indeed, it was one step above squalour, which was kept at bay by what was clearly a determined effort to keep the place clean and tidy. There were two beds; Anthony was sitting on one and on the other, which was Matilda's, was piled the bedding for the two boys, who slept on the floor. There was a simple stack of shelves, on which clothes were neatly folded. In the corner by the window was a sink and the gas burner at which Matilda cooked. Next to it was a refrigerator. The window was paned with glass louvres, every third one missing, and curtained with a piece of cloth suspended from a wire. It lifted and fluttered fitfully in the night breeze. The room was virtually devoid of ornamentation. There was a cheap wall clock, and on the TV stand perched a few gewgaws: a fluffy white cat with a bell tied on a red ribbon around its neck; a small glass vase containing a spray of artificial flowers. Matilda's little touches.

Jimon returned with two bottles of Carlsberg and one of F&N orange crush. He ceremoniously placed them on the floor before us. "Whose is the orange?" asked James. "Raden's," said Jimon, just as his brother walked in, towel-clad, wet-haired and squeak-slippered from his bath. This occasioned some mirth, for Raden was, at eighteen, the elder of the two. Jimon was just sixteen, and knew he wouldn't be allowed to drink the beer without a dutiful admonition from James. But he opened all three bottles and filled glasses for Raden, Anthony, James and me.

Anthony was twenty-eight and worked as a security guard for an office building in downtown Kuching. Raden was in the sixth form of secondary school, Jimon in the fourth, and Matilda was just completing a secretarial course. Their rent was paid by an elder brother working in Sibu, who also gave them their pocket money each month.

James had met the siblings' father in their ancestral longhouse on one of his upriver jaunts the previous year, and had taken to heart the old man's request that James keep an eye on his children in Kuching. "But I tell you," James told me, "Kuching's a helluva long way from Batang Ai."

James feared for the fate of the kids, Jimon in particular. "He wants no more connection with the longhouse, but he's got nothing going for him in the city. He's lazy. Raden and Matilda have a sense of responsibility. Jimon, no. He just wants to drink beer and find people to take care of him. Sixteen years old, already drinking beer. Bugger's going to be an alcoholic before he's twenty." All this was said on that floor, as we sipped our drinks. Jimon smiled, enigmatically. James continued: "This is the reason the Ibans are being left behind. They have no tradition of leadership beyond the customs of the longhouse. They've always been a subject people. All they can do is sit quietly and hope that whoever rules them can take care of them. No ambition. No hope."

But Jimon could see past James's bluster to the soft-hearted man within, and seemed not to take any of this scolding to heart. James took us all out to the Kuching Club for more beers and the continuance of his lecture, and thence to a *karaoke* bar where he treated us to one of his famous Tom Jones impersonations. He bought the beers that Jimon quaffed with pleasure, all the while lamenting this young man's lack of prospects. The Ibans smiled and said little, but seemed to enjoy their night out with their gruff benefactor and his scolding words and heart of gold.

The following afternoon I visited Sim Kwang Yang, deputy secretary-general of the Democratic Action Party and member of parliament for Kuching. He was a chain-smoking, articulate man in his mid-forties, with greying hair, intelligent eyes and a gently supercilious manner; easily forgiven in one who has successfully remained an Opposition politician in Malaysian for some fifteen years. Sarawak's problems were easily stated, according to Sim: corruption, corruption, corruption, and the federal government.

It had gone beyond tragedy, and had entered the realm of farce. But what could be done? A man could do little more than keep his own conscience clear, and try and inspire others to do the same. To stay in his beloved homeland, no matter how many chose to portray him as a traitor and a subversive, and speak his truth at all times. "A man cannot flee his country," said Sim Kwang Yang, "any more than words can flee a page."

I liked that. I liked Sim. There was a nobility about him, a dignity that easily transcended the modest offices of DAP's Sarawak headquarters, on the upper floor of a three-storey shophouse with a coffee-shop at street level and a taekwondo school on the first floor. Our conversation was punctuated with rhythmic stamps and yells from below.

But Sim had been Kuching's member of parliament for ten years; he was a veteran of three general elections, and he was, in his way, secure. Kuching was, after all, a very Chinese town. But as he pointed out, Sarawak's politics were very different from the Peninsula's. "We could be this country's true model of multiracial harmony. No one group in complete dominance. Even our Malays are not as they are in the Peninsula. No difficulties with extremist religion, for one thing. And they would be the first to say they are Sarawakians first, Malaysians second." (Flashback: Angels on the evening flight ....)

"That does not speak well for national unity," I riposted.

"Until Sarawak begins to get the respect we deserve from Kuala Lumpur," said Sim, emphatically parrying the thrust, "don't talk about national unity." Again, that common thread of disaffection. Sarawak was growing up. The last time I had been there, exactly ten years before, it was still very much a forest state. There was Kuching, and there was jungle. Along the coast were a couple of places—Sibu, Bintulu—beginning to emerge as oil and gas terminals. But that was all; there had been little evidence of this strange and exciting new sense of self; this nation-within-a-nation that Sarawak seemed to have become.

After nearly three decades of an unequal partnership with the Peninsula, Sarawak was beginning to come into its own. Once there had been a testy chafing at the myth of Sarawak's "Independence through Malaysia"—to many Sarawakians a contradiction in terms. Now, the state seemed to be regarding its role in the Federation more as a matter of mutual convenience than as a convenient repository of vast natural resources. Sarawak to Malaysia would not be as Sumatra to Indonesia. But whether the quantum leap to maturity would take place while there was still something left of its resources—in particular its fabulous forests—was a dicey question.

"I think we have a working relationship with the federal government," said Sim Kwang Yang. "The state government is nicely hand-in-glove with KL. So Sarawak's doing well, economically." It was obvious: Kuching, though still graceful and green, was clearly richer now than ever before. New buildings, new roads. Rolexed angels flying home from weekends in Singapore. "But the forests are going, and the rivers are choked with mud. Is anyone saying the price is too high?"

Sim Kwang Yang was. I respected him for it, and I wished him well.

I left Kuching the next morning. James came to see me off at the new airport, eliciting a promise that I would come back soon, that we might go on an adventure together to the headwaters of the Baleh River. A firm handshake, and James was gone.

I climbed aboard an aircraft for the flight north to Sabah. The 737's route followed the Sarawak coastline for much of its length; we flew over many river mouths, all of them spewing out thick brown sludge, spilling the primeval soil of Sarawak into the deep green maw of the South China Sea. It was a disturbing sight. Sarawak seemed to be haemorrhaging; arteries burst open, the land bleeding.

Angels were no longer in evidence.

AND SABAH? Sabah was slowly choking; a strangled shadow of the place I once thought I knew.

Not that we hadn't had much to furrow our brows over then: those were the years of Mustapha and Harris, of the gigantic presence of the hugely ambitious, of presumptive god-kings and their courtiers. A decade or two before, Sabah had been a great uncut diamond, laden with the potential of being Malaysia's richest state. But behind the promising facade was a corrupt and shady place; it was almost too easy to draw cynical contrasts between the shining glass tower of the Sabah Foundation's new building, rising proudly to the sky on reclaimed land in Likas Bay, and the subsistence-level lives of the people of the hinterland.

Sabah in the Seventies had been a study in such contrasts: the limousines of Kota Kinabalu and the ponies of the Bajau; the peasant farmers of Ranau and the chief minister's plan to have cable-cars strung up Mount Kinabalu. But now there were no such self-righteous little ironies to be savoured. Kota Kinabalu was a town trapped in terminal deterioration.

The capital of Sabah, once so gleaming, haughty and proud, now felt and smelt like a Sumatran town. The central bus station was a morass of mud and water, stuffed with battered minibuses. Working the crowds were shoals of small children and their mothers, hawking cigarettes and sweets. Such a sight—the barefoot urchins in grubby shorts and tee-shirts, the women squatting on their haunches in the shade of batik headcloths—had been ubiquitous in Indonesia and all but unknown in Malaysia. No longer.

The city's pavements were cracked and collapsing. Roadside foliage spread untrimmed. Grime and dust lay like a shroud on the town; the Kampung Ayer, a cluster of houses built on stilts in the coastal shallows, once so quaint and picturesque, now wallowed in a foetid quagmire of filth and sewage. And all around, floating on the air like alien aromas, snatches of staccato Tagalog, or the broad vowels and trilled fricatives of Indonesian.

The Kota Kinabalu I once knew had died, and what was left had begun to rot. A different, hardier, breed of occupant had gathered to feed off the remains, crawling like vermin in the rags of a mendicant. However much the tramp himself may disagree, such disease seems an unacceptably high price to pay for independence. But what would have been the alternative? Servitude? The immaculate garb of the household staff?

In 1985, Sabahans had sent a message to the federal government: they would no longer tolerate the megalomaniacal excesses of the likes of either Tun Mustapha Harun or Datuk Harris Salleh, the arch-rivals who had vied with each other for the rule of Sabah, each in his turn pledging loyalty to the Barisan Nasional when it suited his needs to have the backing of Kuala Lumpur. Sabah was as polyglot and demographically diverse as Sarawak, with the Malays and Muslims an even smaller minority. The largest single community was Kadazan; the most popular religion, Christianity. But Mustapha and Harris, ingratiating themselves with Kuala Lumpur, had for years pursued what were seen as "Islamization" policies. In 1984, Harris had gone so far as to cede the island of Labuan to federal control. A new party had been formed. The Parti Bersatu Sabah represented Christian and Kadazan interests with Chinese support, and in April 1985, Harris was ousted. Mustapha, whom Harris had defeated eight years before, thought this was his chance to come back. He, too, was thwarted.

So Sabah became the first state in the federation to go its own way under an administration that seemed more a mirror of its people than of the Malaysian ideal. PBS, under chief minister Joseph Pairin Kitingan, conciliatory in victory, applied for membership of the Barisan Nasional. There was the belief that this would soothe the sting of defeat for the nation's ruling party, which had supported Pairin's enemies. Rather than have Sabah under an Opposition party, the Barisan Nasional accepted Sabah into the fold. But it wasn't happy about it. Sabah began to feel a chill wind blow from the Peninsula.

Umno laid plans to open up in Sabah, a state long ignored as not having enough of a Malay population to make the effort worthwhile. Pairin found himself and his family members under intense scrutiny, their business affairs in particular. The PBS felt itself cold-shouldered at every opportunity.

In 1987 had come the Umno split, and three years later the first general elections with a dissident faction of Umno contending as a separate entity. Days before the polls, Pairin took PBS out of the Barisan Nasional and gave his support to Tengku Razaleigh's party. It didn't do Razaleigh much good, but Sabah, retained by the PBS, became an Opposition state. Some of those who had been with Mahathir Mohamad at the time of the PBS pullout said later, with awe, that they had never seen the prime minister so angry.

The squeeze began. Sabah's timber export quota was lowered, decimating the state's principal source of revenue. Tourism was tacitly discouraged; domestic air fares were raised. (For Sarawak, however, there were affordable package deals.) Domestic investment was redirected; foreign investment put on hold. (Sabah was "politically unstable".) The borders grew even more porous to illegal immigration from the Philippines and Indonesia. The local television station was abandoned. Sabah was denied permission to have on its territory a branch of a Malaysian university, as Sarawak did. Pairin was charged with three counts of corruption. Kota Kinabalu became a funereal town.

Illegal immigration went beyond epidemic proportions, and became a fact of life. A thriving black market emerged in the blue identity cards that denoted Malaysian citizenship. In one famous case known to the reporters of Sabah's *Daily Express* newspaper, a woman who spoke neither English nor any Malaysian language was found carrying a Malaysian IC; in her purse was also a document issued her during a recent registration exercise of illegals. She had lacked the wit, or perhaps merely the knowledge, to discard it. Umno, in its recruitment drive, apparently found a good many more Malays in Sabah than had previously been suspected. (Their distinctive accents being simply the natural result of their long historical association with the people of our neighbouring countries.) Within a year, Umno was claiming a Sabahan membership of a quarter-million or more, numbers to rival PBS.

But PBS, according to most, remained secure. Its backbone was the rural populace of the heartland, and those people were still too poor to particularly feel the squeeze that was slowly draining the breath of hope from their capital city.

I was not sorry at all to leave Sabah, regretting only that I had no time to pay my respects to the highest mountain in Southeast Asia. But I consoled myself with the thought that in the decade since I had last hiked up a Kundasang plateau to stare in awe and wonder at the majesty of Mount Kinabalu, no one could possibly have had the time, inclination or money to do anything outrageous to it. ❑

16

AND SO THE YEARS slipped by, and the night that had marked Malaysia's changing of times faded into a largely unlamented past. The nation moved on; those who were disposed to remember would, as like as not, nod sagely and admit that yes, it had been a necessary action. Unsavoury, a shame, perhaps even a tragedy—but, nonetheless, *necessary.* Perhaps (and here a certain resolve would make itself apparent, and their jaws would jut), it had even been a *good thing.*

With the clarity of hindsight, Malaysians came to accept that the authorities had been right to invoke the Internal Security Act that October night in 1987, in what would henceforth be called—when it was talked about at all—"the Crackdown". The tension had been too great. Once again, the Tiger and the Dragon had squared off against each other, and the Malaysian masses had wondered just what it would take to shut some of their politicians up. Something had to be done. And, of course, inevitably, something was. The Necessary Action was taken.

There were those Malaysians for whom that night did not, could not, fade. It had been frozen in time, for it had marked the end of their careers and indeed, for some of them, the end of their lives as Malaysians. They had moved to other countries and begun anew. Many of them had been journalists, and most remained so, for theirs was a profession not easily distinguished from a way of life. But few would continue to write; instead, they worked on the subs' desks of the *Atlanta Constitution* or the *London Times* or the *Sydney Morning Herald*. They married, begat children, became adoptive citizens of their countries of abode. In time, they would cease thinking of themselves as exiles, and shed the notion of ever going home—or perhaps it would be truer to say that they would adopt a wider definition of "home".

It is, after all, where the heart is, and there's only so much room in that romance for heartbreak.

And Malaysia moved on. A new generation swiftly emerged to fill the spaces vacated by the casualties of the Necessary Action, and it was in many ways wiser than its predecessor. The wisdom of holding emotions in check was rewarded with a rising tide of new foreign investment. Wondrous, stratospheric figures: multiple tens of billions. The influx of new money bore out the assurances of those who had insisted that political stability was the prime determinant of investor confidence, and that foreign fund managers and CEOs rarely cared how that stability was achieved.

Two years after the Necessary Action, Malaysia gussied itself up for a year-long harvest of tourist revenue, and reaped more than $2 billion. It was gratifying recompense for having adjusted history so as to have several important anniversaries fall in the same year. History was compliant enough—given the vagueness of 15th-Century records, it was entirely plausible that Melaka had indeed been founded in 1490. It was also fortunate that Kuala Lumpur's sanitation department had been set up in 1890, thus legitimizing the centennial of Malaysia's capital city as "an administrative centre".

There were some quiet grumbles, to be sure, about the peripheralizing of Yap Ah Loy's achievement of more than twenty years earlier, when the redoubtable "Kapitan China" had whipped into a semblance of organization the brawling mining settlement at the confluence of the Klang and Gombak rivers. But such grievances were muted, for the last thing anyone wanted during Visit Malaysia Year 1990 was to be perceived as insensitive to ethnic concerns. The two years that by then had passed since the Necessary Action hadn't been quite enough for the memories to fade completely, and it had only been a matter of months since the last of the detainees had been freed.

It was, however, the subsequent conduct of those men that most emphatically set the seal on the appropriateness of the action that had incarcerated them. Those who had not been utterly broken—and perhaps one or two of the older and frailer ones were—were all the better for their detention. "I never really knew the Muslims," said one Chinese activist, "until I lived with them in detention." And one of the Muslims he was referring to said: "Those guys? They were okay. They didn't insist on eating pork." Mortal antagonists became friends behind bars, recognizing a national camaraderie beneath their ideological differences.

One example: at one stage, the dissident Chinese detainees from the Opposition socialist party had launched a hunger-strike in protest of some maltreatment or other. (They were considerably less than comfortable in detention, of course; as one official smilingly said at the time: "They're not in a hotel.") But the Muslims from the fundamentalist religious party had decided that that was as good a time as any to perform the religious merit-making of a voluntary fast. It demonstrated a sort of solidarity wholly unimaginable outside.

Upon their release, some of the detainees produced little books and pamphlets documenting their experience of the Necessary Action, and in this they served both history and their consciences. But they were careful not to make too big a fuss about it, because they knew it would be a long while before they could be certain that the occupants of the unmarked cars parked outside their homes some nights were as idly innocuous as they seemed.

So the flame-tongued radicals and rabble-rousing hellions who had been swept behind barbed wire emerged more sober, politically, and in the 1990 general elections nine of them won seats on the Opposition benches of parliament.

That was where they had belonged all along, of course, but three years earlier the streets of Kuala Lumpur had seemed so much more spectacular an arena for their contentions.

Those elections were indeed a triumph of Malaysian democracy. Yes, the Opposition carped at the unseemly brevity of the ten-day campaign period, and yes, the ruling National Front government was returned with its precious two-thirds majority intact despite the lowest electoral turnout in the nation's democratic history. Still, Malaysia emerged at the end of October 1990 with a new and in some ways more mature political identity. Two states of the country's fourteen were won outright by Opposition parties. Sabah went the way of its Christian-Kadazan majority. Most agreed that was only to be expected of a territory that had long shifted uneasily in alliance with the Malay-Muslim federal centre. And the Muslim fundamentalists won Kelantan.

Most agreed that that, too, was appropriate: there was a place in the syncretic Malaysian sun for the Islamic extreme, and Kelantan was—indeed, always had been—that place. Without a state of their own to administer, the fundamentalists had woven themselves into the national fabric, sniping from the fringes at Malaysia's unbridled capitalism and the moral decline it engendered. But now they had won Kelantan, and they had a place to call their own and treat as such. One of the first acts of the new state administration was to prohibit night-shift work for women.

That had a less than stimulating effect on the nascent state economy. Kelantan had for many years been a backwater of national development, and the new manufacturing industries which might have turned that around depended quite heavily on round-the-clock labour. But the priorities of Kelantan's new masters were different, and they did not waver from their principles, not even when the national government began re-examining Kelantan's allocations under the federal budget. That had been the threat during the elections: the people of Kelantan had been warned not to expect the continuing largesse of the federal government if they rejected the Barisan Nasional. But they went ahead and rejected it anyway, and seemed content to pay the necessary penalties for the right to reconstruct their state in their own image.

That image would soon begin to alarm the rest of the nation, as Kelantan forthrightly embarked on the transformation of the state's legal codes in strict accordance with what the state government believed was Islamic law. As always, Kelantan would find itself close to the more shadowed centres of the nation's religious conscience. Muslims in other states would say, uncertainly, "It's good what they're trying to do, but is it workable?" If it wasn't, Kelantan would make a fool of itself—and of Islam—in the eyes of the nation and the world. If it was, where would that leave the country's non-Muslims?

The rest of the Malay opposition was left in disarray. The dissident faction that had split from Umno, calling itself Semangat 46, had allied itself with the predominantly Chinese socialist party and the Muslim fundamentalists. They had watched the Muslims win Kelantan on their ticket, then shut the door on their participation in the new state government. The socialists had secured a fair say for themselves on the Opposition benches, and when the elections were over the presumptive Opposition alliance was seen to have been essentially an electioneering device, and it began to unravel. The central core of Umno dissidents remained faithful to their cause, but they were in the wilderness, and many of their fellow-travellers returned to the Umno fold.

So perhaps, in the wake of the 1990 elections, Malaysia wasn't as overtly united as it had been before. But that only meant the new Malaysian political complexion was closer to the truth of the national condition. It was in its way a mark of maturity, and most Malaysians were content to accept it as such, put the elections and the Necessary Action behind them and apply themselves to making the most of the new opportunities opening up all around them.

The mainstream Malaysian media recovered under new management and resumed their traditional roles of sustaining government initiatives, encouraging foreign investment, dutifully criticizing the more egregious opportunisms, and entertaining their readership as best they could. No one asked for more. "It would be good to have better newspapers," confided one of the young stars of the remade Malaysia, "but it's a luxury we can do without for a few more years."

Certainly, the condition of the media had no bearing on the influx of new money—perhaps it had even contributed to the confidence of investors. Malaysian media managers noted that, in Asia, those countries with the most independent media—India and the Philippines, say—were also those with the sickest economies and most turbulent politics. At the other extreme, they pointed out, was Singapore.

And so the money came in, and prosperity reigned in Malaysia. The economy grew at double-digit rates, igniting a heady consumer boom. People bought new cars and moved to better homes in nicer parts of town. The towns themselves spread ever outward; construction was virtually ceaseless and the number of housing starts unprecedented. New hotels and shopping malls sprouted like mushrooms after rain, and fine new highways ribboned out across abandoned padi land.

The twenty-year deadline for the New Economic Policy came due, and there were year-long deliberations on what would follow. The proceedings of these consultations were frequently marred by accusations of "bad faith" on various sides, and Opposition politicians were reduced to making walkout statements. But in due course a new social contract was agreed to by the participants, and this was called the "New Development Policy". Little of the consultations was ever made widely known to the public, so most Malaysians seemed to believe that the NDP was an extension of the NEP, and that nothing had changed.

Malaysia's Indian community, for so long a peripheral element of the central ethnic equation, continued in its silent, disregarded way. Perceiving itself a small and vulnerable community, Malaysian Indians continued to measure the value of their leadership according to how well they got along with the top Malays. In the wake of the 1990 general elections, the Malaysian Indian Congress grew to be more and more beholden to the party president, who was famously loyal to the prime minister, and who was therefore believed to enjoy the prime minister's enduring support. In time, the Indian community would be riven by dissent over the president's autocracy, culminating in a full-blown controversy over the allocation of shares, ostensibly intended for the Indian community as a whole, to three companies in which the president was believed to have an interest.

It would be an ignominious scandal for the Indian community to endure. For all their demographic insignificance, Malaysian Indians formed a vital buffer between the Malay and Chinese communities. It was plausible to argue that without them, Malaysia would be a much more volatile dichotomy of cultures and not an inherently less unstable triumvirate.

But Malaysian politics had continued to evolve along distinctly racial lines, and each community had to attend to its own politics in isolation from the others. Just as the views of the non-Malays were largely irrelevant to Umno's political decisions, so too were those of the non-Chinese to the MCA's and the non-Indians to the MIC's.

The great Malaysian-Chinese business houses, on their part, recognizing that there would be no foreseeable end to their country's preferential policies in favour of the indigenous communities, spread their capital ever further afield, investing in neighbouring countries and throughout the western Pacific Rim. Some Malay politicians tried to depict this as capital flight, accusing the Chinese again of malleable loyalties, but in truth these Malaysian corporations were binding their home economy ever more intimately with the region as a whole. It was, of course, the most economically promising region in the world.

The national leadership, widely admired for its firm steerage of a difficult and plural nation, gained respect in foreign and regional affairs; Asean bent ever more to Malaysia's will. There was room in Malaysia's world-view for a greatly expanded Association of South-East Asian Nations. Vietnam was eager for admission, and Myanmar might have found a place in line if not for the continuing abuse of its people. It was with regret that Malaysia led the call for Myanmar to be less callous with its Muslim minorities. Meanwhile, Malaysian investors flocked to Vietnam and Cambodia in a post-colonial herd, seeking virgin opportunities.

There was considerable local acclaim for the Malaysian prime minister's notion of an East Asian Economic Caucus, and there was even a groundswell of support for the idea of a Commonwealth or United Nations role for him upon his eventual retirement from national leadership. But that would not be for some years yet.

In the meantime, there was still much the Barisan Nasional wanted to achieve. There was the matter of Sabah, for one. A Christian administration in a Malaysian state was a sobering ethnic admonition, and it was a red-letter day for Umno when the party admitted its first non-Muslim member, who happened to be from one of Sabah's many indigenous tribes. That, too, was a welcome acknowledgment of a long-silent truth: one didn't have to be Muslim to be Malay, despite the somewhat awkward definition of a Malay contained in the Federal Constitution. Umno changed its anthem for the occasion, deleting a reference to the Malay "race" and substituting it with one that spoke of Malay "stock" or "roots". What this meant for Sabah, however, would come clear soon enough, as Umno mounted a vigorous membership campaign in that state.

And then there was the matter of the sultans. During the 1983 controversy over the powers of the monarchy, prime minister Mahathir Mohamad had sealed his reputation for what some called courage and others, arrogance. Now, nearly a decade later, there was widespread support for the government's reservations over the business affairs of certain sultans and their families. That the sultans were constitutionally above reproach seemed unfair to many Malaysians, especially in light of the often extensive business interests enjoyed by some of them.

But the government could not be seen to be disrespectful to the sultanates, so venerable an institution were they, and so intrinsic to the Malay identity, so its apprehensions were properly couched in the language of "advice" and delivered to the sultans with all due ceremony at a specially convened meeting, attended by all but two of them.

The judiciary, on its part, did its best to attend to the national good, as defined by the Legislature and the Executive, despite the continuing refusal of the Malaysian Bar Council to grant a vote of confidence in the new Lord President. After all, as the prime minister had been saying all along, the Constitution of a developing country such as Malaysia should never be a straitjacket; it had to be cut from elastic cloth.

And so the years passed, and Malaysia moved buoyantly onward and upward, and there was less and less ambiguity over the true nature and seat of authority in the nation. The Malaysian model of nationhood was seen to be using all the many tools at its disposal. If and when necessary, even the blunt instruments. No one really relished the thought of using them, but they were there, and Malaysia had shown how they, too, could be useful in nation-building. It all hinged, as always, on the sort of nation being built.

The Necessary Action had been given the police codename "Operation Lallang". *Lallang* is the colloquial name for a species of razor-edged wild grass, *Imperata cylindrica,* that can grow in impenetrable thickets on waste ground. "Isn't that what you're supposed to do with lallang?" someone said at the time. "Cut it down to the ground?"

"No," I'd replied. "It will grow back in no time. You have to tend the soil."

The soil has been dearly tended, in what has become a very Malaysian way, and in Malaysia today the ground has become very valuable indeed, and there is hardly any of it to waste on what grows wild and tenacious, untrammelled and free. ❑

The Journey Home

THE VIEW from the windows of the crawling train was extraordinary. Long before reaching the outskirts of Kuala Lumpur, it seemed we were moving towards the epicentre of an enormous explosion.

The ground lay levelled and raw all around; dead trees were scattered like kindling. Thick clouds of red dust billowed and drifted in the wind. Giant yellow machines roared and groaned; teams of workers, mouths and noses scarved against the dust and fumes, laboured alongside the railway tracks.

(Which was why the train was crawling at less than walking pace: the old wooden sleepers were being replaced with new concrete ones. The train swayed and heeled sickeningly as it traversed the rail-works. The project had been underway since the beginning of the year; since then there had been eight derailments. A week after my ride back to Kuala Lumpur, there would be another, particularly bad one. Someone would die. The first reaction of the authorities would be to blame "vandals", but it would emerge that the apparent misalignment of the tracks had been to blame: the engine driver had panicked and slammed on his brakes too heavily. This made more sense. How would a vandal derail a train? By placing rocks on the tracks? Leaping out from behind a culvert and shouting "BOO!"?)

It took an eternity to travel the last twenty kilometres to the capital; a plodding, dusty, miserable ride, causing me to vow never to take the train again. The romance I remembered from my childhood was all gone. Carriages were now either air-conditioned to the point of anaesthesia or open to elements grown uglier; the great old Hainanese and Hakka cooks were replaced by absentee Bumiputra caterers providing barely edible styrofoam food at hideous prices, served by sullen young Malays in little red bowties.

And what of one's fellow passengers? In first class: the arrogant and spoiled, sneering at waiters, ordering food like pashas. In third class: the hoicking masses. I watched oily-mouthed Chinese women blithely tossing indestructible styrofoam packets out the windows to settle on what was left of the landscape like fossil jellyfish, there to lie undisturbed for the next thousand years. For who would care to clear them away? I watched ugly Malay youths abuse the Indian cleaning woman: they held out their empty soft drinks cans to her as she passed along the aisle with her rubbish bag, then, just as she reached out for them with a tentative smile, they bent down to place them very deliberately on the floor. Her face clouded, she kicked the cans violently to the end of the corridor. The youths sniggered, twisting in their seats to mock her bent, retreating, defeated back.

I want to stand up and shout, "YOU BASTARDS! You foul inconsiderate ignorant reprobates!" But that would have been anti-social; perhaps dangerously so.

For I was tired; my journey had been exhausting. Vainly I tried to recall the sweetness of moments spent in almost meditative silence by the banks of the Perak River in Parit, or beneath an arcadian bower of trees in Taiping's Lake Gardens, or immersed in a tumbling forest stream in the foothills of the Main Range. I closed my eyes and tried to imagine the sight of Kedah Peak silhouetted by the sunrise, viewed from the bund of a ricefield. I tried to imagine the mountains, to remind myself that what I was now seeing around me was not all there was of Malaysia.

But it was a futile endeavour, for I realized I was seeking solace in a foreign view. I was not seeing Malaysia the way other Malaysians did. These were the Real Malaysians, these people around me. These sullen, uncommunicative, suspicious, rude, hostile people, each sealed into the private cocoon of self, into which might be admitted only those of their own kind. What had been the most frequent question asked of me on this journey? "Are you Malay or Indian? Are you Eurasian? Are you Muslim? What ARE you?" Everything that emerged subsequently—every comment, opinion and answer—would depend on my response to that question. What was Malaysia? Depends on who's asking. Are you one of Us, or one of Them? What are you? Malaysians were afraid of each other; and resentful that they should be afraid.

Ah, fatigued thoughts. The self-consuming spirals of a tired brain. Why think? Unbidden, an unexpected memory flashed into focus. At the Fisheries Research Institute during the first year of my Malaysian career, I had shared an office with a young USM graduate named Wuan Thong Onn. A man of amazing strength—he lifted weights as a hobby—and professional expertise as a researcher. The one thing Wuan never talked about was Malaysia. Whenever our conversation veered in such a direction, he'd shake his head and turn back to his desk. There was a small placard on that desk, bearing the legend "SUAW". I asked him what it meant.

"Shut up and work," he said, smiling his gentle smile.

Good advice. GREAT advice: look what it was building of Malaysia. Shut up and work. Shut up and make money. Shut up and build this place, build your dream, do what you have to do to take care of your own, make your pile. Shut up and *work*. But shut up.

The prime minister, now sixty-seven years old with a surgically bypassed heart, was looking at the end of a tremendous career. But Mahathir had not finished dreaming. Malaysia was strewn with new signboards extolling his latest vision: "2020". By which year, it was planned, Malaysia would attain the status of a fully developed country. There was an official definition of what this meant. In sum: a self-sustaining economy, serving a populace that considered itself Malaysian first, anything else second. The elimination of race as a function of the Malaysian reality. In Kuching, the DAP's Sim Kwang Yang had dismissed "Vision 2020" as a stunt to get the people to grant the government a blank cheque for the next thirty years.

Not so, I'd contended. Mahathir longed for the ideal of a happy and harmonious nation as much as anyone else and probably a lot more than most. This was just his way of getting to it. Indeed, I thought it deeply ironic that after all he had done to—and for—Malaysia, Mahathir was admitting that he would be long dead before his plans might even begin coming to fruition. We might disagree with his methods, but surely not his motives. And there Sim and I had agreed to disagree.

But to finally see an end to the racial identities of Malaysians! Such a glorious dream!

And then to look around me at my fellow passengers on that train ride to Kuala Lumpur, stirring now to gather their belongings as the train hauled itself like a dying dinosaur towards the station: the Chinese women in their loud nylon dresses and ostentatious jewellery. The Malay youths in their skintight jeans and lurid heavy-metal tee-shirts. The Indian cleaning woman in her grubby tunic, clutching her plastic rubbish bag, standing in the gangway and staring vacantly out the open door at the gathering darkness, her face a dead blank mask of ineradicable weariness ....

To imagine any one of these characters, these stereotypes, smiling at another, saying hello, helping with each others' baggage, exchanging addresses, becoming firm and lasting friends .... Such a mad and impossible fantasy.

So be it. I had never been one for Utopian dreams; I was almost abashed at the emotions roiling within me as the train squealed and clanged to a halt at Platform Four. What have the masses ever meant anyway? Let them carry on as they will; their only relevance comes around once every five years, and even then they've never been much of a bother to the half-a-dozen or so individuals who've always been the only people actually to run this country. To believe that Mainstreet Malaysia might ever be a place of laughter and light, of happy people waltzing around arm-in-arm in their various ethnic costumes, the way they do on the government's billboards and TV commercials, is to be some kind of fool indeed.

No, there was another meaning to racial consociation, and it was one of the more heartening discoveries of my Malaysian journey. The Merdeka generation of Malays—my generation—was proving itself capable of working with their non-Malay countrymen with more grace and confidence than ever their fathers had had. Malay men and women in their thirties and forties were moving into the boardrooms of the national economy, and there they were conducting themselves with expertise and acumen, winning the respect of their colleagues. It was a promising trend. But what if ...

...What if the day might come when there would no longer *be* a "Malay", or a "Chinese", or an "Indian", or an "Other", for that matter? What if the day will come when every second or third Malaysian child, asked to fill in his first school form, looks at the space marked "Race" and goes blank with befuddlement? But my father's this and my mother's that and my grandmother's the other... so what am I? MALAYSIAN! And that's that.

MIX THE BLOODS! Mix them in the most enjoyable way imaginable, which is on a molecular-genetic level, and we need never again fear they might mix in the gutters of our streets, streaming from the mortal wounds we might inflict on each other. Mix the bloods! Unlock the mighty hidden potential of Malaysian genetics; expand the gene pool! Create wonderful new generations of astonishingly beautiful children of indeterminate race, the property of no one culture, and therefore the owners of them all!

Ah, if only. Perhaps we should start by simply eliminating the space marked "Race" on all those forms.

KUALA LUMPUR had gotten real. Which was, in a curious way, a relief. Here was Ground Zero of the explosion that had flattened the land to all visible horizons, turning the Klang Valley into a cauldron of new opportunities, the new housing estates and industrial zones spreading like bacterial cultures on a petri dish, seething with new life-forms or strange mutations of the old. I could barely recognize the place, and was lost as a new tourist on the streets of Kuala Lumpur.

Gone was the shiny showroom sparkle of Visit Malaysia Year 1990, during which Malaysia had invited the world to come and marvel at the smart new nation being built; this gleaming machine on this showroom floor, flanked by pretty girls in *sarong kebayas* twirling cellophane *bunga manggars.* Now the engine was firing on all cylinders, and all that remained on the showroom floor were skidmarks.

Kuala Lumpur was throbbing, honking, smoke-solid, oil-streaked; it smelled of exhaust fumes, melted rubber, heated metal. It was a city in overdrive. Kuala Lumpur was through with preening before the mirror of the world. The city was prowling, growling, feeding. There was serious work to be done; serious fortunes to be made.

Fortunes were undoubtedly being made on the new highways—those billion-ringgit projects so contentious at their outset. Now, seven years after the first stage of the North-South Expressway had been completed in the prime minister's home state, the various sections of the Highway were beginning to link up. They were a joy to ride, slashing through hills and lashing out over abandoned padi land, changing the landscape, revealing new landscapes—the most potent of metaphors for the changing of times.

Seng Keat and I went for a night drive on a newly opened stretch. Pristine tarmac and concrete sped beneath the wheels of his jeep; red and white cat's eyes ribboned into the darkness ahead like landing lights. The highway punched through a granite massif, the slaughtered rock towering around it in jagged cliffs. I said, "When you can chew up the hills and spit them out as highways, man, you got *teeth.*" There was nothing like this in any of the countries around us, I reflected. "Singapore, maybe. A few miles of it. But in Singapore there's nowhere to go."

Seng Keat said, "I guess this country's the cutting edge of Asean."

"The cutting edge? Hell, this country's the *blade!"*

My friend allowed me the enthusiasm, although be couldn't really feel it himself. I had been away; the changes were more obvious to me than to him. Those who stayed, fighting their daily battles with Malaysia's many downsides, saw how far we still had to go more clearly than how far we had come. And Seng Keat was in advertising, an industry close to the source of Malaysian definitions, and therefore in the thick of so much that was wrong. It explained his grittiness; the mist of cynicism that drifted on the edges of his clarity. But he was still one of the clearest-thinking people I'd ever known.

And one of those who gave me hope. I had come to think of Malaysia as a galaxy of stars in a night sky: uncountable motes of brilliance in the dark, each of them shining with an internal light. But each shining alone. Brilliant Malaysians were everywhere: in business, industry, the media, the schools and colleges, the cities, towns and villages. But so many seemed to burn alone, unaware of the existence of the others. The key was to link them. Network them. Let each shining light extend a ray of talent and ability to the others, conjoining, reinforcing, enfolding each individual seed of potential in a nourishing field of support. When that multitude of stars began irradiating each other, when their light began to mingle, then the night would be transformed into day, and their light would illuminate this nation, and not merely glow in the darkness like a constellation of fanciful dreams.

The cool night air, that excellent new road ... I was feeling good. How badly we needed that highway; how splendid it would be when it was completed, and it would be possible to skim down from Thailand to Singapore in six breezy hours and not a whole exhausting day. The Highway was taking a long time to build, but I now saw this as an advantage. The oldest stretch of it, in Kedah, was already sinking and buckling and in need of repair. It had been an unprecedented challenge to build a highway over padi land. But lessons had been learned in the process, and the newer stretches were that much better.

When the Highway was complete, and all the sections finally linked, I imagined something of a *kundalini* unwinding up the spine of this nation; a channel of energy would open that had never opened before, and Malaysia would be radiant.

And what of the destruction? No; we had grown, we had changed. The logging still continued, the dammed waters still rose, but not with as much impunity as before. Malaysia had developed an intelligent and vocal environmentalist lobby, which had achieved its greatest triumph yet over the proposed development of Penang Hill. This had been one of the typically ghastly notions of the tastelessly monied classes: a Disneyland-style theme park atop one of the most beloved hill stations in the country.

The outcry had been immediate, but also *reasoned*. Scientists from Penang's own university had helped assemble terse little documents detailing the consequences of such a project on the wildlife of the Hill. These detailed studies, alloyed with public disfavour expressed through the usual signature campaigns and letters to the editors of major newspapers, blasted holes in the sails of the developers. Moreover, they ensured that presumptive developers would no longer be so dismissively stupid about the innocuousness of their plans—nor would they continue to assume a comparable level of stupidity on the part of the public.

Occasionally, stupidity had gotten through anyway. The rape of Trengganu's Pulau Redang was so total that it was said that the millionaire entrepreneur behind the project was himself aghast at the damage he had wrought.

It would be nice to think so, but no one was counting on it. As those involved in the Save Penang Hill campaign pointed out, the project had yet to be abandoned; all they were succeeding in doing was to have its environmental impact assessment constantly sent back for redrafting. I argued that this was enough of a success: clog up the machinery, throw sand in the works until the developers grew bored with the idea and went looking for something else to desecrate—and then take them on for that, too. There would never come a time when these battles were done; which was why the Good Fight was its own victory.

But the issue had also brought out something else: the most articulate voices raised in defence of Penang Hill belonged to those who actually lived in Penang themselves, and this had made a vital difference. No such connection had worked on behalf of Pulau Redang; the dumb despair of the fishing community there was easily disregarded by those with extravagant designs on their island. There was a lesson in this: environmental protection was not a matter of philosophy or ideology, but of simply caring for one's home. Environmental activists were not "anti-development"; they were merely house-proud.

It had taken a long time for this truth to begin sinking in, but it seemed to have done so, and Malaysia was not yet devoid of wilderness and forests. This was more than could be said for Thailand, for example, or even the Philippines.

Something was saving this country; something so elusive and difficult to define. Dissected to its constituent parts, Malaysia was a hopeless mess of conflicting priorities, mutually unintelligible languages, contradictory cultures and blinkered religions. Malaysia's politics were divisive, its economy exploitative, its pillars of authority buttressed by an impenetrable scaffolding of draconian laws upheld by a parliament in which dominance seemed to matter far more than debate. There was no reason for Malaysia to have survived this far ...

But Malaysia had. Put those disparate constituents together, and something greater than the sum of its parts seemed to emerge. Some strange and magical alchemy was at work, which saw to it that Malaysia was achieving development without wanton destruction, generating wealth without overwhelming inequity, reaching maturity without stumbling fatally into the pitfalls of adolescence. Some have portrayed this as an argument for stern leadership and stringent laws. I choose to see it as a testament to resilience and durability, and perhaps a certain steely apathy; to the presence in Malaysia of sufficient numbers of citizens prepared *not* to die for their country.

I recall now those conversations I had in Jakarta with the woman who had been my childhood schoolmate; how she had so airily dismissed Malaysia as a nation of compliant stooges, lacking fire, spirit, heroism. At the time I was incensed, but only because I could not find the arguments to counter hers. Now I grow thankful. Perhaps Tamalia was right, but could it be that this is precisely why we have been safer than we have a right to be?

Perhaps Malaysia is a nation succeeding by default, and perhaps this explains why there is always such a false and hollow ring to the pious sloganeering that attends politics and nation-building in Malaysia; all these "fights", these "struggles". The truth is: *don't* fight, *don't* struggle. Just shut up and *work.*

One of the few lines of writing I remember from my tenure with *Asiaweek* magazine in Hong Kong was this: "The mettle to succeed is forged in the will to survive." Contemplating the examples of those who built greatness from nothing, it had always struck me that the skills such individuals used to *survive* were precisely what had carried them to success. Durability, diligence, stamina, intelligence—or cunning. But where this success truly *endured,* becoming something worth more than its mere material value, there was always a certain integrity involved. To utilize a more recent buzz phrase: Quality Control.

If the parallel holds true on a national scale—and why should it not?—then Malaysia must surely be bound for some kind of greatness. *Despite itself;* despite the incomprehensible blindness that has had us so fixated on ideals that we have grown all but unconscious of our realities. Yes, many of those realities are unsavoury, but we do ourselves as great an injustice in blinding ourselves to them as to our virtues, strengths and durabilities.

I could not believe that it would take as long as thirty years to achieve the goals enshrined in Mahathir Mohamad's "Vision 2020", not at the rate of change I had seen throughout the country. But without a new commitment to forthrightness and honesty among Malaysians, it might as well take three hundred years. For if all we dared do was talk about what we wanted to be, and not what we *are,* then how would we know when we'd made it? Would we have to have another government campaign, telling us it's okay now, we've made it, we're a developed nation, we're all Malaysians first, racial consciousness is a thing of the past, let's all have a party? And if such be the case, why wait thirty years? Why not do it NOW?

It was in a small house in Ampang Jaya, sitting on the floor in earnest conversation with three young Malaysians of a sort I had never met before, that I finally realized what had driven me to abandon my entire life to this journey. I had come home in search of an answer to the question that had incessantly vexed me during my years away: What was *wrong* with Malaysia? Suddenly, I knew.

All three of them were twenty years old, or thereabouts. Their fathers were Malay, their mothers were not. One was actually a member of the Kedah royal family, a grand-nephew of Tunku Abdul Rahman, although he played down the connection. That they were beautiful goes without saying. They laughingly called themselves "Bumiputehs". They had been educated abroad; they had come home to Malaysia to see what all the fuss was about, and to check out the ripe new opportunities opening up for young Malaysians of their predilections. One wanted to make music, another wanted to make films, the third was hoping to do something in design.

"The changes are coming," said the first, "and they're coming with the music! Listen to it, man, there's something new and special coming out! You guys had better understand what's happening, and not stand in our way."

You guys? I suddenly saw that he was talking to me as a representative of the older generation; a dizzying realization indeed! All right, if that's the way to play it: "Yes, we'll bear that in mind," I said. "But what I hope most for my generation is that we'll be less of a hindrance to you than our elders have been to us. And I believe we will be. You just remember that when you start hating us!"

They laughed at that. I was dazzled by them; by their beauty, their intelligence and energy, their hunger to grow. "Look at you," I said, mostly to myself but aloud. "The true children of the NEP. There's gotta be hope for this country."

The second one said, "What's the NEP?"

I thought he was joking. He was not; he was looking at me expectantly. "You don't know what the NEP is?" The incredulity in my voice intrigued them. They shook their heads, edging closer. I still couldn't believe this. These kids may well have been conceived under National Operations Council rule! "What do you think the initials stand for?" I asked.

One of them hazarded a guess. "National ... Education ... Programme?"

I leaned back against the wall, dumbfounded. Outside, the housing estate went about its evening affairs. There was the sound of television sets tuned to the news, the sounds of cooking in neighbours' kitchens, the occasional car driving by. From somewhere wafted in the fragrance of burning frankincense; in the distance a mosque sounded its call to prayer. I exhaled a long breath. "The NEP," I said, "is the reason you exist ..." but that sounded so ridiculous I had to let it die an instant death. I tried again. "The NEP stands for 'New Economic Policy'. In May 1969 there were racial riots, following the general elections ...," their intent expressions remained, but their eyes immediately began glazing over. I gave up. "You're just going to have to read up on your Malaysian history," I said.

"I'd really like to," said one, "when I have the time." A nice response. At their age, I'd have shrugged and said, "Who cares? History's bunk." I couldn't resist: "Tell you what," I said. "You make sure you get a copy of my book when it comes out."

They assured me they would.

Some years earlier, I had given a talk to a group of sixth-formers, ostensibly to help them prepare for the General Paper of their coming examinations. It had swiftly become a free-flowing dialogue, and I had thoroughly enjoyed the rapid-fire cut and thrust of their questions and opinions. The students were from the top class of a top-flight, multiracial, coeducational school in Kuala Lumpur; they were among the brightest of their generation. It was a thoroughly Malaysian mix of eighteen-year-olds, all races, both sexes. But the two Malay boys were the quietest of all, listening attentively enough but volunteering nothing of their thoughts, not even when the discussion began dealing with the NEP. I asked them, point blank: "Do you think you could survive without the NEP?"

They both shook their heads. "No."

"Why not?"

No answer.

"You know you couldn't survive without the NEP, but you don't know why not?"

No response.

I suggested to them that the NEP's continued existence was proof of its continuing failure. "It exists to help the Bumiputra community stand on its own feet, like the crutches that help an injured person walk again. But once he's healed, he doesn't need the crutches anymore. Or like the scaffolding for a new building being built. Once the building is finished, the scaffolding comes down. It doesn't stay up there forever. The NEP will only have succeeded when no one thinks about it, or talks about it, or believes they need it anymore. The NEP's ultimate success will only come when the emerging generation of Malaysians has no memory of it, no feeling for it, no knowledge of it other than what they learn in history class. Do you think such a day will come?"

They shook their heads again. "No."

"I'm sorry you feel that way," I said, trying hard not to let my exasperation show. "But I believe you're wrong."

I would never have believed, however, that even the glimmer of such a day would come so soon. The three young Malaysians said goodbye and left for a night out on the town. I watched them go with fond amazement. How completely out-of-synch they were with whatever it was the Malays were supposed to be these days; how innocent of the baggage of expectations imposed upon the Malays in the effort to exorcise their insecurities. And how effortlessly, even ignorantly, they exceeded those expectations!

The new generation was here; there it went, off for a night of music and dance and whatever else these kids get up to these days, strong, confident, worldly, self-aware, resembling their fathers not one jot. It was exciting to believe that a new Malaysian definition was emerging, and that it would be devised by the new generation of Malaysians for themselves, in all their blessed arrogance and freedom, and not be imposed upon them by the need to atone for the sins of their fathers.

I looked forward to Omar's music and Adam's films. ("Omar"! "Adam"! Malay names, Muslim names, but names that might belong anywhere.) I looked forward to seeing what Malaysia might look like through the eyes of the NEP generation, as it strides towards its own maturity. If reality was a matter of perception, then surely theirs were the perceptions that mattered most of all. I had found an answer to the question that had brought me home: The only thing wrong with Malaysia is the way Malaysia sees itself.

And it was time to sweep the mirror clear. ❑

EPILOGUE
Kuala Kubu Baru
August 31, 1992

I LIVE NOW on the first floor of a two-storey shophouse in a small town in the foothills of the Main Range, not far from where the road begins to wind up towards Fraser's Hill, and from there down into Pahang.

It is a spruce little place, this town. There has been for many years a police college here, and an army training camp. Perhaps it is their presence that imparts an air of efficiency and orderliness to the area. There are large trees here, and well-tended municipal gardens, and the rain is montane and pristine: it dries clean, not leaving circles of dust behind. It is not as quiet a town as I had hoped when I rented this place to finish writing the manuscript to this book, but the noise is the noise of a working town. The town wakes early; newspaper vans arrive, the rubbish truck does its rounds, the gas shop loads up its lorries with the clangour of pile-drivers, the coffee-shops open for breakfast, all while the sky is still awash with the mauve of dawn.

The street on which I live is very Chinese, and it was occasion for much gossip in the neighbourhood when I moved in—it is unusual for a non-Chinese to want to live in a Chinese part of town. Out here, in the working-class Malaysia beyond the urban centres, the races share a tacit understanding that they shall not impinge too much upon each other. "Why a shophouse in town?" I was asked. "Why not a terrace house in the low-cost estate on the outskirts?" Because I valued the convenience—everything I need is a few seconds away; there's a grocer downstairs and a tailor next door and a stationer next door to him. But also because this is a fine space to have. Its ceiling is high, its walls are white, a good light floods in, a constant breeze lifts my curtains, and in the evening I can climb up to the roof to watch flocks of swifts wheel and dance in the darkening sky before settling down for the night on the telephone lines, orderly as soldiers.

As I write these lines, the minutes tick by towards midnight on August 30, 1992. In a little while, Malaysia will celebrate its thirty-fifth National Day. Not that there's any unusual excitement in town tonight; indeed, it is unusually quiet. My neighbours even seem to have abandoned their mah-jong tonight, which is remarkable. But I speak too soon; even now, that familiar clatter of plastic tiles begins to filter through these stout pre-war walls.

I have grown very fond of this town in the month that I have been here; it has not been unfriendly to me, and not far away there is a multitude of rivers and jungle trails up which I can lose myself when the need arises. That was one of the reasons I chose this town as my writing retreat: all around are forested hills. But I haven't gone into the forest as often as I'd expected; it has been adventure enough assembling this story. When this is done—and it is nearly done—I shall have to pack up my things and leave this town for Kuala Lumpur and the next phase of this task: lawyers, publishers, designers, printers, distributors .... I have not much of a feeling for all that, although I hope I shall be able to work with those who do; for me, this journey is almost over.

I shall be sorry to leave this town, with its gentle shopkeepers and family businesses; it has been instructive for me to learn that many people still spend all their lives in the town where they were born, attending to the family shop, taking it over from their parents, and passing it on to their children. Such continuity is reassuring in a country that is changing so rapidly, so profoundly. I have found this town to be a restful place; a place it would be easy to imagine as home.

But then, I am Malaysian, and only Malaysian, I have been away a long time, and now anywhere in this country feels like home to me. Which is just as well, because nowhere else in the world ever could.

It is now midnight, and the wall clock chimes. The tailor down-stairs has hung a Malaysian flag outside his shop, by the small votive shrine where he lights his joss-sticks each morning. I can see it from my front window. It hangs there in the darkness, the red and white of its stripes catching the headlights of passing vehicles. But there are not many vehicles out and about tonight, and there is a soft and blessed quiet in the street below.

The flag drifts gently in the languid midnight air, and the swifts sleep undisturbed. ❑

AFTERWORDS
February 1993

THE MANUSCRIPT of the First Edition of this book was completed at the end of August 1992. In the six months ensuing, the following developments unfolded in Malaysia, involving some of the people mentioned and trends described in my narrative:

The Prime Minister, Datuk Seri Dr Mahathir Mohamad, completed the political journey begun a decade earlier, and compelled the Sultanates of Malaysia to accept a diminution of their powers and privileges.

It was a most historic moment, catalysed by a high-school hockey coach in Johor named Douglas Gomez, who made a police report after being physically assaulted by the Sultan of Johor. This act by Sultan Mahmood Iskandar, said the Prime Minister in Parliament, was "the straw that broke the camel's back". After more than twenty years, one of the three sacrosanct Articles of the Federal Constitution—Article 181, pertaining to the Sovereignty of the Rulers—was taken down from its pedestal of sanctity for redrafting. The Constitutional immunity of the Sultanates was to be removed. As a consequence, the Sedition Act was also to be amended.

By any measure, the trimming of hereditary immunities was an important step forward in the practice of a Constitutional democracy. But the attendant media spectacle left many Malaysians discomfited, as hordes of journalists descended on the palaces and for month after month newspaper columns and letters pages were filled with denunciations of royal excesses.

Those excesses, as suddenly, torrentially revealed, were often great indeed. We heard of unconscionable business liaisons with unscrupulous tycoons. We heard of profligate extravagance. And we heard what we had known all along but had been legally bound never to mention: we heard of outrageous arrogance; of push-ups by the roadside, slaps in the face, of arbitrary authority wielded with utter contempt for the dignity of law. Or of life itself, for that matter: we even heard of murder.

There was an outpouring of sentiments long concealed, in ringing testimony to the fact that the silencing of speech could never silence thought. There was a tremendous catharsis about this damburst; the relief of a mighty release. But it was expressed in a form and language that seemed to know no bounds. It was unprecedented, and much for that reason profoundly disconcerting. Suddenly, Malaysians were waking up every morning to see their supposedly strait-laced newspapers engaging in what sounded perilously like outrageous sedition.

As there was very little media coverage of the Rulers' responses on any of these matters, there could be no documentary confirmation of the "ill-feeling" allegedly being raised in the heartland by the supporters of the Sultans and Opposition parties.

But a prickly unease did settle on the populace, and there was palpable relief when the Prime Minister announced that the crisis would be over in thirty days (that is, by February 19, 1993) when the Amendments to Article 181 of the Federal Constitution would pass into law with or without the Sultans' assent. (As allowed under the provisions inserted into the Constitution after the crisis of 1983.)

To the surprise of many observers, however, there was no discernible diminution in media coverage against the Sultans, which was the first time in years that the official news media had not responded to a clear cue from the Prime Minister. There could have been only two possible explanations for this anomalous behaviour: Either the news media were acting more independently than they had since mid-1987, or they were taking their cues from someone other than the Prime Minister.

This was fodder for doomsayers, who speculated that a situation was developing which might lend itself to another security exercise somewhere down the road. But the truth this time seemed more closely related to transitions, rather than rebellions, and this would make a difference.

Certainly, however, the stakes were rising in the Umno succession question. A battle for the leadership of Umno had been a central element in the last security crackdown, and now it seemed another battle was underway. While Mahathir remained in office, this would be a second-tier tussle, to be sure. But it was no less portentous for that, for it was becoming clear that Mahathir would not live forever. And neither would anyone else, with or without ambition.

There was also the notion that the expected economic contraction—reflected in the final-quarter figures for 1992 and by most measures a necessary corrective for an overheated economy—would be parlayed into political mileage.

In a significant shift from the rural arena of Umno's past internal contests, the changing political equation was now most dramatically mirrored in big business. While the main pages of the newspapers were dominated by the Monarchy's descent, their business sections were telling the Other Big Story of the Day: developments involving the Renong Group, since 1990 the flagship of Umno's corporate assets.

In the richest management buyout in Malaysian history, ownership of the New Straits Times Group and Sistem Televisyen Malaysia Berhad passed to four senior managers of the NST Press. The deal was worth RM800 million. [The designation "RM"—Ringgit Malaysia—has been introduced to replace the dollar sign for Malaysia's currency.]

The four buyers were: Khalid Ahmad, formerly managing director of the New Straits Times Press; Mohamed Noor Mutalib, formerly NSTP senior group general manager; and

NSTP group editors Ahmad Nazri Abdullah and Abdul Kadir Jasin.

Khalid was subsequently appointed managing director of Sistem Televisyen Malaysia Berhad, operators of TV3, while Mohamed Noor took over Khalid's previous position as NSTP MD. The editors stayed where they were.

These corporate moves were seen as linked to the Umno succession—and the changes were coming too thick and fast, at this writing, for anything more than a speed-blurred impression of what was happening. Sanusi Junid began to make appearances, but Anwar Ibrahim was suddenly showing very strongly. Whether or not this would work to his advantage within Umno, against the form of bedrock support enjoyed by Abdul Ghafar Baba and Abdullah Ahmad Badawi, remained to be seen. As one senior Umno politician noted: "Anwar is not of Umno's roots. He was bud-grafted to the stem."

The Umno General Assembly was scheduled for later in 1993, by which time a clearer picture would have emerged.

ON THE MOVE . . .

LORRAIN OSMAN, the former chairman of Bumiputra Malaysia Finance, was finally extradited from ten years on remand in London to Hong Kong, where he would stand trial on matters pertaining to the BMF scandal of 1982/3. On New Year's Eve, GEORGE TAN, the boss of Carrian and the central figure in the affair, who had been set free on a technicality by a Hong Kong court, suffered a stroke that left him paralysed and incapable of speech. It was not clear if his malady was directly attributable to the news of Lorrain's extradition.

DR MUNIR MAJID, once group editor of the *New Straits Times* and later chief executive officer of the Commerce International Merchant Bank, a featured player in many nationally important financial negotiations, was appointed head of the new Securities Commission.

FAUZI OMAR, formerly Assistant Editor of *The Malay Mail,* became the afternoon tabloid's Acting Editor, with the transfer of his predecessor to the night desk.

THE DATE OF COMPLETION of the Peninsula's North-South Expressway was brought forward six months, to March 1994.

DATUK RAHIM NOR, Director of the Special Branch at the time of Operation Lallang, was now Tan Sri Rahim Nor, Deputy Inspector-General of Police.

IN OTHER NEWS . . .

THE YEAR OF THE ROOSTER made its subdued advent. The word in the Chinese community was: Let's just do this calmly and quietly this year; things seem a little jumpy right now. The Klang Valley was blessedly quiet for a surprisingly long time, as the Chinese New Year was followed in rapid succession by the City Day and Thaipusam holidays. The number of KL folk venturing outstation for the holidays seemed unusually high. There seemed a special need this year to drop in on the Old Folks Back Home.

It should be noted that Rooster Years are very special to this country. The last time the Rooster was here, in 1981, Mahathir Mohamad became prime minister. The time before that was in 1969, when the Rooster Year began just before the riots. The time before that was 1957. And the time before that was 1945.

So: the end of the War and the birth of political consciousness in this country, then Merdeka, the May 13 riots and Mahathir's ascent to the nation's top political office—an office he was manifestly destined to raise to the top, full stop. All in Rooster Years.

Quite clearly, another vintage Rooster was upon us.

(Personally, I was delighted that the First Edition of this book, launched a week before the Lunar New Year, should do so well as to have me at work on the softcover Second Edition by Chap Goh Meh. I am at a loss for words to express my gratitude for the encouragement and support of all those who gave it in such full measure.)

(And the truth was, *alhamdulillah,* just about everyone who mattered, did.)

RR
Petaling Jaya
February 1993

Bibliography

Abdul Rahman, Tunku, *Political Awakening*, Petaling Jaya: Pelanduk Publications, 1986.

Abdul Rahman, Tunku, *Viewpoints,* Kuala Lumpur, Heinemann, 1978.

Butcher, J.G., *The British in Malaya 1880-1941,* Oxford University Press, 1979.

Chandra Muzaffar, *Islamic Resurgence in Malaysia,* Kuala Lumpur: Penerbit Fajar Bakti, 1987.

Comber, Leon, *13 May 1969: A Historical Survey of Sino-Malay Relations,* Kuala Lumpur: Heinemann, 1983.

Fatimi, S.Q., *Islam Comes to Malaysia,* Singapore: Malaysian Sociological Research Institute, 1963.

Fisher, C.A., *Southeast Asia,* London: Methuen, 1964.

Gomez, E.T., *Umno's Corporate Investments,* Kuala Lumpur: Forum, 1990.

Gullick, J.M., *Kuala Lumpur 1880-1895,* London: Malayan Branch of the Royal Asiatic Society, 1955.

Gullick, J.M., *Malay Society in the Late Nineteenth Century,* Oxford University Press, 1989.

Heng, Pek Koon, *Chinese Politics in Malaysia*, Oxford University Press, 1988.

Hickling, R.H., *Malaysian Law,* Kuala Lumpur: Professional Law Books Publishers, 1987.

Hua, Wu Yin, *Class and Communalism in Malaysia,* London: Zed Books, 1983.

Israeli, R., ed., *The Crescent in the East,* London: Curzon, 1982.

Jesudason, J.V., *Ethnicity and the Economy,* Oxford University Press, 1989.

Kitab, Kris and James Ritchie, *Sarawak Awakens: Taib Mahmud's Politics of Development,* Petaling Jaya: Pelanduk Publications, 1991.

Khasnor Johan, *The Emergence of the Modern Malay Administrative Elite,* Oxford University Press, 1984.

Kok Wee Kiat, et al., *The Malaysian Challenges in the 1990s,* Kuala Lumpur: Pelanduk Publications for the Malaysian Chinese Association, 1990.

Kua, Kia Soong, *445 Days Behind the Wire,* Kuala Lumpur: The Resource and Research Centre, Selangor Chinese Assembly Hall, 1989.

Kua, Kia Soong, ed., *Media Watch: The Use and Abuse of the Malaysian Press,* Kuala Lumpur: The Resource and Research Centre, Selangor Chinese Assembly Hall, 1990.

Lim, Kit Siang, *Crisis of Identity,* Kuala Lumpur: Democratic Action Party, 1986.

Loh, Kok Wah, *Beyond the Tin Mines,* Oxford University Press, 1988.

Mahathir Mohamad, *The Malay Dilemma*, Times Editions, 1970.

Mahathir Mohamad, *The Challenge,* Petaling Jaya: Pelanduk Publications, 1986.

Morrison, I., *Malayan Postscript,* London: Faber & Faber, 1942.

New Straits Times, "Elections in Malaysia 1955-1986", Kuala Lumpur: New Straits Times Press, 1990.

Miller, H., *Menace in Malaya,* London: Harrap, 1954.

Nyce, R. and S. Gordon, ed., *Chinese New Villages in Malaya,* Singapore: Malaysian Sociological Research Institute, 1973.

Purcell, Victor, *The Chinese in Malaya,* Oxford University Press, 1948.

Purcell, Victor, *Malaya: Communist or Free?*, London: Gollancz, 1954.

Roff, W.R., *The Origins of Malay Nationalism,* Kuala Lumpur: University of Malaya Press, 1974.

Salleh Abas, *The Role of the Independent Judiciary,* Kuala Lumpur: Promarketing Publications, 1989.

Salleh Abas with K. Das, *May Day for Justice,* Kuala Lumpur: Magnus Books, 1989.

Shaharuddin Maarof, *Concept of a Hero in Malay Society,* Eastern Universities Press, 1984.

Shaharuddin Maarof, *Malay Ideas on Development,* Singapore: Times Books International, 1988.

Shaw, W., *Tun Razak,* Kuala Lumpur: Longman, 1976.

Sowell, T., *Preferential Policies: An International Perspective,* New York: William Morrow, 1990.

Suaram, K. Das, ed., *The White Paper on the October Affair,* Suaram Komunikasi, 1989.

Syed Husin Ali, *The Malays: Their Problems and Future,* Longman Malaysia, 1981.

Turnbull, W., *A History of Malaysia, Singapore and Brunei,* Allen & Unwin, 1989.

Wheatley, P., *The Golden Khersonese,* University of Malaya Press, 1961.

Williams, P.A., *Judicial Misconduct,* Petaling Jaya: Pelanduk Publications, 1990.

Winstedt, R.O., *The Malays: A Cultural History,* Singapore: Kelly & Walsh, 1947.

Zakiah Hanum, *Asal-Usul Negeri-Negeri Di Malaysia,* Singapore: Times Books International, 1989.